Planetary Combination

Revised Edition

Bob Makransky

THE WESSEX ASTROLOGER

Revised edition published in 2025 by
The Wessex Astrologer Ltd,
PO Box 9307
Swanage
BH19 9BF
England

For a full list of our titles please visit www.wessexastrologer.com

© Bob Makransky 2016, 2025
Bob Makransky asserts the moral right to be recognised as the author of this work.

Cover Design by Jonathan Taylor

Typeset by Kevin Moore

ISBN 9781916625396

A catalogue record for this book is available at The British Library

No part of this book may be reproduced or used in any form or by any means without the written permission of the publisher.
A reviewer may quote brief passages..

> *This newly revised edition of 'Planetary Combination' includes interpretations for each and every Ptolemaic aspect (conjunction, sextile, square, trine, opposition) as well as parallels and contraparallels in declination.*

Praise for *Planetary Combination*

"While this book is nominally a series of explanations about aspects between the traditional planets, the degree of character description for each planetary pair is extraordinarily precise. An entire personality is captured within these aspects. In the same way that the author provides highly detailed character sketches for each planetary duo, he gives the same attention to configurations. In addition to the most common shapes, he also provides several pages on shapes that are not found in any other astrology text. An unusually terse and bold reference, Planetary Combination transcends psychological mumbo-jumbo to give you the bare-naked reality of the adult Western psyche."

- CHRIS LORENZ,
Dell Horoscope magazine.

"This is one of the best books on aspects out there. He not only deals with aspects themselves, but goes deep into chart morphology. It is one thing to analyze aspects and quite another to look at the "pictures" - the forms - that the aspects make. Most books on aspects deal with the aspects of longitude. But he also includes the parallels and contraparallels. He has an interesting discussion of orbs, values (strengths of an aspect) and mutual receptions. A student would have to read many books from many authors to get the information that is given here. As always with Bob Makransky's work, the book is interesting and well written, not for a beginner or casual reader, but fascinating nevertheless - especially for a serious student."

– JOSEPH POLANSKY,
Diamond Fire magazine

"*Planetary Combination* is an excellent and comprehensive summary of all the relevant chart factors. ... One has to search hard to find such material! But this is all presented, as is all of Makransky's work, with vigour, wisdom and accessibility. ... Much of the book is taken up – as we might expect – with a very generous coverage of the astrological aspects. I looked up a few of my own and they were spot on. ... *Planetary Combination* fills a gap in the current state of astrological literature. It manages to retain both a sense of firm tradition whilst feeling utterly new and fresh."

– JAMES LYNN PAGE,
author of *Everyday Tarot, Celtic Magic, The Christ Enigma* and *The New Positive Thinking*.

"You are entering a world of verbal complexity and conceptual subtlety. There will be plenty you have not seen anywhere else. You may find Makransky's approach to astrology insightful, delightfully unconventional, or just plain weird. I applaud Bob Makransky and his publisher Margaret Cahill at The Wessex Astrologer for having produced a work of originality and complexity and befuddlement, astonishment and inspiration and irritation."

– JOSEPH CRANE,
The Astrology Institute

Table of Contents

Glossary	1
Introduction	5
Planets	12
Zodiacal Aspects	13
Orbs	17
Well-Aspected vs. Afflicted	20
Parallels and Contraparallels of Declination	23
Disposition	25
Mutual Reception	26
Configurations	29
General Considerations	29
Conjunction Forms	31
Stelliums	31
Close Pairs	33
Simple Configurations	34
Triangular Forms	35
Grand Trines (and two Grand Trines)	35
Fans	38
Wedges (and two Wedges)	41
Square Forms	43
T-Crosses (and two T-Crosses)	43
Mixed Forms	47
Wedge with T-Cross	47
Compound Configurations	48
Triangular Forms	48
Grand Sextiles	48
5/6	49
Square forms	50
Grand Squares (and two Grand Squares)	50

Quadrangular Forms	52
Rectangles (and Bow Ties)	52
Kites	53
Trapezoids	54
Baskets	56
Aspects and Mutual Reception	**57**
The Moon's Nodes	**225**
Appendix: The Natural Disposition	**235**
Bibliography	**243**
Books by Bob Makransky	**244**

Glossary

Zodiac – or *ecliptic*, is the circle of the Sun's apparent yearly orbit around the earth; it is divided into 12 **zodiacal signs** of 30° each.

Triplicity – group of three zodiacal signs considered analogous to the four elements:
Fire Signs: Aries, Leo, Sagittarius
Earth Signs: Taurus, Virgo, Capricorn
Air Signs: Gemini, Libra, Aquarius
Water Signs: Cancer, Scorpio, Pisces

Quadrature – or *quadruplicity*, is a group of four zodiacal signs of similar character:
Cardinal Signs: Aries, Cancer, Libra, Capricorn
Fixed Signs: Taurus, Leo, Scorpio, Aquarius
Mutable Signs: Gemini, Virgo, Sagittarius, Pisces

Ruler / Exaltation – each traditional planet has one or two zodiacal signs which it rules, and another zodiacal sign in which it is exalted (Uranus, Neptune, and Pluto are not considered to rule or be exalted in any signs). These *essential dignities* are considered to greatly strengthen the effect of a planet posited in its ruler or exaltation:

Planet	Ruler(s)	Exaltation
Sun	Leo	Aries
Moon	Cancer	Taurus
Mercury	Gemini / Virgo	Virgo
Venus	Taurus / Libra	Pisces
Mars	Aries / Scorpio	Capricorn
Jupiter	Sagittarius / Pisces	Cancer
Saturn	Capricorn / Aquarius	Libra

Detriment / Fall – are the signs in which planets are considered to be debilitated: detriment is the opposite sign to the ruler, and fall is the opposite sign to the exaltation. Thus e.g. Mercury is in its detriment in Sagittarius and Pisces, and in its fall in Pisces as well.

Disposition – the **dispositor** of a given planet is that planet which rules the sign in which the given planet is located. For example, since Jupiter rules Sagittarius and Pisces, then it is said to be the dispositor of any planets located in Sagittarius or Pisces.

Mutual Reception – when two planets each occupy a sign ruled by the other; or are in the exaltation sign of the other; then they are said to be in **Mutual Reception**. For example, when Mars occupies Sagittarius, Pisces, or Cancer; and Jupiter occupies Aries, Scorpio, or Capricorn; then Mars and Jupiter are considered to be in Mutual Reception.

Aspect – angular relationship between pairs of planets (or a planet and an angle – Ascendant, Midheaven, Descendant, Lower Meridian) as measured in degrees of celestial longitude in the zodiac (ecliptic). In this book only the **Ptolemaic aspects** are recognized, viz.: **conjunction** (0° separation in zodiacal longitude between the two planets), **opposition** (180°), **trine** (120°), **square** (90°), and **sextile** (60°). Other authorities use minor aspects such as **semi-square** (45°), **semi-sextile** (30°), **quincunx** (150°), **sequiquadrate** (135°), **quintile** (72°), and **septile** (51° 26').

Orb – the **orb** of an aspect is the allowable deviation from exactitude permitted in the analysis (this can vary according to context); e.g. with 6° orbs, two planets are considered to be in a square aspect if their angular separation is between 84° and 96°.

Value – the value of an aspect is the integral part of the actual deviation from exactitude; e.g. in the case of a square aspect, if there is between 89°01' and 90°59' angular separation between the two planets, then the value is one; if greater than one and less than or equal to two degrees from exactitude (88°01' to 89°00' or 91°00' to 91°59' angular separation), the value is two; if greater than two and less than or equal to three degrees from exactitude (87°01' to 88°00' or 92°00' to 92°59' angular separation), the value is three; and so on.

Partile – an aspect with a value of 1 (i.e. within one degree of exact).

Applying / Separating – an **applying aspect** is one in which the orb of inexactitude is decreasing at the moment of birth; and a **separating aspect** is one in which the orb of inexactitude is increasing at the moment of birth (irrespective of what occurs in the future due to e.g. retrogradation).

Dexter / Sinister – **dexter aspects** (sextile, square, or trine) occur between the conjunction and opposition (the angle measured from the faster planet to the slower planet increases when progressed); whereas **sinister aspects** occur between the opposition and conjunction (phase angle decreases when progressed). In the case of aspects of the Sun and Moon, dexter = waxing and sinister = waning. This distinction is not described in the present book, but I daresay it is not insignificant: e.g., lunar phases 8 and 22 both refer to Sun square Moon, and both are deeply conflicted; but the dexter square (8) is aggressive and aggrandizing; where the sinister square (22) is passive and appeasing.

Configurations – or *structures*, are complex aspects (of three or more planets) such as: Grand Trines, T-Crosses, Fans, Wedges; Grand Squares, Kites, Rectangles, Trapezoids, etc.

Temperament type – or *chart shapings*, a system of classifying horoscopes devised by Dr. Marc Edmund Jones which distinguishes seven types of horoscopes depending upon the distribution of the planets around the zodiacal circle. For example, all of the planets distributed more or less evenly is a *Splash type*; all the planets occupying but half of the zodiacal circle is a *Bowl* type; etc.

Parallels and Contraparallels – a planet's *diurnal circle*, or *declination circle*, is the apparent daily path of a planet around the earth, which is a small circle parallel to the celestial equator. Two planets which share the same diurnal circle (have equal declinations) are considered to be in **parallel**. Two planets which have equal declinations but of opposite signs (one north of the celestial equator and the other south) are considered to be in **contraparallel**. In this book we allow an orb of inexactitude of 1° declination in measuring parallels and contraparallels.

Antiscion / Contrascion – *antiscion* is a point at a like distance from the nearest solsticial point (0° Cancer or Capricorn) from a given planet. For example, the antiscion of a planet at 14° Capricorn is at 16° Sagittarius. The *contrascion* is the antiscion of the planet's opposition point. Antiscions can be considered a symbolic form of the parallel; they are not considered in this book; but that is not to say they are not effective.

Table of Favorable and Unfavorable Planetary Combinations (per Morinus)

	SU	MO	ME	VE	MA	JU
MO	+					
ME	+	+				
VE	+	+	+			
MA	+	−	−	−		
JU	+	+	+	+	−	
SA	−	−	+	−	−	+

Table of Favorable and Unfavorable Planetary Combinations (per Makransky)

	SU	MO	ME	VE	MA	JU	SA	UR	NE
MO	+								
ME	−	+							
VE	−	+	−						
MA	+	−	+	+					
JU	+	+	−	+	+				
SA	−	−	+	−	−	+			
UR	+	−	+	−	+	+	+		
NE	−	+	−	+	−	+	−	+	
PL	+	−	+	−	+	−	−	−	−

Introduction

"Personality traits are enduring patterns of perceiving, relating to, and thinking about the environment and oneself that are exhibited in a wide range of social and personal contexts."
— *Diagnostic and Statistical Manual of Mental Disorders IV*

In astrology, "personality traits" are symbolized by the planets; and "a wide range of social and personal contexts" are symbolized by aspects and configurations (complex aspects involving three or more planets).

Where strength factors in the horoscope reveal who the native is (and thus are analogous to the Ascendant), aspects and configurations reveal what the native does (and thus are analogous to the Midheaven). Where strength factors arise from within the native (even though e.g. angularity is learned), aspects and configurations are descriptive of external circumstances and relationships (and the native's reactions to same). Where strength factors view the native apart from his or her social milieu (true, angularity indicates how a native addresses his or her social environment; but this is merely a posture or a mask, not an actual grappling with people and events), configurations and aspects show how the environment impacts upon the native and how the native adjusts to it.

For example, a strong or weak Sun indicates how the native shines – or fails to; whereas aspects to the Sun indicate the triumphs or struggles the native engages in to get there (and in particular relations with father and superiors). A strong or weak Venus indicates how the native enjoys or suffers from others; whereas aspects to Venus indicate the ups and downs of personal relationships (particularly those involving women). A strong or weak Jupiter indicates how the native exceeds his or her limits; whereas aspects to Jupiter indicate from whence inspiration and guidance come (with particular reference to money matters).

In a general way, the strength factors reveal the social roles people play – the usual strategies which they employ to "win friends and influence people"; and the aspects and configurations are revelatory of the arenas in life in which these roles are played out: how people make their way in the world, their interactions with their environment, their game plans; as well as the success / failure, ease / obstacles, satisfaction / frustration, that are encountered in this endeavor. For example, Mars-Pluto aspects symbolize a self-certain, intense, and heavy-handed approach to situations and relationships; whereas Moon-Neptune aspects symbolize a soft, vulnerable and naïve approach. Thus Mars-Pluto natives tend to find themselves confronting intense, conflictive circumstances; whereas Moon-Neptune natives find their environments gentler and more sympathetic to their endeavors.

It is the aspects (rather than the strength factors) which are responsible for the recurrence effect: the fact that the same situations tend to happen again and again in a native's life – such as the fact that women who have been raped once are five times as likely to be raped again as are women who have never been raped. Or, for another example, in the cases of Thomas Alva Edison and Woody Guthrie catastrophic fires at different times in their lives completely changed their directions.

Configurations can be considered to be complex aspects – i.e., aspects which involve three or more planets. As might be supposed, configurations symbolize a more complex type of social interaction than do simple aspects. They even seem to take on a life of their own in the sense that they can be analyzed and described without reference to the particular planets involved. Their usefulness in horoscope delineation lies in the fact that they tend to tie a chart together by providing a central theme or game plan for the chart as a whole.

What aspects and configurations show is how people organize themselves and their lives, pull themselves together, gird themselves for action (or dissipate themselves). And, because people create their own realities, aspects and configurations also show how the world organizes itself around them (whether collaboratively or implacably or something in between). Aspects and configurations show both how a native acts in the world and how the world reacts – it's the native's road show, the basic script they've written which they keep repeating over and over. It shows both the *Sturm und Drang* of a native's particular life and also how the native adapts to it, creates it, struggles against it, or wallows in it.

What all configurations (and aspects) show is the *tenor* of the life – not so much the mood (shown by planets in signs of ruler / detriment, exaltation / fall) or expectation (positive or negative – shown by angular / cadent planets). Aspects refer more to outer circumstances, how the native takes other people and the circumstances of his or her life. What this means is harmony / disharmony with surroundings and other people; satisfaction / dissatisfaction with self and environment; whether the person is at home within him/herself or at war with him/herself; whether the native is calm and unruffled or bristling and bustling. Is the native basically accepting, light, and breezy; or is he or she suspicious, combative, easily frustrated, and affronted? What is his or her stance towards the world around them: relaxed or guarded, indifferent or possessive? Do they attempt to fit in; or go their own way?

The well-aspected / afflicted distinction has to do with basic approach to everyday life – as an easy swim, or as a "gird your loins and wade in there" battle. Harmonious / inharmonious aspects and configurations refer to adjustment, adaptation, and attunement to the social environment. It's a phony form of attunement, since it has nothing to do with how at peace one is in one's own heart (that's what aspects show in the Generalized Planetary Hours system), but rather how at peace one is with one's neighbors, society, etc. The aspects and configurations show outer success rather than inner worth.

Which came first – the chicken, or the egg? Do the things that happen to us condition us into becoming the people we are; or, does being the people we are attract the "outside" events which will reflect the karmic choices we've already made ("before" we were born)? The astrological equivalent of "You create your own reality" is expressed as "Character is Destiny"; the point being that who we are, and the things which happen to us, are not essentially different but are merely two sides of the same coin (innate psychological propensities are going to attract certain types of recurring life experiences, which can be read in the natal horoscope. Every horoscope tells a story).

Note that aspects manifest both in terms of personality and in terms of circumstances and events in a life. In this book we shall focus on the "Character" aspect of this identity since personality traits are unitary and simple to describe (the brief interpretations for each aspect in the horoscope given in this book are like snapshots – or better said, caricatures

– of the native at different times, responding to different stimuli); whereas the ways in which "Destiny" can unfold are multitudinous and can take many different possible forms (and in any case, are usually indicated more by the astrological houses than the aspects). Charles Carter does a commendable job of discussing this point in his book *The Astrological Aspects*. The emphasis in this book is on the Character rather than the Destiny because of the paucity of examples of natives whom the author knows quite well. While it is possible to obtain a feel for what a person's character is like without knowing them intimately, in order to learn the details of that person's family and personal history – the events in that person's life, the traumas, joys, successes, failures, hopes and fears – requires considerable familiarity with them. Where the author has seen sufficient examples of circumstantial correlations with aspects – particularly where they accord with astrological tradition – then these will be mentioned. Note that by using intuition it is often possible to deduce specifics from the abstract symbols – for example, that since the Moon symbolizes the mother, the public, health, and travel, then Moon afflicted by Mars in a given horoscope indicates a dysfunctional mother; or public rejection and humiliation; or ill health; or dangerous journeys. In the case of Theodore Roosevelt who had natal Moon opposition Mars, all of the above interpretations were true at one time or another in his life (but he prevailed against all adversity by sheer willpower, since both Moon and Mars were strong by zodiacal sign).

It is assumed that the reader is sufficiently conversant with traditional astrological lore to recognize the types of situations and relationships which are symbolized by the planets in combination (any horary astrology textbook contains this information). Specific prediction depends upon intuition – starting from an understanding of Character – since there are too many possible ways that Destiny can manifest in the material world to be able to arrive at correct conclusions using deductive reasoning alone.

What is meant by a native's "Character"? Who is that person? Consider a woman: her children pay attention to her (have certain expectations of her) in a certain way; her husband pays attention to her in another fashion; her mother, the clerk in the supermarket, the cop who catches her for speeding, the neighbor who can scarcely conceal his lust for her, the evangelist who wants to convert her, the IRS agent who wants to audit her tax returns, all have different expectations of her, pay different kinds of attention to her; and as a result see her and act on her in different ways. So who is *she*? And who does *she* think *she* is when she is primping herself before the mirror for her lover; as opposed to when she is feeling hurt and shame and anger at having been rejected? What exactly does the horoscope tell us about this person? *Who* is this person? Who are *we*?

As I say in my book *Magical Living*, "Not only does the totality of who 'we' are encompass infinite lifetimes in other worlds and realities (which give rise to our customary moods), it also encompasses infinite probable realities within this present lifetime as well as all those others (which give rise to our customary concerns). Not only that, but within the confines of a single probable reality of a single lifetime, which is all we normally pay attention to or consider to be "ourselves", we are still multiple personalities. That is to say, we are not the same person from moment to moment, but in fact shift from one to another subpersonality or thought form, in response to this or that changing stimulus. The only difference between an Eve, Sybil, or Truddi and the rest of us is that their slips are showing: they're acting out the multiple personality role openly, whereas the rest of us are marching around with our dress uniforms – our fear of going crazy – buttoned down tight.

"Most of what we consider to be 'ourselves' – that is, the thoughts, feelings and perceptions which occupy our conscious minds most of the time we are awake; our sense that there is a continuing 'us' there – is just a collection of habits and predilections learned from our parents and society. Each of our habitual thoughts, reactions, beliefs, etc. is a thought form – a learned behavior which is a being in its own right (some authors, such as Richard Dawkins and Daniel Dennett, have used the term *memes* instead of *thought forms*). Most of what we think *we* think, believe, or perceive is actually just what our parents and society think, believe, or perceive; and these thoughts, beliefs, and perceptions have an awareness, a sense of selfhood, and a will to live all their own. We create them with our decisions and we breathe the breath of life into them with our attention."

We can consider that the astrological aspects provide a model to describe a person's customary moods and customary concerns – the matrices which tend to crank out thought forms of a given type (e.g. depressed, giddy, rapacious, passive, irresponsible, angry, lecherous, etc.) which are symbolized by the planets in combination. NOTE: A person does not manifest all of his or her thought forms at the same time, but typically will have Venus trine Jupiter days and Mars square Saturn days (which presumably can be identified to some extent via astrological prediction). Different aspects to the same planet don't contradict – they merely show different "aspects" or facets of the personality. For example, Moon-Venus aspects show how well integrated (or at war within self) the native's anima – or feminine side – is; this is projected outwardly as relationships with women. If Moon squares or opposes Venus this indicates disorder within the person's anima reflected in conflictive relationships with the principle women in the native's life. However, if for example Venus also conjoins North node, then blessings will flow to the native from women; but not necessarily mother-sister-wife-daughter (not the principle relationships).

The reason why I am so enamored of William Faulkner's novels is that he had a genius for portraying his characters in all their complexity, and plumbing their motives to the depths. For example, Faulkner frequently portrayed bad guys (such as Christmas and Popeye) as apparently unmitigated bastards for most of the novel; then suddenly he'd turn things around and show the reader what those guys' childhoods were like; or reveal what was *really* going on under the surface of their supposedly villainous acts; and then the reader understands why these people did what they did: that this is how they learned to deal with their own victimization.

In astrological interpretation there is also the problem of denial. For example, Moon conjunct or opposed Mars or Saturn often points to issues of anger, hurt, or abandonment with the mother; but the native can be repressing these feelings on a conscious level – because he or she fears the mother; or is trying to protect the mother from herself (is in denial to abet the mother's denial). In my book *Topics in Astrology* I discuss sexual signatures in synastry – the horoscope factors which indicate strong sexual attraction between two people (namely a man's Sun, Mars, or Jupiter conjunct or opposed to a woman's Moon or Venus). But, particularly in our sexually-repressed society, it often happens that there is never any open manifestation of what is actually going on "beneath the surface" (that this sexual attraction becomes conscious). The point is that the horoscope indicates potentials – probable realities (what W. B. Yeats termed "*Body of Fate*") – rather than concrete events. The horoscope reveals what is happening on an emotional level; but the extent to which a person is in denial about his or her own feelings is the extent to which these horoscopic indications remain latent (and the extent to which the astrologer's deductive predictions regarding same will be off base).

When interpreting the charts of natives with horoscopic indications of emotional repression (such as Sun conjunct Mercury or Venus conjunct Saturn) combined with indications of violent anger (such as Mars conjunct Saturn or Pluto), then what often happens is that these natives employ passive-aggressive tactics to provoke other people to rage at them openly while they themselves play the innocent victims of unwarranted aggression. In other words, these natives project their inner anger outward onto other people rather than express it openly themselves. This possibility complicates the process of horoscope interpretation: people in denial will always deny, but this doesn't mean that the indications in their horoscopes are incorrect.

Always keep in mind that the horoscope is filtered through the experience and prejudices of the astrologer who interprets it; and if you aren't intimate with the native, how would you know if you're interpreting the thing correctly (except by using intuition)? Intuition is the only way to cut through the morass of symbols to arrive at a correct understanding of who the native is *at this moment* and what their actual problem is (beneath the denial). All astrological technique is merely reaching for intuitive understanding. There is no way that the process of astrological interpretation can be computerized: the reason why computer-generated astrological reports are so useless is because no distinction is made between what is important and what is not. This is also the bane of neophyte astrologers attempting to make sense out of the morass of symbols present in a horoscope. A word to the wise: simplify; simplify; simplify. Look at what is most important (overall configurations and the aspects which compose them) and branch out from there (strength factors).

While there is almost universal accord amongst astrologers as to what the symbols mean (e.g. what Mars symbolizes; or the trine aspect; or the 2nd house), there are a wide variety of approaches to interpreting horoscope charts as a whole. Dr. Marc Edmund Jones promulgated various techniques (of which the Temperament Type is the best-known) for grasping the underlying emotional dynamics of the chart / person as a whole; and then isolating the factors (which he termed "Focal Determinators") which make that chart / person special. My own books attempt to do much the same thing, but with a somewhat different approach – using configurations and aspects rather than Temperament Types to assess the general situation, to get a feeling for who that person is in terms of their social context – what they are out to accomplish; and then using strength factors to highlight what is unique and distinctive about that person.

Note that in all this analysis we are looking at the person – the woman in our example – as a *social* being. She is also a spiritual being, with a particular karma and destiny which have nothing whatever to do with the social context into which she was born and conditioned, and in terms of which she developed her own response to the pressures brought to bear upon her. To see a person in the horoscope as a spiritual being, it is necessary to resort to other techniques (in conventional horoscopy, looking at the Moon and its paraphernalia: the nodes, critical degrees, lunar phase angle, Part of Fortune; in the horoscopy of the future, in terms of Generalized Planetary Hours horoscopes).

> "There are no 'good' or 'bad' people. Some are a little better or a little worse but all are activated more by misunderstanding than malice. A blindness to what is going on in each other's hearts. Nobody sees anybody truly but all through the flaws of their own egos. That is the way we all see each other in life."
>
> – TENNESSEE WILLIAMS

Planets

The Sun and Moon refer to the native's individual destiny and karma, respectively (*Will*).

Mercury, Venus, and Mars refer to the native's personal relationships with the people in his or her immediate environment (*Body of Fate*), and have particular reference to childhood and youth.

Jupiter and Saturn refer to the native's ideals and obligations (respectively): his or her role in greater society (*Mask*), and have particular reference to adulthood and middle age.

Uranus, Neptune, and Pluto refer to the native's response to the *Zeitgeist* or spirit of the time in which he or she lives (*Creative Mind*), and have particular reference to old age.

In this book we will use the following keywords to describe the activity of the planets; these can provide a useful mnemonic for interpreting the effects of the planetary combinations:

Sun symbolizes the native's sense of PURPOSE;
Moon symbolizes the native's sense of ASSURANCE;
Mercury symbolizes the native's MENTALITY;
Venus symbolizes the native's ENJOYMENT;
Mars symbolizes the native's sense of ACCOMPLISHMENT;
Jupiter symbolizes the native's UNDERSTANDING;
Saturn symbolizes the native's sense of RESPONSIBILITY;
Uranus symbolizes the native's sense of INDEPENDENCE;
Neptune symbolizes the native's INTUITION;
Pluto symbolizes the native's CLARITY.

Zodiacal Aspects

"The key to a native's intelligence is found in a study of his oppositions, exactly as a key to his point of view and natural slant upon things will be found in his parallels, and the key to his spontaneous activities and his capacity for performance will be found in his conjunctions."

– Marc Edmund Jones, Pythagorean Astrology

Table of Keywords for Zodiacal Aspects

aspect	glyph	(per Makransky)	(per M. E. Jones)
Conjunction (0°)	☌	Focus (intent)	Activity
Opposition (180°)	☍	Awareness (intelligence)	Awareness
Trine (120°)	△	Stasis (stability)	Creation
Square (90°)	□	Change (conflict)	Construction
Sextile (60°)	✶	Expansion (opportunity/ism)	Production

Here the term "zodiacal aspects" will be limited to the Ptolemaic five (unless otherwise noted) – conjunction, opposition, trine, square, and sextile; and we will arbitrarily adopt 6° orbs of allowable inexactitude in measuring these (however, when I was writing the aspect interpretations in this book, I would sometimes describe an aspect and then think, "Hmmm. This sounds just like Joe." And, upon checking Joe's horoscope, sure enough – he had that aspect, but with an orb of 8° or 9°. This wide-orb effect is most noticeable in aspects which are part of an overarching configuration).

The aspects can be considered to be social roles which provide people with a sense of personal recognition and continuity; as if to say to oneself (by saying to others): "Oh yes, that's who I am! I'm the puckish one – the vulnerable one – the coolheaded one – the shy one – the tough one – the detached one – the jolly one – the serious one – the bullheaded one" – etc. etc. Aspects represent a way of validating oneself by inducing other people to react in some wonted fashion; by contrast, Mutual Receptions and parallels of declination are more abstract, less dependent upon exacting some stock reaction from others (although they do provoke one, that is not necessarily the primary aim).

Aspects reveal how natives move to occupy space – how they spread themselves out in their social environment. Afflicted indications show a war going on with other people and / or the environment; well-aspected indications show ease, acceptance, complacency with regard to other people and the ambience. The reason why the same sorts of experiences tend to recur in a given life is because they are being called up from the same customary moods. People keep making the same decisions and responses over and over; and this brings forth similar situations over and over. The aspects reveal the shaping, this way and that, of natives' characteristic modes of act and reaction.

Sextiles and trines indicate easy, breezy circumstances and relationships. Squares are invariably unfortunate, whereas oppositions can be beneficent (especially when the conjunction is disharmonious – in that case the opposition can be quite favorable).

Conjunctions show a way of plowing on ahead, looking neither to the left or right, but focusing attention on the path beneath one's feet. They indicate concentration, resoluteness, fixity, drive, thoroughness, meticulousness, self-possession, and tenacity.

Oppositions symbolize self-consciousness, and show a way of separating oneself from other people – distinguishing oneself from the herd. Oppositions have a facility for distancing themselves in order to obtain a broader, more inclusive point of view (to get on top of the proceedings). Dr. Jones opined that a lack of oppositions "reveals a definite handicap in the life of the native. ... a completely individual responsibility for the basic equilibriums in the life. This can mean either an exceptional opportunity for shaping the destiny according to the native's desire and vision, or a self-ordering in idle fantasy or wishful thinking and thus a drift to certain self-deterioration." Oppositions often reverse the feeling (light fiber) of the conjunction: e.g. if the conjunction signifies levity then the opposition signifies seriousness; if the conjunction is morose then the opposition is cheerful; if the conjunction is vague, the opposition is definite; and so on.

Squares have to create problems where they otherwise wouldn't exist; they are unable to just relax since they must be constantly vigilant. They take a defensive posture and are discontented with their lot. They are antsy, sensitive, easily affronted, combative, and take things very personally.

Trines are aspects of stability in both positive and negative senses: trines take things as they come, and complacently (unquestioningly) accept things as they are. They don't work themselves into a sweat, but lay back and enjoy the scenery. They have an intellectual or theoretical bent, unlike the sextiles, who are movers and shakers. Sextiles are achievers who are adept at spotting and exploiting opportunities, and in general are on the move with clearly defined ambitions and objectives. Where trines (and oppositions) are moral, sextiles (and conjunctions) are amoral.

As noted previously, people don't show all their aspects all the time. They'll have their Venus trine Jupiter days, and also their Mars square Saturn days (or they'll reveal their Venus trine Jupiter or Mars square Saturn aspects with respect to those particular situations and relationships indicated by these planets' house positions in the natal horoscope).

In general, the best magicians have the fewest aspects. This is because, while other people *can* be manipulated by flaunting some sort of bait at them, in fact the role-playing symbolized by the aspects entangles the angler as much as the fish. Heavily aspected charts symbolize being pinned down into lots of stereotyped roles – being overly dependent upon other people for validation (or rejection, as the case may be) for a sense of self and effectiveness (or helplessness).

By contrast, natives with few aspects are more free-spirited, less encumbered by the baggage of social role-playing, more fluid and capable of being "who" they need to be in a given situation in order to dominate and control it. They are more capable of picking up nuances and capitalizing upon this gut-level knowledge than are natives with lots of aspects, who are compelled to be puckish; or compelled to be vulnerable; or compelled to be coolheaded (whether or not that's what the actual situation requires).

Preponderance of aspects (18 or more with 6° orbs – i.e. at least thrice the allowable orb in degrees): As is usually the case when considering the preponderance vs. absence of any astrological factor, a preponderance of aspects indicates a sense of weight, heaviness, obligation; whereas paucity shows a lightness of spirit: the ability to pull up roots and transplant oneself readily – like Pinocchio, "no strings on me". When there are relatively many zodiacal aspects in a horoscope, the native is spurred to action by a concatenation of causes. Aspects may be thought of as patterns of activity, habitual modes of action and reaction. Therefore, if there are many aspects it means that there are many such patterns: these natives are rigid and possess a strong need for organization – everything in its place. You tend to reduce your daily life to a set of routines and feel rather put out by the unexpected. You don't mind – indeed seemingly welcome – the feeling of being stressed and under pressure; and you are most at home when you are running hither and thither attending to this and that. You have lots of attachments and expectations of other people; as a result, your relationships usually involve struggle: you demand that other people fit in to your prescribed slots and fulfill your personal images of them; and you can be extremely severe and sharp-tongued when they fail. You tend to be distrustful and insecure: you feel a need to justify – at least to yourself – everything that you do. In consequence you lack spontaneity: you tend to be overly cautious, reflecting carefully and taking every possible scenario into account before acting. You carry an air of care-worn weariness – like Atlas, you carry the world on your shoulders.

Few aspects (6 or fewer with 6° orbs – i.e. fewer than the allowable orb in degrees): On the other hand, when there are relatively few aspects in a horoscope, then there are relatively few fixed patterns of activity in your life, so you act in the most simple, direct mode possible. This is not to say that you can't be thoughtful and calculating; but rather that what you eventually do in any given situation is not the product of internal rumination but of knee-jerk reactivity. You are spontaneous, adaptable, flexible, daring, and open to new experience. You are confident in yourself and your ability to meet and deal with new situations. Your relationships are less of a problem since you are emotionally independent and have few attachments to or expectations of people; or at least you do not depend on them to fulfill your images. You are light-hearted, cocky, and cavalier; and when you crash (as you invariably do unless it's all sextiles and trines so you can get away with it), you are able to just shrug things off and try your luck once again (not take misfortune as a personal failure). You always act automatically, or by reflex, so once someone has gotten to know you well they can usually predict exactly how you will behave in any given situation.

When there is a **preponderance of applying aspects** (and by "applying" is meant that the difference in longitudes of the two planets involved – irrespective of signs – is decreasing; i.e., that at the moment of birth they are moving towards completing the aspect), what is shown is a nascent thirst for experience which motivates you in all you do. You are eager and optimistic, and willing to try new activities and to learn new ways of doing things. You take a window-shopping approach to situations which keeps your ego intact even when your (at times) rampant enthusiasm leads you to make serious mistakes. You just pick yourself up, dust yourself off as if nothing had happened, and hurl yourself back into the fray.

When there is a **preponderance of separating aspects** (so that the two planets involved are moving away from the aspect) what is shown is a feeling of ennui or world-weariness, or at least a sense of past history. You are apt to stick to modes of act and reaction which you have found to be tried and true. You may be quite aware that some of the things you do might be done in some ultimately better way, but you feel that it's all been settled long ago as far as you are concerned. You have an air of Eeyoresque pessimism, as if you were carrying some inescapable burden through life or were living under a perpetual black cloud.

Orbs

Although in the discussion of individual aspects we (quite arbitrarily) use a cut-off point of 6 degrees of inexactitude, for the analysis of configurations we will employ rather wider orbs than usual, because the idea is to see relationships in the horoscope. We will allow seventeen degrees orb of inexactitude when the Sun is involved in an aspect; twelve and a half degrees when the Sun isn't but the Moon is; and ten degrees when neither the Sun nor Moon participates in the aspect. Observe, however, that this is but a rule of thumb: for example, one can discern a Grand Trine effect when there are three bodies located in all three signs of a given triplicity, even if they are way out of orb. With respect to Grand Sextiles, 5/6, Grand Squares, and Grand Trines in particular, it isn't necessary to be exigent: it is more important to identify relationships and understand who a person is than adhere to some arbitrary rule. The important point is to tie things together.

The foregoing assignation of orbs is congruent with Dr. Marc Edmund Jones' usage; and it is not too different from that of traditional astrologers such as Morinus (the founder of modern astrology). As Geoffrey Dean explained in *Recent Advances in Natal Astrology*, "At sunset they observed that the planets became visible only when the Sun had sunk about 18 degrees below the horizon. Therefore they concluded that the Sun's orb was a fraction less, i.e. about 17 degrees. If a planet became visible on the horizon after sunset when the Sun had sunk about 10 degrees, the orb for that planet was then 17 − 10 = 7 degrees. In this way curiously precise orbs were defined that varied according to visibility, for example:"

Year	Author	SU	MO	ME	VE	MA	JU	SA
1000 AD	Taijak	15	12	7	7	8	9	9
1600 AD	Morinus	18	12	8	13	6½	8	7

Obviously, what configurations are present in a given horoscope is very much a function of what orbs you decide to use, since a slight difference in allowable orbs will often make a huge difference in which configurations exist. As Dr. Jones pointed out,

"It must be remembered always that the analyst is working out of the natural set of his own mind. He will use the tendencies of judgment with which he classifies to go on into his analysis, and hence he is not apt to go far afield if he is basically competent. The purpose of the over-all perspective primarily is to serve his mental processes. ... The astrologer need not worry over the correctness of his identification when ... in doubt because, as long as he ... (can) see ... one of the types, it will unerringly reveal its whole nature. ... Interpretation is always of a life that someone is living in a very real context, and the astrologer has the task of revealing the potentialities of character in this context in relation to actual events and in accordance with values inherent in both the person and the person's situation."

In other words, it doesn't matter all that much how you look at the chart, what shapings or configurations you see in it, as long as you see something which you can peg your interpretations to. It's rather like looking at abstract art, and just seeing something in it that is meaningful in the sense that it provides you with a *feeling* (this is a point to which Geoffrey Dean took violent exception regarding Dr. Jones' philosophy of interpreting horoscopes. And I take violent exception to Dean's critique of Jones here, since after all, a change in orbs isn't about to turn a Grand Sextile into a Grand Square – i.e. the underlying aspect structure doesn't undergo radical alteration by admitting wider orbs). The fact is that the "science" of astrology – when all is said and done – is merely a system of thought designed to stimulate intuition. This is the reason why it is often possible to make accurate predictions from an incorrect horoscope (e.g. incorrectly calculated for am instead of pm). Again, there is no right way or wrong way to interpret a horoscope, which is why so many different techniques flourish and are found practicable by their devotees.

With respect to the question of orbs, Dr. Jones described an intriguing technique in *Pythagorean Astrology* which I have not yet experimented with, but which deserves a mention:

"The first rule is that every planet must be in aspect with every other planet, and that only the aspect which is closest in degrees of value is to be taken. The second rule is that conjunctions, oppositions, trines, squares and sextiles only shall be carried out to the extreme orb necessary to create an aspect between any two particular planets. The third rule is that semi-squares, semi-sextiles, quincunxes, and sequiquadrates shall be given preference if closer than the aspects given above, but not if of the same value, and never if necessary to use more than a five-degree orb. The fourth rule is that quintiles, septiles, and all more obscure aspects shall not be considered if more than three degrees separate the planets creating these aspects. The fifth rule is that no more than a degree and a half shall be taken for a parallel, and that some other aspect in addition shall always be taken between any two planets that happen to be in parallel."

Dr. Jones' point is that, "From the standpoint of life the man who masters his wide aspects is as already suggested creating a subjective and eternal being, whereas the individual who is only able to respond to his close squares and trines is obviously in bondage to the passing outer realm of objects."

Well-Aspected vs. Afflicted

Hightly afflicted horoscopes refer to natives who are in a great deal of pain. Of course, the events in these natives' lives will usually be more traumatic than average; and deductions can be made as to how these traumas will actually occur in a given life based upon the particular planets and houses involved in the afflictions. However, it is not always true that the natives' lives are so traumatic, particularly if there are counterbalancing indications (other, favorable configurations; many planets strong by sign; many planets conjunct fixed stars etc.). Rather, afflicted horoscopes symbolize internal pain. As Viktor Frankl put it, suffering is like a gas which expands to fill the available space: whether we are only suffering a little, or whether we are suffering a great deal, we believe that we are suffering horribly. Natives with highly afflicted horoscopes regard themselves as suffering horribly, no matter what the actual facts of the case are – no matter how rich or successful they may be, they believe they are suffering greatly.

Note that some natives consciously repress (deny) the fact of their pain; on a conscious level they may tell themselves and other people that they are happy. But on an operational level – the level on which they actually are making their moment-to-moment and day-by-day choices in accordance with their customary moods and customary concerns; on the level of what they lie sleeplessly at night contemplating – they choose pain, whether they consciously permit themselves to feel this pain or not. Denial is always a welcome option – especially when Mercury is near the Sun.

Conversely, largely well-aspected horoscopes refer to natives who don't find life to be basically problematical. These natives are more self-accepting and accepting of other people, hence they tend to find themselves in pleasant rather than painful situations and relationships. Even their failures are less stressful than those of natives with afflicted horoscopes: natives with well-aspected horoscopes don't take things so personally; they don't glory so much in triumph nor take setbacks and rejections to heart.

"Afflicted" charts or "well-aspected" charts are more than just a matter of aspect ratios. Structure is all-important (Grand Trines, Kites, T-Crosses, etc.) – you have to look at the complete chart, not simple ratios of good or bad aspects. Grand Trines, Kites, Trapezoids, T-Crosses, etc. have more to do with whether a given chart, as a whole, is afflicted or well-aspected, than do aspect ratios. Classificatory schemes (such as computerized horoscope interpretations) should be developed based on structure rather than aspect ratios. A straight, unweighted percentage of harmonious versus inharmonious aspects is a misleading indicator because it is evident that some combinations are intrinsically more important than others – e.g. Sun conjunct Jupiter is more powerful than Venus sextile Pluto; and Mars opposition Saturn is more powerful than Mercury square Jupiter. Aspects which compose important configurations (such as Grand Trines and T-Crosses) are more influential than simple aspects by themselves. Also, for most of the past century Neptune has been sextile Pluto, so a typical population sample will be biased in favor of harmonious aspects.

One might say that the difference between well-aspected and afflicted is the difference between eager anticipation and eager expectation. Well-aspected entails knowing how to wait patiently, and then to strike while the iron is hot; whereas afflicted means riding a roller-coaster of eager expectation and crushing disappointment – the only purpose of the expectation is to bring on the disappointment (it's a completely self-defeating stand). Well-aspected horoscope natives know how to wait (anticipate) calmly, with little worry or pother, little sense of ego-stake in the outcome of anything. If something he or she is pursuing crashes, they just go on to something else – they don't get into a big stew about anything. Eager anticipation doesn't cling to one certain outcome, but knows that there will always be other opportunities on other days.

Whereas afflicted horoscope natives always have a clear mental picture of precisely what they want, and whom; and if things don't turn out precisely as he or she envisioned, then they feel put out and ripped off by life. They take setbacks very much to heart, as if the whole universe was just out to hassle *them*. Afflicted chart natives seek conflict and disappointment; whereas well-aspected chart natives prefer calm and ease.

As is the case with most good/bad distinctions in astrology, well-aspected charts are good for material things, whereas afflicted charts are good for spiritual things. The spiritual path (like everything else in life) would be simple for natives with well-aspected charts, but they generally lack the motivation to pursue spiritual ends because they're quite comfortable with things as they are. Conversely, while natives with very afflicted charts find the spiritual path as thorny and heartbreaking as anything else in life, they are nonetheless advised to go for broke for the spiritual, because they'll never find any repose in the material world.

> "It must be noted that any configuration may be considered good or bad from two points of view – happiness and achievement. The benefic planets and aspects undoubtedly are most favourable to the former, but they are by no means good for success or attainment, in and by themselves, since they incline to tranquil and uneventful conditions and the less noble alternative of the 'Choice of Herakles'. On the other hand, a horoscope almost entirely dominated by the malefic planets and by inharmonious aspects will, as a rule, break the native through repeated obstacles and misfortunes. Hence, for achievement, a mixed map is best, affording both opportunity and incentive. ... It stands to reason that, since to achieve anything notable is *ex hypothesi* difficult, the map of the man who does this must contain difficult elements."
>
> CHARLES CARTER, THE ASTROLOGICAL ASPECTS

Parallels and Contraparallels of Declination

Much of life is a struggle to find the proper balance between conforming to society's expectations on the one hand, and freely expressing our own feelings on the other. Our socialized behavior brings us the acceptance and approval of other people, but it provides us with none of the inner satisfaction and joy of feeling that we are valuable beings in our own right. Our personal happiness depends upon both types of assurance: knowing that we are members in good standing of our social group, and knowing that we are unique individuals in the cosmic scheme of things.

The first imperative – the need for emotional validation in a social context – is symbolized by the zodiacal aspects. Aspects reveal areas of adjustment (or lack of the same) between the individual and his or her social environment. The planetary impulses at work operate on a level of socially-conditioned beliefs (fitting in or rebelling). We use these planetary energies in the way our parents and society have taught us to use them. They are creative energies, but they are constrained by the values and judgments of our social milieu and the times in which we live.

The second imperative is the need for emotional validation as a divine being (apart from the opinions of other people), which is symbolized by the parallels (and contraparallels – we will use the general term "parallels" to indicate both) of declination – here taken with a maximum of 1° orb of inexactitude. The parallels reveal a sense of specialness unto self; they go off on their own to find an individual answer to some question in life which the zodiacal aspects address in a conventional, stereotyped, and therefore rather sterile fashion. The parallels exemplify an ideal of individualistic effort – blazing a new trail all alone. They symbolize those areas of life marked by a touch of personal distinctiveness.

In the parallels we have combinations of planetary energies operating in unconditioned fashion, on a level of intuition and feeling rather than one of concepts and thinking. We know how to use these energies without ever having been taught. We use them to express what is in our hearts rather than what is in our minds. Therefore, a parallel shows an inherently more satisfying use of planetary energies than an aspect does. We can thus say that the parallels are of a benefic nature, although they do tend to isolate us within ourselves (cut us off in this area of life from the rituals of reward and punishment which animate most of the people around us).

For present purposes we will consider two planets to be in parallel if the difference in their declinations does not exceed one degree. Contraparallels – two planets within the same degree of declination but with one planet north and the other south of the equator – are also considered to be in aspect if the difference in declinations does not exceed 1°. Contraparallels between two planets are similar in meaning to oppositions: both of these aspects are somewhat more abstract, intellectualized, and objective as compared to the parallels and conjunctions between the planets. Contraparallels are a bit more romantic, idealistic, or whimsical than parallels (which are thoroughly practical and earthy). When both a parallel or contraparallel and a zodiacal aspect exist between the same pair of planets (except, perhaps, for Sun and Mercury which are usually both), you should consider this planetary combination to be of particular importance and interest in the native's life. E.g., look at the houses they are in.

Preponderance of Parallels: Natives who have many parallels in the horoscope (nine or more) are emotionally self-contained individuals who tend to seek isolation. Albeit you are superficially agreeable and pleasing, your natural instinct is to avoid other people or to push them away. You are often self-conscious in social situations because social poise doesn't come naturally to you: you feel you have to fake it somehow (and you are not very adept at phoniness). Thus you shy away from the social commitments and entanglements which people with no parallels eagerly seek out and enjoy. To others you may seem like an oddball, or a real character. You are hypersensitive to encroachment on your private space, and you take an oblique view of your fellows: suspicious, cynical, superior. On the other hand, you have a deep sense of personal integrity. Attuned to your own inner convictions rather than to social acceptance, you are hard-working, thorough, and conscientious.

Absence of Parallels: Natives who have no parallels in their horoscopes are sociable, outgoing, and demonstrative. You go into social relationships in a breezy, nonchalant, matter-of-fact way, and you always make yourself comfortably at home in any circumstances. You seek your own equilibrium by keeping on top of your social milieu in some sort of wonted role (which depends upon what is going on with your aspects) which allows you to fly on autopilot. Whatever part you play to dominate your social environment, you can usually make everyone around you accept you more or less on your own terms (or if your horoscope is afflicted, reject you on your own terms), and thus give you whatever special indulgence you desire. On those occasions when this support system of other people fails you, you feel totally lost, betrayed, and bewildered. You are at your best when you are onstage holding everyone's rapt attention.

Disposition

When planet A is located in a sign ruled by planet B, then B is said to dispose of A. The disposition of a planet symbolizes the orientation of that personality trait vis à vis the prevailing cultural mores; hence it is an indicator of conformity. Disposition has to do with constraints which are put on natives' freedom of action, and the balance between their public and private selves. A planet in good aspect with its dispositor indicates ability to accept the world as given and to play his or her own part in it – at least superficially. A planet afflicted by its dispositor feels like an outsider looking in: there is a difficulty in fitting oneself into the prevailing social norms, but at the same time a lack of initiative in striking out on one's own. Therefore, affliction with dispositor leads to a feeling of being trapped and helpless.

When considering zodiacal aspects one should look at whether one planet disposes of the other, or which is stronger by zodiacal sign or angularity in order to get a grip on precisely how that combination of planetary energies will combine – whether one tendency will prevail over the other, or if they are both strong, or both weak.

When no planets in a horoscope aspect their dispositors the natives do pretty much as they please, and possess little social ambition or need to justify their actions to themselves or anybody else. They are independent, aloof, spontaneous, eccentric, headstrong, self-assured, and explorative. They are always ready to try something new just for the hell of it, with no expectations.

Natives with a preponderance of planets conjunct their dispositors make their own rules and create their own world. They have very private personalities with little concern for what other people think of them. They are driven by a need for power and a sense of complete control over their world and the people in it. They both offer and demand total loyalty.

Natives with a preponderance of planets in good aspect to their dispositors are content to conform to social expectations outwardly while maintaining their inner independence. They are content to follow the well-trodden path (at least externally) because it really doesn't matter one way or the other – these planets obtain their satisfaction privately. These planets indicate worldly ambition and diligence which is duly rewarded by society.

Natives with a preponderance of planets which are afflicted by their dispositors are apt to feel like outsiders, no matter how hard they try to play by the rules. They are not content to follow established paths since they don't feel comfortable or part of the proceedings. They feel a strong need to justify themselves, and they take little pleasure in conventional pastimes and enjoyments. They may be forced by circumstances into unrewarding careers and relationships in which they are the frustrated rebels. They do best as they can to develop alternatives to what they feel they are being pressured into.

Mutual Reception

A Mutual Reception between two planets occurs when they are posited in each other's ruling or exaltation signs. For example, when the Sun is in Cancer or Taurus and the Moon is in Leo or Aries, then the Sun and Moon are considered to be in Mutual Reception. In any zodiacal aspect, the two planetary personality traits work in tandem to secure advantage or protection for the personality as a whole. The major benefic aspects (sextile and trine) symbolize a successful cooperation or clear communication between the planetary principles involved, i.e., one leading to satisfactory results. The malefic aspects (square and opposition) symbolize an unsuccessful cooperation or blocked communication. The conjunction is variable in its effect – benefic when the planets involved are of like or complementary natures, and malefic when they are of contrary or antagonistic natures.

The Mutual Receptions between the planets (hereinafter referred to as MRs) differ from the aspects – even though they can be considered wholly benefic – in that they are more transcendent than the aspects. They symbolize a union of planetary principles which is more self-contained than that of the aspects; they look inward rather than outward to achieve their aims. The aspects symbolize either opportunities or obstacles – something to be seized and manipulated – whereas the MRs symbolize a way of getting through things. They have greater scope or freedom of action than the aspects do because they entail less ego-involvement, less stake in positive or negative outcomes, and less dependence on rewards and punishments as a spur to action. Where the zodiacal aspects symbolize an unconscious, automatic connectedness between different planetary impulses, the MRs symbolize a true joy of collaboration.

The average horoscope will contain one, or perhaps two, pairs of planets in Mutual Reception, whereas it will contain a dozen aspects (with 6°orbs). Thus special attention should be given to the Mutual Reception pairs: these represent at least one area in people's lives in which they have things flowing smoothly and are spiritually attuned to the world around them (for our outer conditions are only a mirror of what is going on inside us).

Preponderance of Mutual Receptions (three or more): You are solid as a rock – very hard to move, and very hard to deflect once in motion. You are introspective and emotionally inaccessible, keeping your distance and maintaining a relatively private life (sharing little of what goes on inside you). You take yourself very seriously, have little objectivity, and can be overly sensitive and solipsistic. You answer to no one but yourself: there is an indefiniteness or cool detachment in your relationships with other people, or a tendency to humor them. You are inaccessible emotionally, keeping your distance; and at your worst you can be extremely wrong-headed and contrary. At your best you possess great determination, and are very concentrated and single-tracked.

Only one possibility of a "Grand Trine in Reception" exists, namely Moon in Pisces, Venus in Cancer, and Jupiter in Taurus, which occurs for a couple of days every 12 years. I know personally of only two such examples, born 6/26/1940 and 7/11/1952; and while such a paucity of examples doesn't lend itself to firm conclusions, my guess would be to say that the Grand Trine in Reception gives an ability to adapt fluidly to circumstances; to not take matters personally; to bounce back quickly after disappointments and tragedies – not as a form of denial or lying to oneself and others, but rather as a true core of inner strength and a cosmic detachment.

Configurations

General Considerations

Amorphous vs. Highly Structured Horoscopes

In a general way, amorphous horoscopes (and those with one, simple configuration such as a Fan, Wedge, or T-Cross) indicate simple people: what you see is what you get; whereas highly structured horoscopes indicate complex, multifaceted people (who are often at war within themselves).

Amorphous Horoscopes: When there are no particular configurations present (which is most likely to occur with Bundle and Bowl Temperament Types) what is indicated is a relative freedom to be and do whatever you please; but at the same time you possess little native motivation or drive. You have a tendency to drift along, to go with the flow, to take little initiative unless prodded, to simply follow in others' footsteps (if there are any footsteps to follow in). This is not to say that you are lazy – you're not at all – but you need direction since you are largely indifferent if left to your own devices. You possess a naturalness and ease of manner which lets you be yourself at all times. You are a simple person (meaning uncomplicated rather than lacking in depth of feeling). You are placid, accepting, and let things pass without comment. Because you are plain-dealing and aboveboard yourself, with little gift for guile, you are nonplussed by subtleties and confused by "politics". Thus while you are friendly and open, you may be a bit eccentric or abstracted – off on your own tangent and unresponsive or unsympathetic (Edgar Allan Poe, the brooding, alcoholic author of the macabre, is a good example). At your worst you are smug, complacent, and fond of a familiar rut. You are not so much unambitious as lacking a sense of urgency – you're in no hurry to get anywhere in particular. You are unabashed and unpretentious, with no need to push yourself to the forefront or prove anything to anybody.

Highly Structured Horoscopes: What is shown when pretty much all the planets are involved in configurations is a more calculated, shrewd, designing mode of self-presentation than amorphous charts. The more structure, the more the native is the prime mover or manipulator in his or her social environment. The native with a highly structured horoscope is like the Stephen Leacock character who "flung himself upon his horse and rode madly off in all directions". You're not necessarily ambitious per se, but you live in a flurry of activity and busyness, and are very intent on yourself and your purposes of the moment. Because you are so headstrong and entirely focused on your own ends, you can be quite gruff, undiplomatic, and blustery – "outta my way, buddy". In relationships you are utterly deaf to anything you don't want to hear, and you will not compromise or be deflected. You are intense, defensive, driven, ill-at-ease and impatient with yourself and other people. You feel a strong need to uphold an image of yourself and make an impression on others, so you are rarely at peace within yourself (less so with lots of trines and sextiles). You need to feel as though you have every base covered, and nothing escapes you. You engage in a constant inner rumination motivated by self-doubt – questioning your motives (less so in triangular charts). You have the capacity for making sudden, drastic changes in your career, lifestyle, beliefs, etc. Your sense of inner balance depends upon constant feedback from others, which can either be back-patting (for the triangular forms) or obstruction and rejection (for the square forms). You are extraordinarily touchy, sensitive, brusque, and tart. You are easily offended, and curtly dismiss anyone who doesn't buy your act. Nonetheless, you are quite a character and make a strong impression on everyone who knows you.

Interpretation when several different configurations are present: When there are several different configurations present in a horoscope which involve basically the same planets, then the meanings of the configurations add to and flavor one another. I have endeavored to illustrate this point in the delineations which follow (i.e., how the interpretations for the more complex forms are "built up" or "blended" from the meanings of their simpler constituent configurations). On the other hand, when there are several different configurations present in a horoscope which involve different planets altogether, then it's more of a Monday-Wednesday-Friday vs. Tuesday-Thursday-Saturday kind of thing.

A good general rule of thumb in astrology is that "contradictory" indications don't contradict – they just manifest at different times, or in regard to different areas of life (as shown by e.g. the houses involved).

Similarly, reinforcing indications tend to "add up" or make the tendency more noticeable and dominant. If there are several recognizable configurations in the chart, pay the most attention to the most complex one (the one involving the most planets). For example, if there is both a Rectangle and a Wedge or Grand Trine, give primary attention to the Rectangle and lesser emphasis to the Wedge or Grand Trine in your interpretation.

Sometimes several different configurations will "aim at" or point to the same planet, which is thereby brought to special prominence. For example, Neptune in the 10th house would rarely be considered an indication of dynamic ambition and drive to succeed; but in Theodore Roosevelt's horoscope the 10th house Neptune is the mediating planet of a Wedge; short leg of an unrelated T-Cross; and one point of a wide Grand Trine in water signs. Thus it is brought to special prominence in both the natal horoscope and the predictions (e.g. transiting Neptune was exactly trine TR's Midheaven two days after he was sworn in as president).

T-Cross same side, opposite side: Compound configurations which contain T-Crosses as a component can be likened to different isomers of the same molecule in that the basic meaning is similar, but when the T-Cross lies on the same side of the opposition as the rest of the configuration then the person is more self-contained, self-cloistering, and prefers to act and work alone; whereas when the T-Cross lies on the opposite side of the opposition then the person is more open, sociable, gregarious, and prefers to act and work with and among other people.

Conjunction Forms

Stelliums

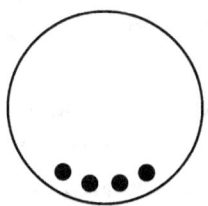

A Stellium is a mass conjunction of at least 4 planets. See whether the adjacent planets combine favorably or not, and whether they are in a good or bad celestial state, to interpret how the Stellium operates (as cheerful stick-to-itiveness or grim, plodding, resignation). Since Stelliums are usually part of larger configurations, look to see what other aspects are made to the Stellium.

You are persistent, tenacious, dogged, and uncomplaining, with a sense of true grit under pressure (real or imagined, depending upon the factors mentioned in the preceding paragraph). You have the ability to hold your own in the face of uncertainty: you are positive and unyielding (with malefics or planets which combine inharmoniously: stubborn, inflexible, clenched up). You possess much depth of character and strength of will, and are able to marshal all your resources to cope with emergencies (hence you are cool and collected under stress). Extremely centered (self-centered), you are like those dolls which are weighted at the bottom so that when they are knocked over they bounce right back up again. Stellium natives tend towards solipsism – fixed within yourself and seeing only your own self-reflection, with little objectivity, scope, or awareness of other people's viewpoints and feelings (which is the negative aspect of your intense powers of concentration and single-mindedness).

You possess a strong sense of dignity and reserve: you keep your own counsel and are somewhat distrustful of other people – or at least you refuse to rely on anyone any more than you absolutely have to. You are secretive and stiffly resent anyone prying into your affairs, or getting too close. You are undemonstrative, with an abstracted, preoccupied air, and you have no need to prove anything to anybody else (just yourself). You are attuned to emotional nuances and take things very personally. It's difficult for you to remain unaffected, to just shake off rejection and failure, to let go of things (such as relationships and possessions). You have good staying power in the face of adversity, and are self-motivated, responsible, and hard-working. Stelliums often appear in horoscopes of geniuses, particularly those working in fields requiring solitary assiduity. You are also moody, broody, and have a dark, self-obsessed side which keeps other people at bay. Louis Pasteur (who had a Stellium in Capricorn in the third house) is an example of a sedulous genius who was also intensely arrogant, combative, secretive, and unjust. You possess a great deal of inner strength and staying power; what you lack is flexibility and adaptability. You have to learn to lighten up and let go.

If the Stellium occurs in a chart with little other structure, you are artless, guileless, and blunt, with great personal integrity and honesty. On the other hand, you are hard to reach, influence, or deflect. You are easily offended and quick to close up into yourself. Albeit pigheaded at your worst, you are also emotionally self-sufficient with a sense of self-esteem which needs little input from others.

If the Stellium occurs in a chart with other structure unrelated to the Stellium then you are breezy, cool, and deft at handling people without becoming emotionally involved or compromised. You are outgoing and sociable without being warm or allowing people to get too close.

If the Stellium occurs as part of other structure in the chart, then you stand on your pride, have firm lines which are not to be crossed, and jealously guard your private space.

Close Pairs

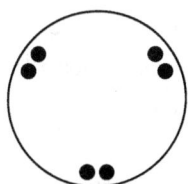

Close Pairs consist of three or more clusters (conjunctions) containing a total of six or more planets. As is the case also with Stelliums, whether the person has an amusing or a grating effect on people depends upon whether the planets in each conjunction combine harmoniously or not (see the Table of Favorable and Unfavorable Planetary Combinations), and whether they are in good or bad celestial state.

Close Pairs reveal a heady freedom of spirit, with a roll-up-your-sleeves, "can-do" attitude. You are spontaneous and unfettered: you talk off the cuff and shoot from the hip (and are quick on the trigger). You are unvarnished and plain-spoken, authentic and real. You're not afraid to call a spade a spade, and you can be quite bluff, blunt, and jarring when speaking your mind. Your indelicacy would tend to get you into trouble were it not for your ability to brazenly stare down and intimidate any would-be adversary. You are very clear mentally and are not fooled by appearances: you can see through (and have little tolerance for) hypocrisy and baloney: you get down to brass tacks with little ado or pother (steamroll over other people). You are completely centered in the now moment – good at taking things as they present themselves, and of making the best use of whatever is available. Dr. Jones describes this as "an unusual capacity both for applying or refining any skills or talents, and for developing a versatility that can win wide approbation. The native always is able to keep the various ramifications of responsibility and self-expression from interfering with each other, and also to give complete and effective attention to whatever may be of importance in any given instance." You are resourceful, flexible, a survivor; like a cat, you always land on your feet. Close Pairs make for good doctors, lawyers, engineers, programmers, etc.

because of their practical, inventive, problem-solving minds. Indeed, the world's first computer program was written in the 1840's by Ada Byron, Countess of Lovelace, who had eight planets arranged in Close Pairs.

Simple Configurations

Simple configurations are those which involve three planets only. They are the basic building blocks from which the compound configurations (involving four or more planets) are built, both geometrically and in terms of interpretation. For example, Rectangles, Kites, and Trapezoids can be considered to consist of two Wedges in different combinations; and they all do have a "Two Wedge" meaning, but with different twists.

The difference between the triangular and square forms (in both simple and compound configurations) is that trine people have got their relationships with other people organized on a truly convenient, superficial level. They're brisk and uninvolved with other people, they avoid conflict and challenge, they don't take setbacks to heart, they're able to pick themselves up and move on to something else, to turn their attention to something which is pleasing, rather than to dwell on the things that make them unhappy. This is also their downfall – they have little tolerance for conscious pain and hence shy from confronting it directly. Square people, on the other hand, have a dig-in-their-heels and tough-it-out stance towards life even when things are going relatively well. They're suspicious of people and circumstances, especially of good fortune; they think there must be some sort of catch to it.

The difference between triangular and square forms is that the former live strategically, flow with the pain; whereas the latter stumble and bumble and struggle against it. Triangular configurations have a facility for transplanting themselves, body and soul, whenever circumstances start getting too sticky or encumbering. Trine is detached whereas square is involved. Triangular configurations avoid getting embroiled in other people's karma; whereas square configurations actively seek to mirror their own inner turmoil in relationships. Trine is loose and easy, whereas square is tense and tight. Triangular configurations let go, whereas square configurations cling.

As might be expected, triangular configurations are better for material things, worldly success and approbation; and square configurations are better for spiritual things. Trines have the ability to make the best of things and not get into too much of an uproar; but they also tend to be complacent, self-satisfied, spiritually lazy. By contrast squares are intense, brusque, jarring, and at war with themselves and their environment, but their discontent is a powerful motive force towards the development of true detachment and wisdom.

All trine configurations indicate natives who are gregarious, voluble, possessing keen analytical minds combined with an irreverent, pixiesque sense of humor. They touch other people very lightly; their presence is like a breath of fresh air. Fans are the most superficially cheerful types: they keep their interactions as frictionless as possible since basically they just want to be left alone, so they put up a mask of sociability. By contrast, 5/6 and Grand Trines truly enjoy being with other people and bring a greater depth to their social interactions.

Triangular Forms

Grand Trines (not involved in a larger configuration)

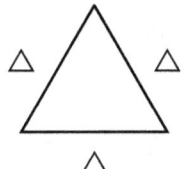

The Grand Trine (120°-120°-120°) symbolizes ease and easiness – inner stability and a facility for weathering any storm (taking things as they come, and being a calming influence on the people around you). You are never at a loss but are quick on your feet with a deft response, a ready retort, a snappy answer to anything. You possess an ironic (sardonic) sense of humor and you are yourself at all times, with nothing to hide or be ashamed of. You remain calm and hold to your own course in the midst of any confusion. You are efficient at handling other people and pursuing your own ends without causing undue fuss or strain. You don't shrink from conflict, but attempt to ameliorate it without making waves or arousing opposition (unlike the Fans who blunder through it or the Wedges who skitter around it). In the case of the passionately eloquent revolutionary purist Maximilien Robespierre (who had a Grand Trine in fire signs), this involved cold-bloodedly eliminating dissent without taking things personally or getting into an emotional tiff. Nonetheless, like the Fan and Wedge types, you are cool and aloof, and don't permit other people to get to you or involve you in their emotional turmoil. You are detached, always maintaining your emotional distance and private space. Other people may complain that you are too distant and impassive in relationships – unwilling to compromise with others, no matter how friendly and superficially sympathetic you may be. You don't take criticism or disappointments to heart, but rather shrug your shoulders and turn your attention toward the things which do seem to be working for you. Even in the face of outside rejection you remain cool, calm, and unruffled – at peace within yourself. You never lose your zest and enthusiasm for life, and your plainspoken candor invites the acquiescence of other people.

As compared with the three other simple configurations (whose descriptions follow), the Grand Trine's embracing of the entire wheel of experience symbolizes a universality of benign interest rather than a pointing in one particular direction (i.e., a point or mediating planet), or a characteristic and specialized modus operandi. You are sociable and outgoing, but you are not driven (as natives of the Grand Square are) to seek approval. Rather, you are able to find a role in the midst of your fellows (symbolized by one of the four elements) in which you can validate yourself. The Grand Trine is the most impersonal, impartial, and just of the simple configurations: at your best you embody a dispassionate nobility of spirit; at your worst you are eccentric and capricious. Dr. Jones said of the Grand Trine,

> "The grand trine or cosmic triangle was considered unfavorable by medieval astrologers because it encouraged a self-diffusion in much the same manner as the Grand Square or X cross. Unless some planet is brought to high focus in a chart containing a grand trine with its subjective emphasis, the scope of experience frequently is narrowed through an unrealized self-pampering. The native escapes this only as he capitalizes on the particular emphasis of his psychological inwardness, such as from the night of time has had convenient identification through a symbolical correspondence with the elements of the ancient physicists. Fire, water, air and earth."

Grand Trine in Fire Signs: This is the mark of a real character – unabashed, flamboyant, ironical and irreverent. You like being in the limelight and holding forth at center stage, and delight in letting it all hang out. Although you can at times play the vain and prissy prima donna, at your best you are able to uplift others with your impish good humor and sense of delight. As Dr. Jones said, "A marked fire emphasis in the horoscope indicates an accentuation of effortless self-adequacy. ... The special genius of these three signs is a capacity for bringing an unimpeachable distinctiveness to some particular and personal manifestation."

Grand Trine in Earth Signs: You are earthy, practical, and self-pacing. You hold to your own orbit without letting yourself be knocked off your stride. You are like the tortoise in the famous race – slow, steady and plodding, but also optimistic and never losing sight of the ultimate goal. You are thorough and dutiful, and enjoy serving others (rather than playing to an audience). While you tend to be overly conservative – even stodgy or fond of that comfortable rut – you are practical and deliberate, and keep on an even keel no matter what's going on around you. Dr. Jones said, "A marked earth emphasis indicates an accentuation of genuine practicality in character. ... The special genius of these three signs is a capacity for standing firm under pressure, and for revealing the fundamental integrity of human nature by championing the right and good."

Grand Trine in Air Signs: You are soft-spoken but masterful; careful in your speech and actions but authoritative once you have made your decision. You are alert, knowing, and quick to pick up on and address openly whatever feelings are in the air. You have a wry sense of humor, which on the negative side can make you overly fascinated with your own perspicacity, and hence dogmatic and opinionated. But you are never at a loss for words, and are a good communicator because of your earnestness, common sense, and insight. In Dr. Jones words, "A marked air emphasis indicates an accentuation of high flexibility in character. ... The special genius of these three signs is a capacity for taking chances or accepting risk, and thereby demonstrating that the resourcefulness of the human spirit is ever fluid in its final effectiveness."

Grand Trine in Water Signs: You are dignified and conscientious, and try to live up to high standards of comportment. You hold your head up high and are not afraid to look anyone in the eye. Your honorableness disposes people to accept you on your own terms, and to indulge you in your quirks and overlook your smug sense of rectitude. You win others over with your high-minded integrity and seriousness of purpose. Dr. Jones said, "A marked water emphasis indicates an accentuation of pure or unquestioning self-completeness. ... The special genius of these three signs is a capacity for a psychological and intellectual reconciliation of every possible sort of divergence or inharmony in human character and affairs."

Grand Trine Across Line of Signs: You do not possess the particular slant or coloration of Grand Trines whose planets are all in the same triplicity, but you have a wider scope and outreach. You are less fixed upon your own designs and more conscious of (and willing to address) the hopes and needs of other people. You are shrewd and convincing, with good communication skills and a facility for manipulating others to your own point of view. You win people over with your openness, idealism, and straightforwardness.

Two Grand Trines (not interlaced):

You are suave, adroit, and fluid: perfectly at ease in – and on top of – any situation in which you may find yourself. You are flexible and adaptable, capable of fitting yourself in to any environment and facing any audience; and without seeming to try to, you soon come to dominate (or at least strongly influence) your milieu. Like the single Grand Trines (all triangular types, actually) you maintain your distance with an impersonal reserve; but in contrast to the spontaneous single Grand Trine types your actions are considered and shrewd. Where the single Grand Trine types are self-validating, you bask in the glow of other people's attention and are adept at manipulating the proceedings your way. And in contrast to the Grand Sextile types, who are balanced within themselves, you seek your equipoise in the approbation you receive from your ambience. You possess a pragmatic point of view, good verbal skills, and are a diplomatic arbitrator and advocate.

Fans

One Fan (only)

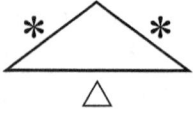

Obviously, single Fans (60°-120°-60°) are most often encountered in Bowl and Bundle Temperament Type horoscopes. You are very simplistic: not in the sense of being unintelligent, but rather naïvely optimistic, ensconced in your own little ivory tower, and oblivious to that which is not true, honest, just, pure, lovely, or of good report. You are not so much other-worldly as not altogether here in this one: you're a bit of a space-out, off on your own tangent, hipped on your own ideas and fixed on your own ends, always buzzing with a bee in your bonnet (which does have its childlike appeal in the proper moment; but can also result in other people not taking you seriously when push comes to shove). Or who knows? Maybe you're the only realistic one and everyone else is being weird, since you usually do manage to get away with what you want (Queen Victoria, who had a Fan with Jupiter point, is a good example). You keep your commitments to other people as convenient and perfunctory as possible. You deal with others impersonally, like shuffling and dealing cards, so people sometimes feel that you brush them and their feelings aside. You tend to gloss over problems rather than grapple with them; for this reason, Fans are often found in the horoscopes of politicians (e.g. Augustus Caesar, Benjamin Disraeli, Benito Mussolini, Nikolai Lenin) for whom expedience is the watchword. This is not to say that you are a shallow or superficial person, or laissez faire, but rather that your first and main concern is yourself and your own goals. Since the world by and large does tend to rearrange itself around you, and other people usually yield to you with little pother on your part, you tend to be smug and complacent, with something of the Great-I-Am about you; nonetheless, this is more good-natured than overweening. You possess a characteristic gift or genius on which you can always pin your hopes; a source of confidence and delight; a pert, saucy, winning quality with which you look other people in the eye to gain their acquiescence (if not support) – which is symbolized by the planet at the handle of the Fan. In the case of a conjunction of two or more planets at the point, use the interpretation for the conjunction, but in its harmonious or favorable sense.

Point Planet(s) of Fan

Sun – You project Confidence: candid, natural, positive, buoyant.

Moon – You project Tenderness: soft, gentle, respectful, solicitous.

Mercury – You project Sincerity: sensible, practical, logical, glib.

Venus – You project Vulnerability: cordial, gracious, soft-spoken, inviting.

Mars – You project Alacrity: jaunty, hearty, unfazed, can-do spirit.

Jupiter – You project Disinterestedness: impartial, altruistic, benevolent, just.

Saturn – You project Integrity: idealistic, honorable, resolute, earnest.

Uranus – You project Irrepressibility: whimsical, lively, independent, elusive.

Neptune – You project Serenity: calm, unbothered, unruffled, blasé.

Pluto – You project Pertinacity: unshakeable, singleminded, steadfast.

Two Fans

On the surface natives with two Fans resemble the single Fan type: idealistic and head-in-the-clouds. But here there is a canniness beneath your wooliness – a method to your madness. Your quixoticism is stylized – not so much feigned as studied or mannered, or performed for the gallery (like John D. Rockefeller ameliorating his rapacious robber-baron image by passing out nickels to waifs in the street). You take an avuncular interest in your fellow bipeds, and you enjoy the role of impartial advisor or arbiter. You have a philosophical detachment which keeps other people at a distance. Like the single Fans you refuse to get involved or committed, not because you are so fixated upon your own devices, but rather because you are above-it-all and refuse to take others (or yourself, even) seriously.

You are not as focused on yourself and your goals of the moment, but rather have an ironically humorous (or at your worst, patronizing) point of view. While by no means lazy, you are not particularly ambitious or (like the single-Fan types) obsessed with your own ends. You don't just barge ahead on spontaneous instinct and blind faith; you consciously play the innocent naif card to your best advantage, to disarm people and render them harmless and pliable. As a result you lack the wholeheartedness of the single Fan type: you don't reveal what you're really thinking and feeling and just barge ahead on instinct, but rather you hold back and watch how people react before you make your moves. But you possess the same devil-may-care panache as the single Fan type, and are usually as successful in getting things and people to bend around you or to give way.

Wedges

One Wedge (only)

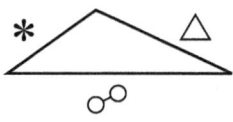

Wedges (60°-180°-120°) are confident, cool, and cheeky; with a facility for making yourself right at home wherever you find yourself. You are frank, simple, candid (outspoken), and aboveboard (not posturing, like T-Cross types); with a simple practicality. You are cocky (also blunt and bluff), and – like all triangular types – smug and self-satisfied. Brisk, efficient, and jaunty, you don't take things to heart but breeze over difficulties (and other people), and don't permit circumstances (or people) get to you or knock you off your pins. You are never disconcerted, but take things in your stride. You prefer to slither around obstacles rather than dig in your heels and confront them directly, as the T-Cross types do; or pretend they don't exist and bluster your way through, as the Fans do. And unlike the oblivious Fan types, you take a realistic and sensible approach to problems and conflicts (indicated by the mediating planet). You are nonplussed by conflict and subtlety, and have an urge to simplify and be out front; but as a result you can be annoyingly unbothered and unreachable.

Where Wedges differ from the Fan types is in your thoughtfulness and need to get an intellectual perspective on your life. The opposition aspect endows the Wedge (and the T-Cross, whose description follows) with a higher degree of self-awareness than the solipsistic Fans or the lofty Grand Trines. You are attentive and reflective (rather than off on your own tangent or above-it-all), and have an idiosyncratic philosophy and a highly original vision and point of view. Beneath the surface you have a wild, maverick streak (e.g. pioneer aviator Charles Lindbergh, who had a Sun-Mars conjunction mediating his Wedge); and a cynical or ironic opinion of your fellow beings; and you can be rather taken with your own cleverness and perspicacity, which on the negative side can make you superior and deaf to other people. You tend to seek a comfortable niche in life in which you are supreme rather than compete with other people, exert yourself unduly, or to actually put your ideals on the line. You are not so much lazy as complacent: you possess a characteristic forte – a winning quality on which you can always rely to finesse around other people and get your own way – which saves you and helps you get by with a minimum of effort on your part; and this ability is symbolized by the mediating planet. In the case of a conjunction of two or more planets at the sextile / trine vertex, use the interpretation for the conjunction, but in its harmonious or favorable sense.

Mediating Planet(s) of Wedge

The source of the natives' conviction – what they rely on; "from whence cometh my help"; their arsenal or bag of tricks; their facility for keeping the "me" out of what they do (where the short leg of a T-Cross shows how the natives inject "me" into what they do).

- **Sun** – you rely on your Authoritativeness: calm, assured, firm, uncompromising.

- **Moon** – you rely on your Instinct: watchful, deliberate, circumspect, knowing.

- **Mercury** – you rely on your Reasonableness: inquisitive, approachable, prudent, fair.

- **Venus** – you rely on your Naturalness: simple, ingenuous, unvarnished.

- **Mars** – you rely on your Resourcefulness: pragmatic, outspoken, doughty, no-nonsense.

- **Jupiter** – you rely on your Idealism: diligent, purposeful, dedicated, humanitarian.

- **Saturn** – you rely on your Dignity: scrupulous, self-possessed, unbothered, untrammeled.

- **Uranus** – you rely on Improvisation: irrepressible, opportunistic, undaunted, self-sufficient.

- **Neptune** – you rely on your Intuition: dispassionate, receptive, original.

Pluto – you rely on your Gumption: thoughtful, discerning, persevering, resolute.

Two Wedges (not involved in larger configuration)

Like the single Wedge type, you are relaxed, natural, and completely yourself at all times, with a down-to-earth pragmatism. But you are more self-conscious than the single type, and concomitantly more conscious of other people, and concerned for their sensibilities. You are politic rather than complacent: two Wedges don't quite "flow" as easily as one because you try hard to please or reach a consensus. You don't take as much for granted as the single types, and thus are a bit less flippant (albeit no less brash, and no less breezily optimistic). Two Wedges are not as self-serving as single Wedges – you are more humane and conscientious. There is a hesitancy here – "Am I doing the right thing?" – which is notably absent in the brassy, sassy single Wedge types. The tendency to seek a niche is heightened: a self-cloistering, which is here more a protection or defensive maneuver than it is a springboard from which to operate (e.g. Friedrich Nietzsche, who had Moon and Neptune mediating his two Wedges, and who in the end retreated into insanity). But you have the same happy-go-lucky geniality and hopefulness.

Square Forms

T-Crosses

One T-Cross (only)

Like the Grand Square, the T-Cross (90°-180°-90°), or *T-Square*, is a configuration of intensity, of holding feelings under tight control. But unlike the Grand Square native, you make no pretense of superficial tranquility to disguise the war going on inside you. Where the Grand Square is pulled in all directions at once, you T-Cross types have one aperture (the short leg) through which all your frustrated energy can be focused.

You are serious-minded and goal-oriented: you possess a grave, unsmiling demeanor and a cool, businesslike manner. You are forthright, bold, and direct, which makes other people pause before crossing you or confronting your no-nonsense intensity (e.g., Oliver Cromwell, who had Jupiter on the short leg). You are concentrated and intent upon the path beneath your feet, and you will not be deflected. In the words of Dr. Jones,

> "What is shown primarily is a simple directness of effort or a persistence of aim and endeavor ... The life tends to be characterized by a practical if varying unification of energies and ends in view (which) brings the interpretation of the wheel to simple and gratifying coherence. ... somebody very definitely trying to be something or to go somewhere in a process of self-discovery."

When you use your considerable force of will creatively – when you put it at the service of your dreams and ambitions – you can accomplish great things in the world by exercising courageous and effective leadership (Albert Einstein, who had Pluto on the short leg, is an example). Thus on the positive side your T-Cross is your dynamic, determined, indomitable, risk-taking side. But there is also a tendency to puff yourself up; to go through empty motions to prove your point; to get a lick in rather than to reach agreement; to be insistent rather than persistent; to fan the breeze with vague discontent (particularly in the area of life shown by the house position of the short leg of the T-Cross). That's why you are so easily frustrated, no matter how much effort and good faith you put forth: what is most important to you is not accomplishment per se, but rather insisting on your own terms. As Dr. Jones put it, "If possessions are the final incentive they are always a token of achievement, and with him any accomplishment often proves empty the moment it has exhausted its basic potentials." The message of the T-Cross, like that of the Grand Square, is to lighten up, to drop the thorny, easily-offended posture, the automatic pulling away from other people and into yourself.

The short-leg of the T-Cross represents where you stand; how you make your stand; what you stand for; and what you will not stand. It reveals how and what you are defending, which on the positive side can be your forte but on the negative side a stumbling block; a hindrance rather than a reliance; a defensiveness instead of a facility. The short-leg can indicate a pushy, overreaching, or overdone deployment of the given planetary energy, particularly when the planet is in good celestial state (if the planet is in bad celestial state, what is shown is a felt deficiency of the symbolized trait which leads to an overcompensation), which puts you out of synch with the speed of your environment. Because this is the focus of struggle in your life, it can also be (as Dr. Jones put it) "in its own nature and through its place by house and sign it identifies the area and conditions of experience as well as the facets of selfhood that create the potential of more than average achievement in a given nativity.". In the case of a conjunction of two or more planets at the short leg, use the interpretation for the conjunction(s), but in its inharmonious or unfavorable sense.

Short Leg of T-Cross:

Sun – you stand on your Authority: autocratic, condescending, final.

Moon – you stand on your Sensitivity: self-righteous, pouty, easily-offended.

Mercury – you stand on your Dogmatism: obdurate, pontifical, deaf.

Venus – you stand on your Insouciance: unbothered, unhurried, blasé sang-froid.

Mars – you stand on your Pride: haughty, supercilious, noblesse oblige.

Jupiter – you stand on your Breeziness: trifling, patronizing, above-it-all.

Saturn – you stand on your Stubbornness: uncompromising, unapproachable, brusque.

Uranus – you stand on your Independence: free-thinking, hard-headed, lone wolf.

Neptune – you stand on your Aloofness: abstracted, reserved, unreachable.

Pluto – you stand on your Insistence: dogged, tenacious, self-willed.

What is the difference between having a planet as the short leg of a T-Cross or mediating planet of a Wedge as compared to, for example, having that planet conjunct the Ascendant, sole dispositor, or planetary hour ruler? The answer is that these different horoscopic criteria show different facets of the personality. Planets conjunct the Ascendant reveal strategies for dominating / taking control of casual, tête-à-tête relationships; sole dispositors show how natives take command of their own lives and the people around them, and aggrandize themselves in the world; planetary hour rulers show how people act when everything's clicking for them and their luck is flowing. By contrast, short legs of T-Crosses show a severe, hard-nosed manifestation of the planetary energy: the way people close up into themselves to get their own way; and mediating planets of Wedges reveal a positive, flowing manifestation of the planetary energy: the way natives open themselves up to new avenues and possibilities in order to get their own way.

The house positions can be suggestive, but are not as definitive as traditional astrology holds them to be. That is to say, the house positions of the point planet of a Fan or mediating planet of a Wedge can indeed indicate the circumstances in life wherein the natives shine; and the house holding the short leg of a T-Cross can reveal the circumstances of greatest concern.

Two T-Crosses (not involved in Grand Square or Bow Tie)

Where one T-Cross symbolizes a driving intensity, two of them can have a leavening effect. Precisely because you do feel so heavily burdened or torn in two different directions, you are able to pull some of the obsessive energy out of both of them and take a detached, philosophical overview of yourself and your situation in life. Two T-Crosses are not as stern and focused as the single T-Cross: you are more aloof and abstracted, with a sense of being embattled or on the defensive rather than trying to prove something to yourself. Although heavy in spirit, with a self-coddling tendency, you nonetheless possess a sensitivity and attunement to your environment which is usually absent from the concentrated single T-Cross type. As Dr. Jones puts it, two T-Crosses are an "indication of some exceptional division of labor in the psychological make-up, such as often becomes an ineradicable or deep-seated rift in the harmony of selfhood as a whole. This situation in an astrological wheel calls for an adjustment in the life with a potential end result of a redoubled force of self-projection, and also perhaps an unusual ability to reconcile differences in others if only it does not slip off into some unhappily eccentric distortion of the native's own character". At your best, your personal struggles have given you a delicacy and restraint in your dealings with others and the world around you; and you find you are best able to keep your emotional balance as you are soft, sympathetic, and gentle in relationships.

Mixed Forms

Wedge with T-Cross (not Bow Tie)

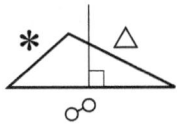
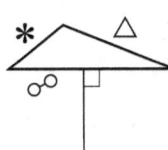

This configuration combines the intensity, ambition, and drive of the T-Cross with the broad intellectual outlook of the Wedge. You are clever, versatile, and possess a forward-looking, can-do spirit. You are a person on the move, someone who is striving for accomplishment and trying to go places in life (which can be suggested by the house position of the short leg of the T-Cross); yet you are also idealistic and thus try to fit your endeavors into an overarching philosophy – you need to feel that your efforts are helping humanity or the world as a whole. You develop some particular area of competence or expertise (your reliance – which can be shown by the mediating Wedge planet and the house in which it lies), and use it as a base from which to operate. You are able to adapt to the changing vicissitudes of circumstances and capitalize on whatever situation you find at hand, and can be both cunning in manipulating or finessing around other people, and indomitable in asserting your own will over them. Sigmund Freud, whose T-Cross had Saturn (discipline) as the short leg and whose Wedge had Mercury (mind) as mediating planet, is a good example. You play the game only by your own rules. You are quite capable of cutting other people off cold, or dropping a responsibility or relationship like a hot potato when you believe it's no longer serving your ends; hence others can find dealing with you a rather bruising experience even though they respect your leadership and nobility of spirit.

The difference between the T-Cross and Wedge on the same side of the opposition as opposed to opposite sides of the opposition is that the same-side natives are more focused on their own ends, on their own goals and purposes; whereas the opposite-side natives are more outgoing and sociable, more solicitous for the feelings of other people, and more willing to listen and respond to them. Same-side natives seem to emphasize the T-Cross more – they are intense to the point of being grim, thorny, caustic and girded for anything; whereas opposite-side natives seem to emphasize the Wedge more – they are expansive, sociable, and intellectually inquisitive.

Compound Configurations

Triangular Forms

Grand Sextiles

Grand Sextiles (60°-60°-60°-60°-60°-60°) subsume all the quadrangular configurations (since they contain three Rectangles, Kites, and Trapezoids). You are a person who has a relaxed, laid-back approach to life and to other people: not so much scattered as utterly indifferent and blasé. You are on your own wavelength and have little worldly ambition, but instead tend to go along with whatever is happening: as W. B. Yeats put it in his *Autobiographies*, "Nature made me a gregarious man, going hither and thither looking for conversation."

It's not that you are lazy or aren't punctilious in carrying out assigned duties; but you seem faintly annoyed by mundane affairs and have little initiative, largely because there is nothing you care enough about to work up a sweat over. You take whatever befalls you philosophically and adapt as best you can. You are by no means irresolute or a shrinking violet: while you're not going anywhere in particular, you stoutly resist being forced or inveigled, and can be maddeningly remote and mulishly obstinate when you feel you are being pushed. While cheerful, optimistic, and cooperative, you are exasperatingly indifferent. You are self-sufficient unto yourself, and basically just want to be left alone. The Grand Sextile differs from two non-interlaced Grand Trines in that the former are more removed and self-contained, with less native drive; whereas two Grand Trines not interlaced are subtle and cunning, and use their imperturbability and patience as the means to achieve their designs.

5/6

The difference between 5/6 (60°-60°-60°-60°-120°) and a Grand Sextile is that the former are more dynamic and enthusiastic – not as sedate and retiring. You are positive and hopeful, with a live-and-let-live attitude towards other people and life in general. You are forthright and direct – even outspoken – but with an inviting personal manner. You make good eye contact and are frank, candid, and self-assured without being pushy or overbearing. You are carefree, light-hearted, without a care in the world (5/6 contains two Kites); the mischievous and humane good humor of Anthony Trollope is an example. You have a faith in basic goodness which is not the product of naïveté, wishful thinking, or superficial cheeriness (such as often characterizes the simple Grand Trine sans oppositions), but rather is an unshakeable conviction of the heart. You possess a true sympathy for the trials and tribulations of others, but with no pity or superficial "helpfulness": you don't go out of your way for anyone, but merely offer a quiet presence and understanding. You are detached without being stand-offish (like the Grand Sextile). Your complete sincerity and honesty are the natural byproducts of your equanimity, rather than an attempt to prove something to other people. You are wholly trustworthy and reliable (5/6 contains a Rectangle); yet you have little worldly ambition or desire to get ahead in life.

I've tried to find an effect when a transiting or progressed planet moves into the position of the "missing" planet of a 5/6 configuration (which presumably would indicate some sort of favorable bringing things to completion); but have not found this to work in practice.

Square forms

Grand Squares

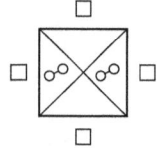

The Grand Square (90°-90°-90°-90°) can be considered to consist of two interlaced T-Crosses, and thus it takes on a more aware, self-conscious T-Cross meaning. Where the T-Cross natives are stern and intent, and make no effort to disguise their aggressiveness and sense of being driven, the Grand Square natives are (on the surface, at least) outgoing, glib, even a bit cheeky. There is something of an "Aquarius" quality about you: friendly, democratic, nonjudgmental, interested in other people, a good listener; but at the same time, cool and aloof. In fact, your blithe, carefree exterior belies a cosmic *Angst*: to intimates your grin can seem more like a grimace. In fact, you hold yourself under very tight emotional control, and as a result – in spite of your outward friendliness – you radiate intense vibrations that other people can find a bit daunting or forbidding. And, just as you have yourself tightly reined in, you tend to bend the people around you out of shape as well (Poet Laureate Ted Hughes comes to mind here; although it could be just coincidence that two of his partners committed suicide – or perhaps it's merely that he had a penchant for suicidal women). If the rest of your horoscope indicates leadership, then susceptible people can fall under your domination and willingly and eagerly become your fervent disciples (or slaves). As a leader you can be dynamic and inspiring, with considerable gumption and stick-to-itiveness, and you never say die. On your negative side you can be a petty dictator: touchy, prissy, and unduly smug and self-satisfied (one thinks of Captain William Bligh, whose crew on the *Bounty* mutinied against him; who later faced revolt in the Spithead and Nore Mutinies; and who eventually, as governor of New South Wales, was forced to flee from the Rum Rebellion against him. Obviously, he had a talent for pissing subordinates off. On the other hand, his incredible self-discipline and bravery brought 18 sailors set adrift by the *Bounty* mutineers in a 23-foot long launch across 4000 miles of uncharted open sea to safety). In other cases, intimates or subordinates can find you oppressive and energy-depleting to be around, since your heavy moodiness can be exhausting to bear. In spite of your gregariousness and loquacity, you are actually quite secretive about what you are actually thinking and feeling beneath the surface. Underneath you are tense, ill-at-ease, insecure around people; hence cautious and guarded, as if under siege. You feel assailed by life, barely able to keep your head above water – treading endlessly to keep your composure afloat, constantly having to prove yourself, prove yourself, prove yourself. Although you project a playful, nice-guy image, you are the furthest thing from easy-going – an unsympathetic cold fish. You hide behind a mask of smiles and joviality, but are ever suspicious and vigilant; always on edge; never relaxed. On the other hand, you are extraordinarily perceptive and have a keen insight into the motivations of other people (if not always your own). The message of the Grand Square is to learn to lighten up; to not take yourself so seriously, as if the whole world somehow depended on you. Your lesson is to learn trust – in yourself first of all – and to relax your grip on both your own feelings and your relationships with others.

Grand Squares can be analyzed further by quadrature – that is to say, by whether they are posited in cardinal, fixed, or mutable signs. However this discussion will be subsumed under the rubric of the Natural Disposition (see Appendix) since the quadrature meanings are basically the same for Grand Squares and Natural Dispositions (albeit applied in different contexts: the former is descriptive of how the native establishes and maintains control, whether by means of projects, ideas, or relationships; and the latter is descriptive of the native's slant of interest and enthusiasm in everyday life). Note that it is quite possible for a Grand Square native to have a Natural Disposition (by negative indication) in a different quadrature from that of the Grand Square. Carlos Castaneda, for example, has a fixed Grand Square, but a mutable Natural Disposition by negative indication.

Two Grand Squares: I've only seen this once, a person born on 6/17/1962: a remarkable individual – dynamic, serious, hard-working, and dedicated: a natural-born leader and passionate crusader – who made a powerful (positive) impression upon everyone who ever met her. However, at the same time a very conflictive person in intimate relationships, who never married or had children.

Quadrangular Forms

Rectangles (not part of Grand Sextile or 5/6)

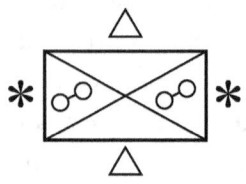

All the compound quadrangular forms (Rectangles, Kites, and Trapezoids) can be considered to consist of two Wedges, thus they are all pragmatic, realistic, and down-to-earth: people who go their own way and do their own thing with little pother or wasted motion, and who depend on their own pluck rather than on other people.

Rectangles (60°-120°-60°120°) are dignified, punctilious, self-contained, upright, reserved, and proper (King Charles is a good example). You have high ideals and you do your best to live up to them. You are a rock – solid, stable, honorable. You shoot straight and play by the rules, and you keep your cards close to your chest. You are unmoved and unmovable – not in the sense of being cold or pigheaded, but rather in having a true disinterestedness and dispassion. You are pensive – a thinker who reaches for understanding, and is little concerned with making an impression. There is nothing subtle or diplomatic about you; indeed you can be blunt and brusque to the point of rudeness. In spite of your tremendous strength of will, self-control, and inner discipline, you are basically at ease within yourself and have the ability to put other people at their ease as well. Albeit outgoing and sociable – a thoroughly pleasant and boon companion – ultimately you stand completely alone. You are careful not to tread upon other people's space, and you are quick to retreat into your own space whenever you feel you are being imposed upon. You are respectful – of other people and the world around you – because at core you respect yourself. You don't need other people's back-patting to reassure you of who you are, so you don't waste energy in empty motions of trying to win other people's acceptance. You aren't blind to your own faults, but have found a way to accept yourself (rather than make excuses for yourself), and thus you are able to accept other people for what they are as well.

Bow Ties

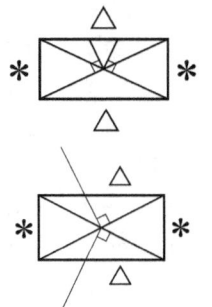

The Bow Tie consists of two T-Crosses on a Rectangle, and so accentuates the calmly detached and rational aspects of both types, and also the self-coddling and self-seriousness. You are idealistic, eccentric, whimsical, and march to the beat of a distant drum. You are definitely on your own wavelength most of the time, and can be obdurate and pigheaded as if for sport. You are scrupulous and fastidious, and are observant of the smallest details and nuances; on the negative side, you are quick to take umbrage. You are resolute and determined without going anywhere in particular (you are not especially ambitious or driven). You are extremely self-contained and do not share what you are really feeling with anyone, and you stiffly repel any incursion into your private space. While by no means unsociable, you hold firmly to your own orbit, making as few waves as possible and avoiding unnecessary involvements. You basically just want to be left alone and go your own way in peace. When the short legs of both T-Crosses are on the same side, you are more sociable, outgoing, and companionable (yet still a watcher rather than a doer). When the short legs are on opposite sides you are dreamy, other-worldly, or dedicated to abstract ideals and lofty goals.

Kites (not part of Grand Sextile or 5/6)

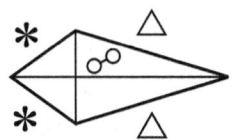

Kites (60°-60°-120°-120°) can be considered to consist of two Wedges; but they can also be considered to consist of a Fan on a Grand Trine. Kites fly: they're light and airy and breezy. You are blithe, loose, cheery; and you possess a sardonic sense of humor. You are not so much easy-going or laid-back as light of touch. Where Rectangles assert their independence, Kites are blissfully oblivious and indifferent: you are not very well grounded but are always up in the air. You may listen to other people just to be polite, but everything goes in one ear and out the other. Although you have an ingratiating manner, you keep yourself aloof and fancy-free and are very difficult to pin down. You are competent, self-assured, and ironic; but on the negative side can be insufferably smug. Where the other quadrangular types manifest their free-spiritedness in terms of personality, Kites tend to manifest it in terms of choice of lifestyle – you're not so much a nonconformist per se as someone who simply goes your own way and lives your life very differently than most people do; or than what you were brought up to do. ("Am I not right to follow my own instincts? It's because I know who I am that I realize what I can be one day." –Jules Verne, remonstrating with his father who urged him to give up writing to practice law). You follow your own star wherever it leads you, and pursue a basically solitary existence even in the midst of people. You are easily transplanted into new environments, and are able to fit right in wherever you are.

Trapezoids (not part of Grand Sextile or 5/6)

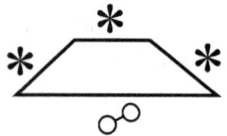

Like all double-Wedge quadrangular types you are friendly, practical, and down-to-earth; but you Trapezoids (180°-60°-60°-60°) are well-grounded (unlike Kites), and relaxed and at ease (unlike the stiff Rectangles). Unlike Kites you tend to favor a conservative lifestyle, and to play by the rules and not make waves; unlike Rectangles you are laid-back and nonchalant, with nothing to uphold or prove to anyone. You are plainspoken, unadorned, and non-demonstrative, with a self-effacing and unassuming manner. You are able to make the best of any situation in which you find yourself: to be realistic, to relax and take things in stride, and to capitalize on whatever resources you find at hand. You are bland and phlegmatic, gentle and genteel. You are not at all dynamic or decisive (unless there's a lot of Aries or Leo involved); and on your negative side you can be overly cautious or compliant – unwilling to make a stand. You are rather vulnerable emotionally, and wear your heart on your sleeve. Like all triangular types you are aloof; but here the aloofness manifests as a withdrawing and closing up into yourself rather than holding yourself above it all. There is a sincerity and plaintiveness about you which inspires trust and arouses the sympathy and support of others (e.g., Wolfgang Mozart). People find your presence soothing and inviting, and you are everyone's confidant and shoulder to cry on. Your calm stability provides a dependable reassurance for the people around you.

Trapezoid With Axis (Trapezoid on T-Cross) – **Same Side**

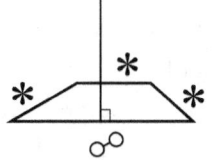

Trapezoids with an axis on same side of the opposition are more intent and determined to accomplish something meaningful in life as compared with simple Trapezoids, who are not going anywhere in particular. Like the simple Trapezoid, you are outgoing, gregarious, and quite sociable; but in this case you are also intensely competitive, a careerist with definite goals and ambitions. You cultivate some special area of expertise in which you truly excel (often shown by the axis planet and its house position – e.g. the Sun-Venus rising in the case of T.E. Lawrence, which gave him the artless charm which won over his Arab allies); and you are motivated by a strong need for recognition and approval for your cleverness from your fellows. Albeit friendly, you don't reveal what you are actually thinking and feeling. There is a secretiveness and touchiness here absent in the simple Trapezoid type. You are definitely out to prove something to somebody (yourself, mainly) and advance yourself in life. You consciously project your Trapezoidal "regular fellow, nice guy" image as a tactic to disarm people and win their support in order to further your own ends (sort of like an "Aquarius MC" meaning as compared to an "Aquarius Asc" meaning for the simple Trapezoid).

The interpretations for the Axis planets are the same as those for the short leg of a T-Cross (listed above).

Trapezoid With Axis (Trapezoid on T-Cross) – **Opposite Side**

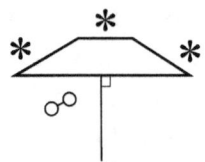

You carry the gregariousness of the Trapezoid to an extreme: you are quite the social butterfly, and you spend most of your time hanging out with and relating to people, engaging them in animated conversation. You are not especially intimate per se – you keep your distance with an avuncular bonhomie. Like all Trapezoids you are genuine and unaffected; but unlike the Trapezoid with axis on the same side, there is nothing you *need* from anybody – you merely enjoy holding court or playing to an audience. You are sassy and brassy, not so much a leader as the cynosure or the star of the show. You are liberated from convention in thought, speech, and action – quite willing and eager to strike out on your own (often shown by the axis planet and its house position). Where Kites are free-wheeling (dictate their own sui generis lifestyles), you are free-thinking: your life is conventional enough outwardly, but what's going on inside your head is not. You use your Trapezoid "regular fellow, nice guy" persona as a front to cover your wild, crazy streak. There is something of an "Aquarius – Uranus" meaning here. You are more independent than Trapezoid natives whose axis is on the same side: they retreat into their own space, whereas you create your own space.

Baskets

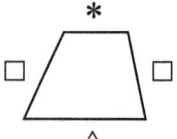

Baskets (90°-60°-90°-120°) are simple rather than compound configurations, but they are listed here because they are quadrangular. It's pretty rare to find a Basket alone (without accompanying configurations).

Baskets are friendly enough outwardly, but are actually the least sociable of the quadrangular types. Albeit polite and civil on the surface (you are not combative or rebellious per se), you are completely focused on the path beneath your feet – you just go your own way and do your own thing without sharing your thoughts or plans with anyone. You are conscientious and thorough, and take pride in your competence and independence. You are serious-minded and are basically a loner – very self-contained and self-sufficient, with something of a fortress mentality. You are easily affronted; are quick to dig in your heels or pull your wagons into a circle; and you are always perfectly willing and ready to stand alone and take complete responsibility for the proceedings. You are a visionary with a unique (even quixotic) take on life and people – Mark Twain is a good example – but you are too private a person to be much interested in leadership or drawing undue attention to yourself (unless there are lots of angular planets or more dynamic configurations present). You don't need recognition or a pat on the back from anyone for self-validation, but are able to sustain and validate yourself.

Aspects and Mutual Reception

Sun – Moon Aspects and Mutual Reception

Soli-lunar aspects are but one lens in a horoscope through which the synodic angle between the Sun and Moon can be viewed and analyzed (the house position of the Part of Fortune is another). In my book *The Great Wheel* I discuss the angular separation between the lights in terms of 28 lunar phases: Phase 1 = the day following the new Moon (i.e., conjunction); Phase 8 = the day following the 1st quarter (dexter square); Phase 15 = the day following the full Moon (opposition); and Phase 22 = the day following the last quarter (sinister square). The interpretations given below are rather different from those given in *The Great Wheel* – not that there is any sort of contradiction, but rather that when a symbol is viewed through different lenses it reveals different facets. For example, Sun conjunct Moon encompasses natives of both Phase 28 and Phase 1; but the former express their Sun-Moon-conjunction love of challenge and proving their mettle in terms of self-discipline and self-limitation – they are ingenuous; whereas the latter express it as opportunity for individual achievement and approbation – they are impetuous.

Natives who have Sun aspecting Moon have a knowing (or know-it-all) gleam in their eyes, a bit of swagger, of chutzpah; they are never nonplussed or at a loss, but possess a saving resiliency and a knack for bouncing right back after any contretemps. Their self-possession is the product of a hearty ego – a sense of invulnerability or exceptionalism, as if the usual rules don't apply in their case since they make their own rules (which can lead to difficulties for the disharmonious aspects). They are single-minded and straightforward; proud, independent, and free-thinking (eccentric); and they make a direct beeline for whatever they are after at the moment with no shame or apologies or diplomacy or niceties. Dr. Jones says that "The Sun and Moon not in major aspect indicate a lack of real ordering of the vitality, and suggest a great tendency to waste energies on the one hand or on the other to fail to direct them into experience adequately enough for any ultimate self-fulfillment." I would say, they lack the spark and sparkle – the pizzazz and zest for life – of the soli-lunar aspect natives.

Traditional theory holds that the (felicitous or conflictive) aspects and configurations involving the lights in a horoscope reflect what was happening in the parents' marriage at the time of the native's conception and birth. I haven't enough evidence to confirm or contradict this assertion.

Sun conjunct Moon is bold and unselfconscious. You are poised and self-possessed, with something of a cocksureness or swagger – as if you are in the know, on the inside track, have a secret all your own. You are energetic, resolute, daring, and adventurous, with a great intellectual curiosity which drives you forward. You seek out the unusual, the path less traveled; and you push yourself (or drive yourself) to the max in your pursuit of self-perfection and significant achievement. You possess a can-do willingness to trust in your impulses, and a disdain for all restraint (you like to push the envelope, be on the forefront). You charge straight ahead looking neither left nor right (brusque and bruising). You possess a spirited freshness and spontaneity, and a jaunty individualism which enjoys holding the limelight – or at least being the one who runs the show. You are brash (bumptious) and insistent (presumptuous), with an impatient bravado which doesn't suffer fools gladly; and you are by no means hesitant about speaking your mind. You don't need or wait for anyone's permission but just leap blindly ahead, and you have an infectious (reckless) optimism. You cultivate some area of expertise and competence to lend yourself a voice of authority and to keep yourself grounded; but you are basically an irrepressible spirit who goes your own way and does your own thing unfettered and free, and you provide levity and hope to others when the going gets tough.

Sun sextile Moon: You possess an ease of manner and effortlessness of delivery which assumes without presuming. You are natural and real; personable and agreeable; and you project a winning alacrity which enlists the whole-hearted cooperation and support of others in implementing your own projects and schemes. You are able to just be yourself and immediately make yourself at home in any environment; and your infectious enthusiasm is an inspiration and surety for the people in your circle – they look up to you and gladly and gratefully follow your lead. You quickly take charge of any proceedings with your unabashed straightforwardness and self-certainty, particularly when others are disorganized or confused – your unflagging eagerness gives the impression that you always know what you're about. On the negative side, you tend to shy away from undue involvements, complexities and conflicts, preferring to keep things moving along smoothly on an even keel. As a result, you refuse to listen to anything you don't particularly want to hear; and you maintain your buoyancy with a noncommittal vagueness or perfunctoriness when you are being subjected to unwelcome demands. In spite of your gregariousness and apparent concern, you basically go your own way and use your social milieu as a springboard for your personal designs, which, however, are usually noble and idealistic.

Sun square Moon indicates a person who always has to do more or be more: it's possible that your parents were in conflict around the time of your birth, and as a result you never quite know where you stand. You always feel an underlying insecurity in just being yourself, with a concomitant incumbency to prove your worth over and over. You possess a plaintive or beleaguered air; are not particularly relaxed within yourself; and thus tend to drive yourself (and other people) unmercifully to feel that you are on top of things. You have a shrewd sense of the politics of everyday society and relationships, although you are the furthest thing from being diplomatic. You call a spade a spade and think nothing of brushing other people aside or giving them the cold shoulder as you go about your business. You become huffy, dogmatic, and self-righteous when thwarted, rather than reaching out or seeking some sort of rapprochement – you either withdraw into yourself or strike out in some new unimpeded direction. Other people can find you callous and bruising, and therefore they tend to give you wide berth rather than confront you directly if they can avoid it (which suits you fine). On your positive side you are very aware and incisive in your judgments; have considerable panache; and bring off your coups with flair and style.

Sun trine Moon shows a person who is comfortable and relaxed within yourself, and therefore adept at putting others at their ease as well. You are unabashedly *real* and down-to-earth; and you project a sympathetic and obliging interest in other people while maintaining your own personal space and distance. You make direct eye contact and are a good listener, with a warm and empathic manner which invites the confidence of the people who know you. Your unfeigned concern and nonjudgmental objectivity makes you the sort of person others instinctively turn to for advice and guidance. You take pride in your work and are punctilious in carrying out your responsibilities – more interested in acquitting yourself honorably than in receiving any particular reward or recognition for your efforts. On the negative side, your above-it-all insouciance, and tendency to shrug your shoulders and walk away when confronted with criticism or blame, can create a distance in intimate relationships: you scrupulously avoid having to deal with what you consider to be other people's issues; and they in turn can find it frustrating trying to pull you down off of your cloud. Nonetheless your ability to not take things personally makes you a rock of stability and surety in any group of which you are a part.

Sun opposition Moon natives are more steadfast and grave than are flighty new Moon people. Where new Moon instinctively gravitates towards groups, full Moon instinctively pulls away and watches from the outside. Your parents may have been pulling in opposite directions around the time you were born, which left you with the immutable feeling of standing alone. You withdraw from others to do your own thing with little concern for issues of approval or rejection; and you depend on no one else for support or succor. You are independent and resolute, and you dig in your heels and tough it out as your first, middle, and last recourse. Where the new Moon people are light and irrepressible, you full Moon natives are staunch and unconquerable. You actually prefer isolation and seclusion to human society since you feel little security that there is anything that can be depended on outside yourself. You prefer solitude to collaboration; or at least to any sort compromise unless it places you in a position of undisputed control. You possess infinite patience and are capable of beating a strategic retreat when necessary, willing to wait for a favorable turn of events rather than expose yourself unnecessarily. Because you are so wary and suspicious, and try to take into account all factors that must be reckoned with, you are far more alert to the possible ramifications and repercussions of your actions, and to other people's feelings (at least intellectually / strategically), than new Moon natives are. However, you are by no means warm or sympathetic – rather you are emotionally distant ("cold fish" is a good description – in comparison with new Moon people, who are charismatic). You may be a responsible spouse, parent, and citizen, but this is more a response to your own concept of where your duty lies, and to your (extreme) sense of personal honor – your fitness as a human being – than it is a spontaneous outpouring of affection, or a sense of real concern for the welfare of your family or society. Guided by your own abstract philosophy of what is moral and dignified, you are immoveable. You don't belong to any group, really; your acute awareness of what everyone around you is unquestioningly taking for granted makes you the perennial outsider. In all events you keep your own counsel, and share nothing of what you are truly feeling inside with anybody. In spite of your seeming self-sufficiency, full Moon natives are often torn with self-doubt precisely because you are too distrustful of others to accept their feedback: you become huffy, feisty, and obtuse as a defense when your plans go awry and you are called to account, or when your considerable poise and élan fail you. Since you care not a fig for what others think of you, you are basically a law unto yourself, and recognize no authority but your own.

Sun parallel Moon makes for a person who is natural, out front, and intent on the path beneath your feet. Unlike the effusive zodiacal aspects between Sun and Moon, you parallels are warier, more reserved, less inclined to barge in upon the scene with a handshake and a "Howdy!" You are just as direct, frank, and self-validating as the aspects, but without the clatter, effusiveness, and self-conscious grandstanding. On the contrary, you are all business: you know who you are; you know what you are about; you know what you want from life; and you know how to get it. Therefore, you are ultimately more convincing and sincere than the demonstrative and showy aspects – you win people over by your seriousness of purpose and complete dedication to all that you do. But because you tend to indwelling, and march straight ahead with little concern for how others perceive or react to you, your tendency is to go your own way and do your own thing without much sensitivity for other people's sensibilities, or the ultimate consequences that your actions and decisions may have on others. You are a law unto yourself – for better or worse – and other people therefore tend to fall into line behind you.

Sun contraparallel Moon indicates a person who is unhurried, self-possessed, and completely at ease in any social setting. You have a keen sense of personal style and flair, and – unlike the Sun - opposition Moon natives whose insularity and indwelling makes them socially oblivious – you are quite aware of the effect your casual insouciance and seeming inconsequence has on everyone around you. You win people over with your ironic, self-mocking sense of humor and appreciation for the underlying incongruities in what everyone else seems to be taking for granted. Your inviting manner puts people at ease: the conspiratorial twinkle in your eye, and your glib, off-hand remarks and tongue-in-cheek patter, are a source of amusement and entertainment for all who know you. You are shrewd, practical, and sensitive to nuances; and are unabashedly revealing about your own motives. On the other hand, your self-delight and vague aloofness can grate on people when it is time to be serious and get down to business: you just go your own way and do your own thing come what may.

Sun–Moon Mutual Reception, like the aspects between Sun and Moon, is easy-going, self-assured, and completely yourself in any social setting. But you MRs are less animated by a need to prove yourself or to make an impression than are the self-coddling aspects: you evince a seriousness of purpose and concomitant humility that contrasts with the preening and self-delight of the aspects. There is a greater sense of attunement here to the ebb and flow of life's energies; a deep faith in yourself and a reliance on the basic goodness of the universe; an adaptability and facility for modifying your goals in response to changing realities; and a concomitant willingness to just go with the current rather than to be frantically paddling to get somewhere in particular. You dominate the proceedings with your simplicity of manner and utter *realness*. You naturally assume the role of cynosure in any group without especially trying to because of your disarming frankness, honorableness, and sincerity

The Inner Child

The relationships between the Sun and Mercury and Venus – taken together – are referred to as the Inner Child, since it is the patterns symbolized by the inner planets which are first imprinted upon the infant. The Sun symbolizes the parent(s) and Mercury and Venus symbolize different aspects of the infantile psyche: namely mind and desire, respectively. Mercury symbolizes the infant's sense of being separated and unique, which later enables the person to make reasoned choices and decisions for him or herself. Venus symbolizes the infant's sense of belonging and being appreciated, which later becomes the person's self-esteem and self-worth. When the Sun (parent) is conjunct (overpowers) Mercury or Venus, the parent treats the child as but an appendage of the parent; and what then develops is a thrall or bondage to the parent which is inculcated by fear and seethes with internalized resentment (self-blame), which may follow the child and color his or her relationships for the rest of the life.

All parents who have several children know that their relationships with their various offspring are quite different – some more affable, others more problematical; and how the various siblings react / relate to their parents is quite different as well. In the case of dysfunctional parents the children will devise survival strategies according to their individual natures, which can be read from the degree of angular separation between the Sun and Mercury, and the Sun and Venus, in their natal horoscopes; and also from their order of rising on the day of birth.

The order in which the Sun, Mercury, and Venus rise in a horoscope can be indicative of the natives' self-projection – three levels of communication, or three stages of intimacy. The leading planet (which rises first; i.e., is behind the others in the zodiac) symbolizes the face that the natives show casual acquaintances; the central planet symbolizes the face that they show their friends; and the trailing planet (which rises last; i.e. is ahead of the others in the zodiac) symbolizes the face they show their family. Here "intimacy" is taken to mean degree of emotional interchange: the people in whom natives invest a great deal of emotional energy (the ones they think about or have strong feelings for) are considered to be intimates whether they are liked or disliked. In this context enemies are considered to be as much intimates as are partners (indeed astrology does not distinguish between the two since both are ruled by the seventh house of the horoscope).

The leading planet takes on a benefic meaning because it symbolizes the natives' mode of advancing themselves and their interests; what they expect of other people; and how they seek to sway or influence them. If the Sun leads the natives want other people to respect them: they try to convince through their earnestness. If Mercury leads the natives want other people to agree with them: they try to convince through their cleverness. If Venus leads the natives want other people to indulge them: they try to convince through their poise.

The central planet symbolizes the natives' mode of holding their own, particularly noticeable in situations of conflict. If the Sun is central the natives rely ultimately on stubbornness and stonewalling. If Mercury is central the natives rely ultimately on logic and argument. If Venus is central the natives rely ultimately on maneuvering and finesse.

The trailing planet takes on a malefic meaning because it symbolizes the natives' mode of retreat; their last defense when routed; that which they will not surrender under any circumstances. If the Sun trails the natives protect themselves from compromise: they salvage their self-respect and honor; they go down with their ship. If Mercury trails the natives protect themselves from contradiction: they salvage their prejudices; they won't admit to error and insist on having the last word. If Venus trails the natives protect themselves from rejection: they salvage their ambitions; they won't be deflected (when the dust settles they're still plumping for whatever it is that they wanted all along).

Sun-Mercury-Venus conjunct: The triple conjunction is the sign of a wounded inner child, usually because of cold, uncaring, or unfeeling parents (or abandonment). Triple conjunction natives are sad people, like bewildered little children lost in the forest with no inkling of how to get home. You are humble and unprepossessing: subdued, non-demonstrative, soft-spoken, and reticent. But you also have your defensive side – insecure and ever prepared for attack. You often feel yourself to be haunted with no respite, no repose, nowhere to turn, and no one you can really talk to. You try to obey the rules; but the rules keep changing on you. You are a pleasant, harmless, complaisant person who has been trained from infancy to go along to get along; and to never raise the question of whether you are happy or fulfilled. Perhaps your parents wouldn't permit you to express your feelings; so you learned to keep your mouth shut and keep things under wraps. You go through life under something like a black cloud, or onus; seeking some sense of redemption or salvation or whatever the leprechauns have at the end of their rainbow. You would benefit by talking to a Jungian psychologist (someone empathic but objective) since there is no one in your circle with whom you feel comfortable discussing your inmost feelings. Indeed, you don't really know what these are yourself (ergo the need for disinterested, outside counsel). Although you are basically a good, kind person, you don't see that because you feel beleaguered, always vigilant, striking before you are struck at, anxiously manning the barricades. The message here is to lighten up and relax as best you can; and to know that your sufferings are what make you stronger (as Nietzsche said).

This contrasts sharply with the situation when both Mercury and Venus are elongated from the Sun, in which case the Inner Child has fully separated from the parent. These natives are aloof; coldly detached, and efficient. They take things in their stride and let nothing get under their skin: they just go their own way and do their own thing and let the devil take the hindmost.

Sun – Mercury Aspects and Mutual Reception

Sun conjunct Mercury: Purpose and Mentality merged may make for little in the way of clear-thinking discernment, with reliance upon gut-level survival instinct serving in lieu of objectivity and reason. You are wary and self-conscious, always heedful of the impression which you are making on other people. It's very important to you that you fit in and belong – or at least, that you are always in the right – and so you affect a smooth, debonair ease of manner or unconcern in order to conceal your underlying insecurity. You don't reveal your true feelings to anyone, thus your intimates may criticize you for being closed-up and uncommunicative. Your seeming insouciance is belied by the quickness with which you take huffy umbrage and strike back, or close down shop at any perceived censure or reproof. You tend to be a closed-minded and emotionally repressed individual, with blinders which only permit you to see what you want to see; and you are critical and disapproving of anyone who doesn't measure up to your own prejudices. As I say in my book *Thought Forms*:

> You tend to operate on instant, gut-level impressions and responses rather than on reflection and thinking things through. You rely more on intuition and cunning rather than logic: you have an unerring sense of where your own advantage and other people's weaknesses lie. You possess powerful concentration and focus: once you have made up your mind about something, you are indomitable. You don't examine your motives or reasons, but rather charge ahead in the sure and certain knowledge that "God" (i.e., your parent and society) is on your side. Thus your decisions have great power and force of will behind them, but evince little objectivity, discernment, or depth of understanding. You have great personal force because you stand by your decisions and opinions come hell or high water; and standing by one's decisions is indeed the key to all personal power and success in life. The problem with Sun conjunct Mercury is that the decisions you stand by are usually not your own, and therefore are not necessarily in your best

interests. You cling tenaciously to those thought forms which you created as a child; even in adulthood you hew very closely to the thought forms your parents inculcated into you. You were a "good" and obedient child; and later on became a "good" and obedient citizen. Mercury conjunction natives are the backbone of society.

Probably one or the other of your parents was a harsh, dominating, or repressed individual who gave you very little in the way of true love – acceptance of who you were (note that approval for a job "well-done" – meaning done the way the parent wanted it – is not true love or acceptance). And you feel constrained to uphold this role in turn for your parents – to approve of them unquestioningly, and to expect unquestioning approval from others in turn. The only thing you are consciously aware of is that you loved your parents; you can't see objectively how they programmed you and how much anger you may feel towards them beneath the surface. Your parents never permitted you to express feelings of anger at them openly, hence you never learned how to handle anger within yourself. Instead, you pretend that you're not angry – that everything is copacetic; you don't have any emotional problems, and the people who do have such problems are just being self-indulgent.

You cannot conceive of disagreement in good faith. Your constant assumption in any relationship is bad faith – that someone has to be the winner, and someone the loser – and you'll be damned if that's going to be you. You assume that if the other person disagrees with you, then ipso facto they must be acting in bad faith. This is because the bad faith model of relating to others – scoring little victory points instead of listening to the other person's feelings – was the only model you had as a child. Your parents stamped you out; so all you know is stamping other people out (before they can stamp you out).

Mercury conjunction natives have what it takes to be truly successful and happy in life: decisiveness, conviction, and determination. With a modicum of thoughtfulness and understanding (which are obtained by *listening* to the people you are intimate with) you can take your place as a role model of sobriety, self-denial, and true righteousness.

Sun parallel Mercury possesses the same low-key personal manner as Sun conjunct Mercury; and has the same discriminating watchfulness and savoir-faire; but you are far more accepting of yourself and hence more relaxed with other people than are the nervous, defensive conjunctions. Where the conjunctions project a public front of urbanity or being in the know in order to seek approval (or rejection, if the conjunction is afflicted), you are less inclined to be assertive because you have nothing to prove to anyone (i.e. your parent) or to yourself – your confidence arises from within rather than from upholding some exalted image of yourself, or needing to always be in the right. You can see yourself clearly and objectively, and you withhold judgment from yourself; this in turn makes it easy for you to be non-judgmental with others. Where the conjunctions distance themselves from people in fear, you parallels distance yourself (maintain your own integrity / separatedness) by granting other people their due space, and insisting upon you own in return.

Sun contraparallel Mercury is clever, earnest, and full of interesting ideas and conversation. You excel at communication because you are sensible, down-to-earth, and truly enjoy company and sharing views with other people – learning from them as much as impressing them. You are attentive, positive and upbeat; and always look for the best in other people and the situations you encounter. Others readily go along with you because of your whole-hearted yet disinterested take on things. You are an original thinker, and are quite willing to strike out in new directions with complete confidence in the product of your mental clarity and instincts. You have altruistic impulses, and at the same time are staunch in defending what you believe is right – which on the negative side can at times lead you to be peremptory or even dictatorial in asserting your opinions. But your willingness to take chances and fly with your intuition endears you to everyone who knows you.

Sun–Mercury Mutual Reception differs from the Sun–Mercury conjunction in its willingness to reach for understanding rather than agreement (forced or unforced). The conjunctions feel that they must always be in the *right*, even when (especially when) they know deep inside that they are not. You Sun–Mercury MRs, by contrast, have little sense of stake in how others perceive you, or in upholding abstract standards for their own sake, but rather you strive to achieve the best results possible in any situation rather than score some little point of your own. You are a great listener because you find that what other people have to say to be illuminating and worthy of attention (and might be useful to know). Because your assurance – your sense of what is right and true – arises from within rather than from the approval or applause you receive from others, when you lose patience you can at times reveal a dictatorial tendency, riding roughshod over other people's sensibilities. Your sense of self-respect arises from your ability to respect yourself, rather than from enticing or coercing obeisance to some exalted image of yourself that you are projecting.

Sun–Venus Aspects and Mutual Reception

Sun conjunct Venus people fancy themselves to be emotionally independent individuals, projecting a façade of blasé insouciance; but in truth this is but a defense to protect yourself precisely because you feel so vulnerable and susceptible to hurt. At root you are a good-hearted soul, with good primary impulses and a great deal of love to give, but nevertheless you feel uncomfortable accepting expressions of love in return. You shy away from intimacy because you feel unworthy of being loved or being too happy. You are guarded and ill-at-ease around people: your natural tendency is to hold back, to trim, to avoid giving offense or opening yourself up to rejection. You never feel a secure sense of belonging or of being on a sure footing, but need be ever on the alert for incursions into your space and territory. You are very vulnerable, without the normal defenses, thus you are quick to react to any slight – real or imagined – and quick to take up the cudgels. Albeit timid and wary in normal mode, you can be quite sharp-tongued and derisive when you feel that you are under attack. Because you are highly suspicious of people, it's hard for you to just relax and enjoy their company – you have to be vigilant every second. Other people puzzle you: they seem to be moving too fast or too slow – as the song goes, "Everyone's talking at me – can't hear a word they're saying". You try to play by what you perceive to be the rules, but it seems you always wind up holding the bag or getting hurt. You allow others to impose on you or to exploit you, and then you feel used and abused. You may get angry and rebel, perhaps, but you can't leave your frustrated desires behind you: you carry them on your back like a bank of loudspeakers which perpetually blare forth the message in the voice of your parent, "NOT WORTHY! NOT WORTHY!"

You feel a driving need to do more or be more than is humanly possible, to prove your worth by being overly conscientious (Venus direct) or overly exacting (Venus retrograde). You will nourish and protect dependents (perhaps by being overly protective and smothering, until they are forced to push you away; or, if your Venus is retrograde, until your "Don't touch me!" pushes them away); but you will not permit yourself to become emotionally dependent in turn: you have no more trust in the motives and desires of other people than you have in your own. You strive and struggle, but you have made an ethic of striving and struggling and deferred gratification instead of satisfaction; and then you wonder why you are never satisfied. Instead of accepting what other people offer you freely, you insist on an undying allegiance or guarantee of security which is impossible to fulfill. Thus you set the stage for the very rejection and humiliation you fear; and when it occurs you are assured that you were right all along: this relationship was not to be trusted.

Venus conjunction natives live in a fantasy world of your own devising in which everything is perfect, and thus you tend to be easily put out by the intrusions of harsh reality. Pygmalion was indubitably a Venus conjunction native (and indubitably Galatea immediately dumped him for a less needy dude). You have to keep messing around this way and that, trying to manipulate or change other people to fit your expectations (e.g. your children; like your parent did to you); which can be extremely bothersome to them. You get hooked on some obsession and keep pouring energy into it long after it is apparent that you are accomplishing nothing. It's extremely difficult for you to admit that you're in a rut, or to cut your losses by just walking away from a futile situation; to your logic this would entail a loss of self. Your goal in life is not personal happiness or satisfaction (no matter what you may be telling yourself), but rather exculpation, so that it cannot be said by anyone, least of all yourself, that you did not do your best.

Yet you *don't* do your best. You never make a total commitment: you hold yourself back even when you think you're giving your all so that you can never be ultimately compromised – so that the ultimate fig leaf can never be stripped away from you, thus revealing you in all your naked worthlessness. You purposely thwart yourself by your own inhibition: it is easier for you to feel undeserving of happiness than to feel happy and then to lose it. And in refusing to take responsibility for your failures – you prefer to believe them preordained – you preclude the possibility of success. You lack the courage of your convictions, the force to carry things through. You are too easily wounded and quick to withdraw into yourself.

You Venus conjunction natives cannot see that there is some enduring intent which exists beyond momentary success or failure; that your very being is not on the line with every passing issue; that there is no need for such a sense of stake in every outcome. As is the case with Mercury's conjunctions, the fear here is of death: the conjunctions are the death points of the cycles. Of course, all creatures fear death, but nowhere is the awareness so acute and the dread so manifest in every situation, in every rebuff or possible rebuff, as it is at the conjunctions of Mercury and Venus with the Sun. On the other hand, you possess a conscientiousness motivated by conscience which keeps you on the straight and narrow, and gives you your tremendous capacity for self-denial. Your readiness to make heroic sacrifices and to comport yourself with honor gives you a purity of purpose and a nobility of aspiration which brings out the best in other people.

Sun parallel Venus possesses the same sense of obligation to do your best and shine as the conjunction types, but you are far more accepting of yourself than the nervous, insecure conjunctions, and therefore you are able to be who you are without any guilt or apologies – to just relax and make yourself at home – in any milieu. You are straightforward, unassuming, down-to-earth, unabashedly *real*. You have a smooth, pleasant self-possession and a light touch. Your intimate candor puts people at their ease and inclines them to accept you on your own terms, and to gladly accede or give way to you. You have truly democratic impulses because you know you are any man's equal; and you are not ashamed to take your rightful share of the good things in life. Where the conjunction natives' moods go up and down according to the approval or disapproval they receive from others, and they quickly close up to protect themselves, you parallels are self-contained and self-validating to start with: your unshakeable sense of your own inner worth as a person keeps you on an even keel no matter what is going on with the people around you.

Sun contraparallel Venus is genuine, self-assured, and relaxed in any social group – you know how to just be yourself, and to thereby take everyone around you along with you. You are independent in thought and action – a real original – and your confidence in yourself and your own ideas leads you to strike out in new directions with a gaggle of followers who cannot resist your brash intrepidity and panache. You reach out to people with an inviting sense of adventure and fun, and can turn your keen insights into human nature, and the politics of everyday society, to good advantage in order to pursue your dreams with the willing support (or at least acquiescence) of everyone you know. Although you can be impatient – even curt and dismissive – with those who don't particularly buy your act – your earnestness and sincerity win you the trust of everyone who knows you. You tend to find yourself in positions of leadership – or at least at the center of attention – without seemingly trying.

Sun–Venus Mutual Reception differs from the conjunction between these two planets in that the conjunction types tend to frustrate themselves by both reaching out for the rewards of life and pushing them away at the same time – they are too caught up in feelings of unworthiness and guilt. You MRs possess the same sensitiveness and vulnerability as the conjunction natives, and the same need to protect and nurture others, but you are not as agitated and torn apart within yourself with issues of self-esteem. You possess an abstracted, far-away wistfulness – a retreat into yourself as a refuge from the world – which is neither defensive (conjunction) nor self-validating (parallel), but rather is an instinctively optimistic thinking the best and reaching for the good. Your childlike naïveté and disarming openness tend in turn to bring out the protective or indulgent impulses in other people. You are soft and gentle, with a conciliatory, ingratiating manner which allows you to move through and amongst people without bumping into them or bending them (or yourself) out of shape. You don't allow yourself to become too stressed-out, or to permit yourself to be brought down or sucked into other people's turmoil; thus you are able to keep your distance and maintain your equipoise when everyone else is tearing their hair out.

Sun–Mars Aspects and Mutual Reception

Sun-Mars taken together symbolize the Animus, or male side of the person (n.b. the terms "Animus" and "Anima" are employed here in a somewhat different sense than Jung used them). The Animus refers to masculine sexuality, which is fundamentally electric and heterosexual in nature; and also to the largesse of manliness: *bushido*, *omerta*, Sunday afternoon football, and the way men think and talk about women. The relationship between the Sun and Mars in the horoscope symbolizes how accepting the native is of his or her own masculine energy; and by extension how well (or not) the person relates to men. If the Animus is at war with itself, this will tend to be projected onto relationships with male friends, lovers, and partners (not so much the father, which is usually shown by Sun and Saturn). Sun-Mars combinations are cool, impersonal, brisk, dynamic, and staunch. They are quick to act and react; are never nonplussed or at a loss; and by hook or crook they get their way.

Sun conjunct Mars makes its natives bold, daring, and self-reliant. You are independent-minded and are quite capable of striking out on your own and pursuing your own course in spite of what anyone else might think; but you do prefer an audience. You are brassy and outspoken, with a gift for the grand gesture or master stroke. You love to be onstage and the center of attention, and you bring off your coups with considerable personal flair and panache (particularly when Sun or Mars is strong by sign). It's not so much a matter of getting your own way (Mars conjunct Ascendant) as making certain that your voice is heard and your presence duly acknowledged. You may cultivate some special area of expertise in which your authority and superiority are unquestioned; or you may just do without the expertise altogether. But you need to have the last word or the tit for tat; and on your negative side your overweening assertiveness and ex cathedra judgments can be quite withering and dismissive. Nonetheless your irrepressibility, mischievous good humor, and ability to shake off setbacks and disappointments with a shrug of the shoulders lends you a boyish charm (even if you're a girl) which delights other people – or at least disposes them to indulge your peccadilloes.

Sun sextile Mars makes you gregarious, outgoing, and self-assured, with something of a pixiesque swagger or flip bravura which lends you a winning charm and entices other people to give way to you. You are not so much interested in making an impression or taking a stand for its own sake as you are in convincing other people and enlisting them on your side (or in your service). You are a good talker, and you reach out to people with an inviting alacrity to share your interests and enthusiasms; hence you make a good teacher, mentor, or salesperson. Your sanguine optimism and devil-may-care cheerfulness are infectious, and incline people to go along with your schemes. Since you are so hipped on your own ideas, you may at times breeze past people, or rudely brush them aside in pursuit of your own ends, which can lead to bruised sensibilities. But your unvarnished enthusiasm for your own plans and projects is usually an inspiration to others as well.

Sun square Mars tends to stubbornness, orneriness, wrong-headedness and a self-defeating running around in circles. You possess the know-it-all hubris of Sun-Mars but without the joie de vivre of the other aspects: you are thin-skinned, easily offended, brusque, tactless, and critical. You shoot from the hip, speak before thinking, and thus give needless offense when a bit of delicacy might have ameliorated a delicate situation. Your need to constantly prove yourself and assert your superiority trips you up: your intensity either overreaches or misses the mark altogether. You lurch from brooding, taciturn disgruntlement – an air of being put out or put upon – to an overbearing officiousness, with little middle ground of savoir vivre. There's an engine driving you that knows no rest or repose. You back and fill, allowing other people to invade your space or bend you out of shape until you erupt and snatch whatever it is that you wanted with huffy indignation. You flare up quickly, and are a master of self-justification and stonewalling. There is a definite need here to lighten up and chill out, because in its proper moment your headstrong tenacity and resoluteness are a stabilizing influence when the people around you are confused.

Sun trine Mars makes you shrewd, insightful, and discriminating, with a wry good humor. You are quick to pick up on unspoken vibrations and the political machinations underlying everyday situations and relationships, and are able to take advantage of your insight to seek accord, find common ground, and advance your own plans and ends thereby. You are a glib speaker, projecting complete self-confidence in your own ideas, and are a master of adapting yourself to any particular audience. You are also a good listener, with a sincere interest in understanding other people's viewpoints and refining your own thinking and opinions. Your hallmark is your unpretentiousness, earnestness, and complete candor. On the negative side there can be something of a self-satisfied complacency or overweening smugness about you – things tend to come your way easily, with little exertion on your part, so you don't much go out of your way for anyone or anything. But your poise, easy-going manner, and ability to take things in your stride provides a sense of stability and strength which calms and assures other people in turn.

Sun opposition Mars stands tall and stands alone, isolated in orneriness and dogged non-involvement. You possess all the self-assurance and decisiveness of Sun-Mars, and the same intrepid enterprise, but you don't play to the crowd or much care what kind of impression you are making. On the contrary, you are super self-serious and focused on your own ends; and you cow other people with your stern, grim, forbidding demeanor and your complete indifference to approbation or censure. You keep your own counsel, go your own way, and do your own thing. You tend to be distrustful of other people, or at least refuse to become dependent on anyone for anything; nor do you much care for others clinging to you. You gird your loins and dig in your heels at any perceived incursion into your private space. While you are judicious, thoughtful, and observant, you are often quite deaf to other people's feelings and indifferent to their sensibilities. You don't deliberately mean to be churlish, but haven't the patience for finesse or tact. On the other hand, your unique point of view and complete self-dedication to everything you do arouse admiration and respect, and incline people to take you seriously.

Sun parallel Mars endows you with a calm, unflinching determination (as opposed to the demonstrative absolutism of the aspects). You are as bold and saucy as the Sun-Mars aspects, but are by no means as peremptory, thorny, and sharp-tongued. Like the aspects you are shrewd and calculating as to where your interests lie and how best to realize them; and you are ever ready to stand and stand alone. However you lack the rebelliousness and contumacy of the aspects, and are not as scrappy and pugnacious. You strive for agreement where possible; and for finesse (rather than throwing down a gauntlet) otherwise. You have an ironic sense of humor and lightness of spirit, and you are good listener: you possess a quiet, low-key manner which invites rather than demands. You try to influence people with your own earnestness and seriousness of purpose rather than by exhortation or fait accompli. You are a trouble-shooter rather than a trouble-maker: more concerned with getting the job at hand done with dispatch rather than proving yourself or your point. You don't choose combat as your first resort, but rather find that seriousness of purpose works quite well by itself, with no need for added histrionics.

Sun contraparallel Mars is similar to Sun opposition Mars in its plowing a solitary path through life looking neither right nor left, nor relying much on others for support or succor. But you are more free-spirited and open to whatever presents itself as compared with the bull-headed, "outta-my-way-buddy" opposition. You follow the road less-traveled, allowing your instincts and whims to be your guide, and seek to enjoy the path beneath your feet every moment rather than hunker down with a fixed destination in mind. Your curiosity and willingness to follow your impulses dares to go where most people fear to tread, just for the sake of novelty (rather than for personal advantage, which is the motivating engine of the Sun-Mars aspects). There is an intellectual seeking here often missing in the Sun-Mars aspects: a desire to learn and understand (rather than to control), and your original thinking and view of life makes you a good teacher and an inspiration to others.

Sun–Mars Mutual Reception makes for an idealistic assiduity and dedication. You possess the same tenacity and grit as the Sun-Mars aspects, but none of the self-will and insensitive despotism: you are disinterested rather than self-interested. You are just as free-spirited and emotionally independent as the aspects, with the same dominating presence and self-assurance, but you possess an intellectualized view of life which motivates your striving; and you view success or failure in terms of how well you have lived up to your own abstract standards of fairness and justice. You are a natural-born leader – purposeful rather than self-aggrandizing, and just rather than jockeying for personal advantage. You have a governor on your impulses which permits you to thread your way through life and around obstacles instead of just butting your way through. You are able to compromise with other people without feeling that you are compromising your own integrity, and you are thus better equipped than the Sun-Mars aspects to realize your goals without creating friction and bad feelings.

Sun–Jupiter Aspects and Mutual Reception

Sun-Jupiter natives are broadminded and just, with a strong sense of fair play and an incumbency to uphold the highest moral principles in their everyday comportment. They welcome new learning experiences, and they reach out to people in a spirit of good fellowship and camaraderie. They possess a refreshingly candid bearing which inspires trust and puts people at their ease – they are natural and genuine in all surroundings.

Sun conjunct Jupiter makes you mild-mannered, easy-going, and positive. You are guided by a philosophical or religious intellectual system which allows you to take things in stride and maintain a hopeful, optimistic outlook; and which makes you an articulate advocate for your beliefs. Your incisive pronouncements make perfect sense; and your spontaneity and complete sincerity win people's enthusiastic support and acceptance. Thus you are usually able to further your own plans and projects in a spirit of cooperation and good cheer. Your unhurried, avuncular manner and impartial objectivity make your presence quite relaxing and comforting. You possess the self-confidence of a person who is fundamentally at peace with the world. Unless the conjunction is severely afflicted, money is not such an issue for you as it is for most people, so there always seems to be more than enough for your needs. On the negative side you can be rather abstracted and up on a cloud much of the time, with an aloof, self-satisfied impassivity. You are true to yourself under all circumstances, so you readily win the confidence and good wishes of others.

Sun sextile Jupiter gives you a simplicity of manner which enables you to immediately fit yourself into any social group. You make good eye contact and have a mischievous twinkle which is both saucy and inviting. You are laid-back and accepting, with a hail-fellow-well-met alacrity. You are not afraid to fly with your impulses; you are experimental and open to new ideas; and it takes quite a bit to bump you off your stride. You are something of a visionary, but you are adept at blending in and not making waves while you pursue your dreams and follow your own idiosyncratic path in life. There is a quixotic nobility – a naïve purity of motive – about you which people find delightful. Notwithstanding, you can be extraordinarily stubborn and set on your own designs. You live in a world of your own making, and you readily find Sancho Panzas throughout your life who will loyally support you, come what may.

Sun square Jupiter makes you something of an adamant know-it-all. You possess the same unvarnished candidness and spirited ingenuousness as do natives of the other aspects between these two bodies; but you are rather more mercurial and headstrong, and thornier for other people to have to deal with. You tend to take issues of the utmost seriousness lightly and unconcernedly, and to blithely breeze over other people's sensibilities in the process. You possess a damn-the-torpedoes dash and heedlessness, together with a flippant self-delight which can become overweening. You are a glib talker and a convincing salesperson – you *do* have a refined self-presentation when you endeavor to impress – but otherwise you can be capricious to the point of pig-headedness; and your adamant arbitrariness forces the people around you to walk on eggs. Your brazen insouciance and ironic take on life incline other people to defer to you – taking you more or less on your own terms or seeing things your way – since you are indeed quite clever (too clever for your own good much of the time). If they don't, however, you have no qualms about pursuing your goals and dreams without asking or needing anyone's by-your-leave.

Sun trine Jupiter endows you with a patient forbearance and tolerant disposition. You don't hold grudges, and you are able to let bygones be bygones, which enables you to focus on ultimate ends rather than the transient frustrations and imbroglios of everyday life. You have an abstract or philosophical take on life and your fellow men which guides you unfailingly through difficulties and confusion, and makes you a practical problem-solver and calm voice of reason in any group. You are realistic and centered in the present moment: you just live and let live, and are usually able to defuse confrontation with your patience and evenness of temper. Your emotional detachment and unwillingness to involve yourself in issues can at times make you annoyingly remote and noncommittal when something more than benign nonchalance is called for; but your calm sang-foid makes you a rock of stability when other people are at a loss and don't know where to turn.

Sun opposition Jupiter is something of an oddball or misfit. You have a bland, open manner and are courteous and subdued, with an abstracted, otherworldly wistfulness that inclines people to let you do your own thing. You easily fit in and adapt to any company in which you find yourself, but you keep aloof and uncommitted so as to maintain your private space and prerogatives (which intimates might perceive as a stiff-necked, dictatorial streak meant to hold others at bay). In spite of your affability and your facility for being your inimitable self in any milieu (oblivious, gauche), you are basically quite cagey and guarded, rather than naturally relaxed with people. You possess a moody, brooding side in which you isolate and protect yourself and armor your vulnerability. You are a visionary whose eyes are always scanning the horizon, and you choose to follow a distinct path from the one into which you were born, or to which you are expected to conform.

Sun parallel Jupiter is very undemonstrative and low-key. Where the Sun-Jupiter aspects employ their native attitude of cheerful good will and laissez faire indolence to wend their way through life and to extract maximum collaboration from their milieu, you parallel natives are not as gushing, nor are you as smug and complacent. You possess a personal effectiveness and economy of action based upon a cool-headed pragmatism and distaste for needless emotional expenditure: you are more interested in finding a modus vivendi rather than demonstrating your personal prowess. Your sobriety, soft demeanor, and impassive air of introspection result from your needing little in the way of recognition or reassurance from anyone else in deciding what to think. You are sagacious, judicious, and you base your judgments and choices on prudent and well-reasoned reflection. You are basically a humble, down-to-earth person; or at least you lack the supercilious swagger which so often characterizes the Sun-Jupiter aspects; and you keep your opinions and judgments to yourself. Your conscientiousness, dedication, and considered judgment are based upon your own analyses and original thought, together with a keen sense of what is right and true.

Sun contraparallel Jupiter makes for a clear-sighted detachment and sober objectivity. Where Sun opposition Jupiter tends to pull away from people and self-cloister, you are outgoing, voluble, and gregarious without losing your sense of self-at-center, or compromising your own impartiality and disinterestedness to play to an audience. You care little about what other people think of you: you are not particularly out to impress or win followers. Rather, you have high standards of comportment to which you hold yourself, and a well thought-out guiding philosophy and sense of purpose in life to which you maintain your fidelity through thick and thin. But you are not at all pushy or proselytizing; nor do you need anyone's stamp of approval upon your efforts. You are something of a romantic, like a knight of old venturing forth in search of the good and true, and your unselfish idealism and sense of honorable acquittal is a model for everyone who knows you.

Sun–Jupiter Mutual Reception, like the Sun-Jupiter aspects, is easy-going and sociable, with an optimistic and hopeful attitude. But where the aspects seek recognition for their perspicacity and brim with good advice for everyone, you MRs are watchers: reserved, self-contained, and attentive. You possess the directness and humanitarianism of the Sun-Jupiter aspects, and you can be quite as complacent and self-satisfied. But you are more cerebral than you are exuberant, and are more interested in learning about people and enlarging your own scope of experience than in pontificating or striking a pose. You listen to other people rather than lecture them; and your soft, unpretentious, *real* manner beckons to them (rather than being designed to impress them). It is not so much agreement or support that you aim for; rather, your reach is for dispassionate, objective thinking; and thus you tend to be more dedicated and conscientious than the aspects, who are forever seeking shortcuts and ease.

Sun–Saturn Aspects and Mutual Reception

The Sun–Saturn combination is serious-minded, responsible, and punctilious. Its natives tend to be stiff, severe, austere, and demanding (intolerant) of other people. These aspects can indicate something of the relationship with the father (whether cordial in the case of the harmonious aspects or problematical with the disharmonious ones).

Sun conjunct Saturn makes for a no-nonsense practicality. You are serious-minded, hard-headed, and hard-nosed: quite willing and able to strike out on your own and make your decisions for yourself without needing anyone's permission, help, or support. You must be your own boss since you chafe under direction. You don't just drift through life or take other people's or society's expectations as given, but rather are determined to "get somewhere" and carve out your own niche by your own efforts. You are sedulous and thorough, and don't shrink from hardship or sacrifice. How outgoing and sociable you are depends on the sign in which the conjunction is located (amongst other factors), but in any case you are basically self-contained: you keep your distance and vigilantly maintain your own private space against any encroachment (thick-skinned). You have firm lines which are not to be crossed, and you possess the inner discipline to work harder and dedicate yourself more fully than most people do. As a result there can be a tendency towards superiority and arrogance, and little in the way of native sympathy or compassion for other people's failings (especially not your father's). On the positive side, your single-mindedness and unswerving allegiance to your ideals lend you a certain nobility of character which compels the respect of everyone who knows you.

Sun sextile Saturn is cheerfully duteous and dependable. You pay close attention to details and are assiduous and thorough in your efforts. You are conscientious in your work habits and punctilious in discharging your routine obligations. You have pleasant manners and are patient and reliable, and you truly enjoy being of service to other people. You are a good teacher / mentor since you are patient and forbearing, and you enjoy explaining things (and learning new things yourself). You have a facility for problem-solving and trouble-shooting, and you can usually find a modus vivendi or collaborative compromise to get past or through any impasse. You prefer harmony and concord in your relationships and you strive for a peaceful, frictionless environment – even if that means turning your back and walking away from unpleasant involvements. On the negative side, you can be quite blind to anything you don't want to see, and quite deaf to anything you don't want to hear. But your probity and positive attitude, and your willingness to do more than your fair share, gain you the trust of other people and win their benediction upon your efforts.

Sun square Saturn tends to a self-defeating wrong-headedness and hubris. You are unvarnished, blunt, and bluff, and possess very little tact or discretion (curt and thorny). You readily say what's on your mind and let the chips fall where they may. There is something of a disgruntled air about you: a sense of being put out or put upon, or a tendency to crab and complain. There might have been conflicts with your father (who may also have been rather picky and critical; or else absent or ineffectual). You possess a stubborn pride and a huffy, dig-in-your-heels defensiveness: you will never admit that you're in the wrong, but are always ready with a self-exculpating excuse. It's difficult for you to just relax: you exist in a constant flurry of activity rushing here and there, hastening to adjust this, that, or the other. You are easily frustrated and tend to fall into a rut – a feeling that you're not accomplishing anything or getting anywhere, that all your struggles are unappreciated or in vain. On the positive side your unpolished naturalness allows you to just be yourself no matter what company you find yourself in; and, in its proper moment, your rough-and-ready bravado and gutsy willingness to tackle anything inspire admiration.

Sun trine Saturn is hard-working and responsible, and quite willing and able to exceed routine expectations and go the extra mile to fulfill your own high standards of comportment and honorable acquittal. You are meticulous and thorough, paying close attention to detail and not allowing any loose ends to escape your notice, nor permitting yourself to be satisfied with a careless "that's good enough". You set high goals for yourself, and aim directly for them without glancing right or left. But unlike the bullheaded Sun-Saturn conjunctions who plough straight ahead, you are politic and expedient – able to modify and adapt to changing conditions and the vicissitudes of human frailty; more inclined to use cogent reasoning to win people over rather than to simply run them over. On the negative side, your ivory tower idealism can make for a smug superiority and sense of infallibility which do blind you at times to your own personal motives; but your mastery of the art of the possible and mental clarity make you a natural-born leader.

Sun opposition Saturn makes for an extremely exaggerated sense of dignity and fastidiousness. You are prim and proper; stiff and stand-offish. You are very sensitive to imagined indignities, and quickly close up into yourself with testy umbrage at any perceived slight. You project a lofty discrimination, or an abstracted perfunctoriness, which holds people at arm's length. You do not invite intimacy but rather keep others at bay with a touchiness that throws them off balance since they never know how you are going to react. You may cultivate some special proficiency which gives you a standard of comparison for measuring your worth and which vindicates your own native superiority (especially vis à vis your father); in any event, there is some exalted self-image that you feel you must uphold. You never fear to stand up for yourself and to stand alone. You take considerable pride in your competence and are scrupulous in fulfilling your obligations with diligence and thoroughness. It can never be said of you that you shirked a responsibility, or did not do your very best to live up to your own highest ideals.

Sun parallel Saturn indicates a formidable earnestness. Where Sun-Saturn aspects are grave and not to be trifled with, possessing a sedate hauteur which holds itself apart from people, you parallels are more humble and unprepossessing. Like the aspects you are concentrated, hard-working, and scrupulous, but your focus is more a matter of accountability to your own conscience and moral sense rather than proving your prowess. You parallels are just as dependable and serious-minded as the aspects, but you are more laid-back and much less demanding of acknowledgement and respect. You are not as manipulative, nor as petty in scoring little power points for yourself. Rather, you work steadily at a relaxed and satisfying pace; and you know that anything you're supposed to have will come to you of its own accord. The emphasis with the parallels is on acceptance and acquiesence to the common good rather than upholding some sort of struggle ethic. True discipline is not an onerous limitation imposed from without but rather arises naturally and joyously from within when you know you are doing a good job for its own sake with no thought of reward.

Sun contraparallel Saturn is serious-minded and intent, with a clear sense of what you are capable of and how to use your native abilities to move yourself forward through life. Unlike the stiff and haughty Sun opposition Saturn, you are readily approachable and gladly reach out to share your thinking and dreams with other people, and to appreciate theirs as well. You are hard-working and responsible, but not especially ambitious in the usual sense of pushing yourself upward toward some abstract goal. Rather, your aspiration is to always do your best and be happy with what you have, rather than to impress or to measure your worth in terms of comparison with others. You feel you have done your duty as you are able to keep yourself on an even keel, and thereby be a steadying influence and a model of equanimity no matter what is going on around you.

Sun–Saturn Mutual Reception enables taking a long view and putting matters into a proper perspective. Where the aspects between Sun-Saturn make their natives attentive to their obligations and zealous of their reputation as dutiful members of their milieu and society, you MRs – albeit just as diligent as the aspects – are less exacting (of yourself and other people), and are more practical and down-to-earth. Your deliberateness and caution may seem to be a bit plodding or hesitant in comparison with the stiff-necked surety of the Sun-Saturn aspects because you ponder and consider the realities of a situation before plunging ahead. You MRs are matter-of-fact rather than demonstrative, and practical rather than authoritarian – you always seek an accommodation or quid pro quo with as little pother as possible. You have a higher sense of accountability than merely fulfilling your end of a bargain; and you try to take everyone's point of view into account in reaching your decisions. You may project a fatherly image – the sort of person others instinctively turn to when they need advice and guidance – and your composure and imperturbability is calming and reassuring. You have a gift for taking things as they come and striving for the best result possible rather than the best possible result.

Sun–Uranus Aspects

Sun–Uranus is idealistic and true-to-self, but also can be whimsical, fickle, and incapable of fitting in or taking direction. These natives usually possess great personal flair and magnetism, and strongly influence (or bend out of shape) the people around them. Sun-Uranus afflictions suggest conflicts with / abandonment by the father and often put tension and stress in all relationships with authority.

Sun conjunct Uranus is unboundedly Promethean. You are devil-may-care and fancy-free, with a highly original personal style and charisma. You are not nonconformist or rebellious per se – you simply do your own thing and blaze your own trail through life rather than follow well-trodden paths. There is something of the Don Quixote about you: idealistic, noble, and spontaneous; and ready to charge off impulsively with nary a fare-thee-well. You are unafraid to take risks (without even thinking them so); and you are animated by a bold intellectual curiosity and a love for exploring new frontiers. Your opinions and viewpoint tend to be on the cutting edge of your social milieu: at least you don't look at things the way the people around you do – you always have your own unique take on any subject. You are unabashedly outspoken and blunt (irascible); and while not combative per se, you are quick to stand up and fight for what you believe in; or turn your back and go off on your own rather than compromise or waste time with explanations. Since you basically follow your own impulses you can be very difficult to influence, so intimates may regard you as being overly distant and noncommittal. But your gung-ho optimism and can-do cockiness make you a most enjoyable and fascinating companion.

Sun sextile Uranus makes for free-spirited intrepidity. You are blithe, plucky, and game, with a great sense of fun and a readiness to rise to any new challenge or adventure. You are daring and a bit reckless, and are perfectly willing to go to any extreme just for the hell of it. You are highly competitive, thrive on attention and adulation, and you love showing off and proving your mettle. You take pride in your fitness and competence; and indeed there is some area in which you are very gifted and in which your talent and superiority are unquestionable. You possess a sassy, irreverent humor and a cynical and ironic view of your fellow men and their peccadilloes; and sometimes your associates may feel that you are patronizing and not taking them or their feelings seriously. You are audacious and sharp-tongued, and have very little patience for what you perceive to be stupidity (i.e., disagreement with your point of view). You're not one for diplomacy, but rather barge right ahead and damn the torpedoes.

Sun square Uranus is both ingenuous and capricious. You are artless and true – unabashedly yourself in any milieu, with nothing to hide or be ashamed of. You possess high ideals which inform all your actions with cleanliness, economy, and nobility. At the same time, you can be too focused on your own ends or in too big of a hurry to bother much with social niceties. You are not deliberately rude – indeed, you can be quite deferential and respectful when you happen to think of it. But much of the time you are off-hand and brusque, which can grate on people – rub them the wrong way. There's no persuading or arguing with you: you have your own agenda, and either other people fit into it somehow, or to heck with them. Your heedless naïvete and lack of social grace actually do lend you a certain flighty charm which others admire; and which inclines them to defer to you (so that they don't get bowled over). You are never at a loss: even in a maelstrom you hold your own, and thus you are looked up to as a model of steadfastness and uprightness.

Sun trine Uranus shows a person who tends to go with the flow and live in the moment rather than by prearranged plan. You have an astute, ironic take on life and your fellow bipeds, and are not easily fooled by appearances. You are shrewd, insightful, and diplomatic in your handling of people, and in trouble-shooting life's difficulties. There is an objective, analytical approach to life here which is absent in the other Sun-Uranus aspects, who tend to barge right on ahead impulsively; rather, you are cannier in threading your way through life while nonetheless maintaining your independence of thought and action. You are able to slither around obstacles rather than blasting your way though them, avoiding needless confrontation while by no means being a shrinking violet. Your remoteness and noncommittal stance can irritate people when you regard their demands as limiting to your freedom to just do your own thing: you just smile, shrug your shoulders, and go your own way.

Sun opposition Uranus is a sign of a bullheaded self-will. You are private, dogged, and remote, harboring your own personal vision and following it unerringly wherever it may lead you. You possess the courage of your convictions and an uncompromising single-mindedness and tenacity. You pace yourself at your own speed and will not be hurried, budged, or caught up in other people's hustle-bustle. You always maintain your own freedom of action and cannot be deflected from the path beneath your feet. You are basically solitary in your habits and permit no one to hem you in or jostle you off your stride – you always manage to keep your own psychological elbow room and space. In spite of your considerable verve and personal magnetism (when you choose to turn them on), your whimsicality can also smack of a smug and above-it-all self-congratulation. You don't much care how you are seen by other people, and they in turn may find you remote, capricious, and wrongheaded. But your staunchly individualistic idiosyncrasies and sui generis view of life – in their proper moment – can be a source of considerable delight.

Sun parallel Uranus is the mark of a spunky gumption. Sun-Uranus aspect natives have a freewheeling, unpretentious, California kind of style: eager, broad-minded, experimentative, tolerant of other people, with an attitude of live and let live. You Sun parallel Uranus natives are just as emotionally detached and independent as the aspects, but you are more self-contained. You maintain your freedom of action not through a battering ram, hell-bent-for-leather, damn-the-torpedos attitude; nor by a sidestepping strategy of avoidance; but rather by being collected and in possession of yourself come what may. Hence, you are difficult to move or influence; loose and nimble, you carefully avoid being pinned down or emotionally committed, and thus are able to preserve your freedom of action at all times. While friendly and outgoing, you can also be maddeningly vague, distant, and noncommittal. You are truly an original – a pioneer who is never afraid to go your own way and follow your own heart, and who possesses an equanimity born of fearless conviction. You are not as glib as the aspects, but you are more placid, analytical, and penetrating.

Sun contraparallel Uranus makes you both wildly individualistic and yet truly humble and sincere. You tend to be isolated in your own world, in which things are pure, lovely, and of good report; and not even the ugly vicissitudes of harsh reality can shake you from your chosen path. Your free-spiritedness and inability to dissemble or play games often leads you into muddles of disturbance and bewilderment (especially if Sun and Uranus are also in opposition); yet you are always able to emerge with your blithe alacrity intact. You have an uncanny ability to say or do or be the right thing at the right time, without particularly trying to; and somehow the hurricanes of life tend to whirl around you, with you always standing impassively in the eye. On the negative side, your obliviousness and tendency to view life through rose-colored spectacles can be the source of imbroglios which a modicum of objectivity and discretion might have obviated (again, particlulary when the two planets also oppose); yet you always seem to have a divine protection and benediction on your efforts.

Sun–Neptune Aspects

Sun-Neptune is high-minded and sincere, but somewhat out of synch with the social environment. These natives are not so much nonconformist as misfits – congenitally incapable of belonging or playing by the accepted rules: they learn early on that the expected rewards for acquiesence to prevailing norms and canons will not be forthcoming in their case, so they have to find some other foundation for a sense of self-esteem than the approval of other people. Hence they go their own way and do their own thing without much of a plan or regard for consequences. The aspects between Sun and Neptune often give considerable psychic ability (for the better if a favorable aspect; for the worse if unfavorable).

Sun conjunct Neptune is both visionary and quixotic. You are truly inspired – psychic, sensitive, and extremely vulnerable to whatever feelings are in the air. You also are a bit other-worldly and naïve, and the "real" world can be a bit too real; too harsh for your delicate sensibilities. As a result your outward manner appears preoccupied or worried, and you are cautious and wary – reflexively withdrawing into yourself or taking counsel of your fears when disconcerted. On the other hand, you have a powerful spiritual or artistic bent, and you possess strong religious or philosophical convictions which motivate you in making your decisions. You are also very idealistic and strive to manifest in all your relationships the highest standards of honor and aboveboard behavior. You live in an ivory-tower dream-world of your own devising wherein your imagination holds sway and where there is assurance of divine benediction upon your efforts. To other people you can seem annoying vague and indefinite at times, particularly when you are off on your own tangent and unwilling to be deterred or listen to reason. But your impeccable aspirations lend you a virtuousness and nobility which is commanding in its innocence.

Sun sextile Neptune is feisty and game. You are spunky with an irreverent sense of humor, a conspiratorial twinkle in your eye, and a pixiesque naïveté. You are positive, upbeat, hopeful, and keep your eyes on the horizon. You possess a quick and agile mind – always ready with a clever, ironic retort; and you have no hesitation about speaking your mind and flying with your impulses. As with the Sun-Neptune conjunction types, you possess much native psychic ability and are quick to pick up on and address whatever vibrations are in the air. You dislike complexities, and indeed have little gift for guile or the ability to conceal what you are thinking and feeling: when you are annoyed, everyone gets the message loud and clear. You can be impatient and brusque – completely without tact; and you usually prefer doing things your own way in solitude rather than depending on anyone else or compromising your own dreams one iota. But your plucky, can-do spirit wins people over and inclines them to grant you indulgence.

Sun square Neptune: You possess a strong moral sense which is couched in terms of high religious or spiritual principles, but you find it difficult to bring these standards to bear upon the harsh vicissitudes of your everyday life and the politics of your relationships. Because you believe the best of people, you are easily victimized or deceived. Your sensibilities are too delicate and refined, and the world is just too inexorable and predatory – not obeying your rules, or caring much about your rights or feelings. Things happen too fast for you to keep up with, so you frequently find yourself swept along or acceding helplessly to oppressive circumstances, rather than taking arms against a sea of troubles and by opposing end them. You usually find yourself on the defensive because your fear of rejection invites other people to abuse your good faith and decency, and invade your space or bend you out of shape. On the other hand, your impeccable probity is a model of right-thinking and action for everyone who knows you; and your deep-felt need to acquit yourself honorably no matter what the consequences arouses admiration and sympathy.

Sun trine Neptune is both intuitive and judicious. You have the ability to cut across pretense and gamesmanship and to see things very clearly; and as a result you tend to hold to very strong, unshakeable opinions; and to be quite judgmental. You are very sensitive to emotional vibrations and the unspoken feelings which underlie everyday society and relationships. You also have a nuanced manner of sending messages yourself: you are subtle and oblique rather than blatant; and you prefer to employ tacit communication and maneuvering to avoid obstacles rather than direct confrontation, or to allowing yourself to be pinned down. You just shut yourself down, and shut out anything that you don't want to see or hear. As a result, intimates may complain that you are vague and noncommittal – off on your own cloud or tangent, and abstracted when a definite response is required. But your high standards of honor and correct comportment are a model of right and righteousness for everyone who knows you.

Sun opposition Neptune makes for a cocksure personal style. You are bold and brassy, with an ironic point of view and a flair for the grand or magnanimous gesture (on the negative side: swaggering or condescending). Like all Sun-Neptune aspects the opposition follows the dictums of its own heart and does its own thing, but you are more down-to-earth and grounded in everyday realities than the oblivious conjunction types. This opposition is not so good for worldly achievement (which you tend to eschew, since you are basically solitary), but rather for putting your personal touch or original stamp on everything which attracts your attention. You have a great intellectual curiosity and love discovering new ideas and learning new skills. Like the Sun-Neptune conjunction types you possess a keen understanding of the motives of other people, and a feeling for unspoken emotional undercurrents; but where the conjunction is nervous and flighty, the opposition is circumspect, suspicious and secretive. You cannot be budged or stampeded, but instead slow everything down to your own speed until everyone else is in synch with you (or else you just go your own way). You insulate yourself not by withdrawing from this world but rather by focusing on that which is of good report, and deliberately ignoring everything else.

Sun parallel Neptune makes for inner certainty and unerring decisiveness. The Sun-Neptune aspects march to the beat of a distant drum: they are part visionary and part space-out, with a well-developed set of spiritual ideals and an inclination to view the world through rose-colored glasses. Because they are so attuned to subtleties they possess a taste for the abstract or mystical, but at the same time they are also subject to disquieting fancies and morbid imaginings. You parallels are similarly high-minded and willing to operate on the basis of your own inner promptings, but you are not as blindly optimistic and naïve on the one hand, nor as torn by self-doubt on the other. You rely on your personal touch with the abstract to guide you rather than permit it to dominate you; thus you are able trust your own impulses, take the initiative, and deal with other people in a frank and above-board fashion (rather than deny painful realities or indulge unreasoning fears). In contrast to the fluttery aspects you are more steadfast and stable, maintaining a level-headed integrity and seeking practical, just solutions rather than aiming for some sort of utopian perfectionism.

Sun contraparallel Neptune is similar to the opposition between these planets in its deliberation and self-pacing: you are focused on the path beneath your feet and you move at a slower speed than most of the other people in your environment. It's not merely a matter of caution; nor of marching to the beat of a distant drum; rather, you weigh and measure your decisions against a benchmark of correct thought and action based on your own abstract standards of fairness and truth. You are incapable of guile or gamesmanship – what people see is what they get. You give your full attention to the people you encounter with little thought of impressing them or of what might be gained from them. Nor are you particularly interested in vaunting yourself or advancing your position in life: you tend to take it one day at a time, and (unless more dynamic aspects dominate) you have little worldly ambition except to do the best you can. There's something of a Sad Sack about you; yet your unswerving allegiance to your high ideals wins people's trust and allegiance.

Sun–Pluto Aspects

Sun-Pluto aspect natives are astute, tenacious, and indomitable. They are self-assured, headstrong and they must always have the last word or get in the last lick. They are not so much gauche as oblivious to social niceties in their drive to get whatever it is they want; and while they can be temporarily stymied they never abandon their goals – they regroup themselves after any setback and go on as before as if there were no interruption. The hard aspects (conjunction, square, and opposition) can bring complete Sisyphean wipe-outs or Damascene, 180° about-faces from one day to the next, which necessitate a completely new beginning in life.

Sun conjunct Pluto is intense, single-minded, and very difficult to influence from without. You are utterly focused upon the path beneath your feet, and are driven by an engine that never rests. You have tremendous fortitude and power-in-reserve, and cannot be knocked off your pins for long. You are extemely nimble at rolling with events and taking advantage of opportunities as they present themselves, and you are quite ready to uproot yourself and sever all your connections in a trice. At intervals throughout your life you arrive at a dead end and make a Saul of Tarsus-like conversion, or a complete reversal of direction: you are forced to release your obsessive grip by being annihilated emotionally or financially, and must then start all over again from scratch (this is also true of the opposition). You are not necessarily ambitious in a worldly sense, but rather are animated by a strong need to carve out your own niche or make your own mark. You are basically a loner – suspicious of other people's motives and never quite comfortable in a social setting unless you are somehow controlling the proceedings. You can be highly arbitrary and dictatorial; and when thwarted you dig in your heels and indulge in a huffy, self-exculpating self-righteousness. But your fearless and unswerving fidelity to your principles assures that you are taken seriously.

Sun sextile Pluto is clever and subtle with an astute sense of the politics of everyday society. You have a bland, undemonstrative manner and placidly accept the situations you encounter as given, rather than get into an uproar or create a fuss. Nonetheless you possess tremendous staying power, inner discipline, and shrewdness. You carefully watch what is going on before you act or react, and no detail escapes your critical scrutiny. You generally prefer to slither around obstacles rather than confront people directly, but you are no shrinking violet and you will take and hold your ground till hell freezes over. You can be irascible and bluff when your hand is forced, but you possess an ironic or sardonic view of your fellow humans which leavens your controlled intensity; and you are always ready to make a peace. You are a keen observer of the passing scene; are highly attuned to subtleties and nuances; and thus you are usually able to get your own way without creating needless conflict.

Sun square Pluto is capricious, willful, and always on the go. You possess a fidgety, high-wire energy which has to be talking or acting all the time. Listening to other people or thinking things through are not your strong suits: your starry-eyed credulity and wildcat impetuosity charge off half-cocked and brook no moderation or interference. You are admirably staunch and intrepid – once you grab onto an idea or a plan, you just won't let it go – but you possess no tact or diplomacy whatsoever. Instead, you have a keen sense of just how much you can get away with, and you brazen out any opposition with unreasoning pigheadedness. You actually seem to relish combat, and rely upon wearing your opponents down with unyielding vociferousness and illogic. Because your gung-ho optimism so often has little basis in reality, you can get easily frustrated and tend to run around in circles without getting anywhere. But you are quick to pick yourself back up when you are knocked down or out, and jump back into the fray.

Sun trine Pluto gives you considerable intellectual detachment and the ability to hold fast and hang on through thick and thin. You have a good intuitive grasp of the underlying vibrations and feelings of the people around you; and a philosophical approach to life which allows you to ameliorate difficulties and resolve disagreements without bending yourself or other people out of shape. You are punctilious and meticulous, and discharge even onerous responsibilities with uncomplaining élan. However, unless other, more dynamic indications contradict, you are not especially ambitious in a worldly sense, but rather have a laissez faire attitude which prefers enjoying the scenery rather than getting anywhere in particular. Your imperturbability can at times grate on people who need a deeper commitment of your attention and energy than you are willing to grant. However, your single-minded determination to go your own way and do your own thing lends you a nobility of spirit which others look up to.

Sun opposition Pluto is mercurial and headlong. You are animated by a simmering discontent and a fitful restlessness, so you are never quite at peace or in repose but always on your guard and scouting around. You are sharp mentally and sharp of tongue: quick-witted, and quick on the trigger. Your nervous, petulant manner bristles with impatience and automatically dismisses bothersome people and situations to oblivion. Your outspoken pugnacity and intolerance for any sort of stricture (especially being dictated to) gives you an embattled air. You possess a true pioneering spirit and are ready to fearlessly strike out on your own whenever you are blocked, or when things have come to a dead end or point of frustration. Indeed, it is likely that in the course of your life you must (or voluntarily choose to) give everything up and begin anew. Although you are intolerant of contradiction and steam-roll over anyone who gets in your way, your willingness to go to any extreme and follow your own star wherever it may lead you wins the respect and deference of others.

Sun parallel Pluto is astute and perspicacious. The Sun-Pluto aspects are self-absorbed and bent on their own designs; hence they tend to take a shortsighted view of the world around them. They are given to wishful thinking and to making black and white judgments. Albeit courageous and determined, they can also be adamant to the point of unreason: their willfulness and obstinate self-certainty make these natives very prickly to deal with. You parallels exhibit the same flashes of crazy eccentricity as the aspects; and you can be every bit as mulish; but you have a greater sense of proportion and detachment from your own value judgments. You are not quick to act or react, but rather are sober and reflective, and arrive at your conclusions and make your decisions only after subjecting them to thorough analysis and refining and redacting them. Your conviction is based upon careful deliberation and patient forbearance (rather than constantly proving your mettle or shooting from the hip); thus you feel little need to impose or impress your views on others. Your pertinacity is intellectual rather than histrionic; it is tempered by a self-restraint absent in the wildly passionate aspects.

Sun contraparallel Pluto is as knowing and attuned to subtleties as the aspects between these planets, but you are rather more phlegmatic and inclined to watch and wait rather than act on impulse. You possess a deep moral sense which informs all your actions; and while you can be as stubborn and unyielding as the Sun-Pluto aspects, and as difficult to move or deflect, your allegiance is more to ultimate aims and objectives rather than to momentary obsessions or personal benefit. You seek to find meaning in the events of your life rather than strategic advantage; in consequence, it may seem to other people that you don't really accomplish much or get anywhere in particular, but are always standing on square one. However, your inner conviction, purity of motive, and strength of purpose is a model of honorable comportment, and you are a rock of stability on which other people instinctively depend in times of doubt and confusion.

Moon–Mercury Aspects and Mutual Reception

Natives with Moon aspecting Mercury are practical, insightful, and adroit (know-it-alls). They pride themselves on their competence, and are highly proficient at what they do (particularly mental pursuits). They are people persons (rather than loners) – skillful conversationalists who love holding forth and expressing their opinions and viewpoints to persuade others. Traditionally, Moon-Mercury aspects imply much travel or moving about.

Moon conjunct Mercury is astute, original, and clever. You are acute, glib, sharp-witted, and snappy – quick to pick up on nuances, quick to see through pretense, and quick to react with a ready retort. You are nimble, cagey, and politic, deft at handling people because of your straightforwardness and plain speaking (inability to dissemble). You possess strong opinions, but you have an inquiring mind and are open to new ideas and are constantly refining your thinking, learning new skills, and honing your proficiency. There may be a love of roaming – mentally if not around the world – and you follow the road less-traveled in your search for some system of belief or standard of behavior with which you can orient yourself and upon which you can base your choices: you set high standards for yourself on correct belief and comportment. You thoroughly dedicate yourself to whatever you do, and you pride yourself on your good judgment and perspicacity. You are not afraid to speak your mind and on the negative side you can be curt, blunt, and dogmatic. Your high ideals and serious-minded practicality assure that you will be heard and believed.

Moon sextile Mercury makes for a blithe, cocky optimism and sparkle. You are cheerful, positive, and forward-looking, and you try to see the bright side of any issue. You have a highly original point of view, strong opinions, and you love to lecture and teach. You are offhand and glib, and are a good negotiator. You have an enthusiastic good humor which refuses to take setbacks to heart or negative criticism seriously: you merrily go your own way and do your own thing, and refuse to allow other people's issues to entangle you or bring you down (flippant). There may be something of the fastidious dilettante about you: up on your own cloud looking down upon the passing scene with supercilious nonchalance. Your cool detachment may at times lead other people to complain that you are unconcerned and uncaring – not there for them when serious commitment is called for. But your infectious mood of hopefulness buoys any group of which you are a part.

Moon square Mercury makes for a doctrinaire cantankerousness. You are self-certain and trenchant – nobody's fool – with a penetrating, analytical mind. But your view of life tends to resemble that of Eeyore: you are skeptical of what everyone else is taking for granted, and are highly suspicious of the rationales of your fellow bipeds – always looking for the angles and hidden motives for their actions and reactions. You are fond of argumentation, especially the picking of holes in other people's reasoning; and, as it turns out (fortunately or unfortunately), you are quite often in the right. The dogmatism common to all Moon-Mercury aspects here reaches a zenith of pontifical smugness; but where the other aspects are concerned with clear communication, you tend to prance and preen, and always make sure that you get in the last word – "I told you so". On your positive side you are in fact a highly original, daring thinker with a unique slant on life which differs markedly from the commonly accepted wisdom of your milieu; and you are courageously ready and willing to put your ideas to the test.

Moon trine Mercury is an indication of a judicious mind which scans ahead and is able to pick up potential difficulties and nuances of meaning which escape most people. You try to take things calmly and collectedly, and you have a gift for problem-solving and trouble-shooting. In contrast to the bouncy, quick-on-the-trigger sextile between these two planets, you analyze and try to foresee consequences and repercussions before committing yourself. Your optimism and buoyancy are based on the conviction that you will be able to handle and deal with whatever comes your way (rather than merely crossing your fingers and hoping for the best). Because you are so sure of your mental powers, you may not always heed or take seriously other people's plaints – you isolate yourself in smug self-certainty. Moon and Mercury both symbolize travel – but even if you never leave home you possess a restless spirit which is always reaching upward and outward beyond the known horizon in search of knowledge and understanding.

Moon opposition Mercury makes you visionary and aloof, with a nervous, high-strung energy that is always on the go. You possess a fertile imagination that bursts with original creative ideas, and there is very little that escapes your attention (you are thorough, meticulous, and good at details). Like all the Moon – Mercury aspects you have a clear insight into other people's true motives, but you are disinclined to involve yourself either by exploiting this knowledge for your own advantage (as the sextile / trine types do), or by considering yourself superior to them (as the squares do). Albeit sociable and outgoing in casual relationships, you like to keep loose and thus may feel contstrained by intimacy (at least by having to take other people's views and feelings into account). You therefore tend to hold people at arm's length and live your own life as you will. This may involve moving around quite a bit till you ultimately find your secure resting place (indeed, your life can be said to be a search for one). You hold to your own course and follow your own dreams wherever they may lead you; and your refreshing, unselfconscious audacity and alacrity is an example of free-spiritedness for everyone who knows you.

Moon parallel Mercury makes for a cocksure self-possession which is never disconcerted or at a loss for words. Like the Moon–Mercury aspect types, you parallels are quick to pick up subtleties and make the right intellectual connections; and you act with little need for pretense, embellishment, or concern for maintaining appearances. But you use improvisation and seat-of-the-pants cleverness as a guide rather than thought-out rationales: you are breezy, matter-of-fact, and quickly adapt yourself to (and can speak confidently in) any social milieu in which you might find yourself. You rely upon your spontaneous ingenuity rather than on reasoning and you finesse or snake your way around opposition rather than try to convince or prove your point to anybody. You possess a clear sense of the art of the possible and a realistic appraisal of how to achieve your goals with the least pother necessary. Albeit usually off on your own tangent and impervious to other people's reasons (deaf to entreaty), you are able to hold to your own course with admirable èlan.

Moon contraparallel Mercury resembles the opposition between these planets in its determination to figure things out for yourself and go your own way without worrying too much about what other people think. But there is a considered prudence or intransigence here in place of the quickness of thought and decision of the Moon–Mercury aspects: you won't permit yourself to be harried or stampeded (which others can at times find frustrating when they are antsy and nervous and demanding a response). While you are intellectually perspicacious and attuned to the nuances and subtleties in what people around you are doing and saying, you staunchly hold fast to a strong sense of dignity and detachment with which you hold yourself apart from conflicts and other people's turmoil. This is not so much a shrewdness or finesse on your part as it is not particularly giving a damn. You go your own way and do your own thing and leave other people free to fall in with you, or get left behind, as they please.

Moon–Mercury Mutual Reception makes for a calm, unhurried heedfulness. For the Moon–Mercury aspect types, life is a search for some system of belief or behavior through which they can orient themselves and justify their choices. They possess an optimistic faith in the rules of the game: in the value of common sense and good faith to resolve any problem, no matter how irrational or intractable. You Moon–Mercury Mutual Reception types are more self-analyzing than the aspects, hence less dependent on stable conditions outside yourself for a sense of inner equipoise. You are more detached (less urgent) in your dealings with people, and move at a deliberate – self-chosen – pace (you cannot be rushed or stampeded). You possess as quick an intellectual grasp as do the aspects, but you are more reserved and self-validating – not as explanatory and self-justifying, nor as dependent upon winning other people's agreement or support – because you don't speak or act until it feels right to do so; and then you are a rock. You have a self-critical, self-mocking faculty not usually present in the aspects, and thus you are able to take a calmer, deeper, more philosophical view of life than the aspects do.

Moon–Venus Aspects and Mutual Reception

Moon–Venus aspects symbolize the Anima – the female, receptive facet of a native's personality – magnetic and fundamentally homosexual. Reference is to the person's soft, vulnerable, emotional, accepting side; and how successfully (or the reverse) this sensibility engages the outside world. A male who has Moon–Venus conjunct or in favorable aspect is one who understands and is popular with women, and who enjoys successful relationships with females in general (hair dressers, beekeepers, dairy farmers). Conversely, males whose Moons square or oppose Venus usually find their relations with the opposite sex to be vexing and conflictive. Contrary to popular belief, not even those with the good aspects of Moon and Venus make happier marriages than anybody else; but there is less tendency to divorce here because the overriding concern for harmony in relationships leads these natives to endure more for the sake of peace.

Moon conjunct Venus makes for gentility and delicacy of feeling; and for a positive, optimistic attitude. You are softspoken and sensitive, and possess a pleasant, gracious disposition which exudes good fellowship and cheer. You are a sympathetic listener, possess good judgment, and are eminently reasonable, fair, and just: you lean over backwards to take other people's feelings into account. Your calming influence on other people leads them to instinctively seek you out when they are in need of comfort or nurture. Moon conjunct Venus makes for popularity, especially with women. You also love children, and they are immediately drawn to and won over by your playful and inviting manner. In any group you are the one who keeps things light and relaxed: you don't let mishaps or setbacks knock you off your pins, but are able to take things in your stride with even-tempered good humor, and to deal with whatever must be done without undue pother or fuss. Your insistence on doing your own thing and refusing to be drawn into other people's turmoil can at times make you seem remote and standoffish; and your pleasure-loving nonchalance can verge on complacent self-indulgence. But you are a rock of stability when things seem to be chaotic and confusing – able to keep your head when others around you are losing theirs.

Moon sextile Venus is light and breezy, with a happy-go-lucky optimism. You are frank, forthright, and sincere. You make direct eye contact and are a good listener and a good talker: interested in other people and what they have to say, and in learning their points of view and what they are doing with their lives. You have your own strong opinions which you are delighted to impart to all and sundry, but you are not officious or doctrinaire – you are merely animated by the strength of your convictions. Nonplussed by contention, you much prefer to confer and convince, and to reach a harmonious consensus, rather than to score little points for yourself or to impose your position on others. You shy away from unpleasantness, and on your negative side you can be lax and perfunctory, letting things slide rather than confronting exigencies realistically. But your winning good humor and personal élan lend a mood of general jauntiness to any group of which you are part.

Moon square Venus is gruff, controlling, and inflexible in pursuing its ends. You are unvarnished, blunt, and abrasive – utterly lacking in the graciousness which characterizes the harmonious aspects between Moon and Venus. Forthright and out front, you are not afraid to get your feelings off your chest and speak your mind. It is difficult for you to let others take the lead, or to let things unfold of their own accord (heavy-handed). You pride yourself on your bluntness; and you blithely steamroll right ahead and grab whatever it is you want with little tact or awareness of other people's sensibilities. You tend to attract conflictive relationships, or else you create them yourself with your adamant stonewalling (where a little ameliorative diplomacy might have easily achieved better results without all the stress). You are fundamentally suspicious of other people and their motives (perhaps because you are so conscious of your own); and you tend to feel uncomfortable when you are too secure or happy. On your positive side you are plucky and possess an admirable true grit; you mean what you say; and you are not afraid to stand up for what you believe in.

Moon trine Venus is friendly and outgoing, with a kindly disposition and deep respect for yourself and others. You are a thoughtful, sympathetic listener, truly concerned for other people and willing to go out of your way to help and be of service in any way you can. Unlike the prancing and preening sextiles between these two planets, you are unassuming and self-effacing; more interested in reaching for understanding than making an impression or pushing an opinion of your own. Your behavior is governed by a deep sense of accountability rather than by allegiance to an abstract philosophical or religious point of view: you are realistic rather than optimistic – a master of the art of the possible. You avoid being sucked into other people's issues and turmoil not via a strategy of avoidance (like the sextiles between Moon and Venus), but rather by being staunch and true to yourself, with an unshakeable sense of self at center which is a rock of stability in the midst of doubt and confusion.

Moon opposition Venus makes for a divine discontent and disgruntlement, particularly in personal relationships (especially with women). You are diffident and self-effacing; brimming with vague yearnings and wistfulness. Things are never quite comfortable or perfect; your expectations are never quite realized; there is always something just outside your grasp which eludes your pursuit of happiness. There is a faint sense of annoyance and distraction about you: you are easily put out and are never quite at your ease or present in the now moment. Your life tends to be a flurry of busyness – hastening hither and thither attending to this or that – with little sense of respite, fulfillment, or just recompense for your efforts. Your relationships are unsubstantial or disappointing (and you may tend to seek indifferent or rejecting partners). You may make a virtue of self-denial; or go out of your way to do more than is really necessary to vindicate yourself; and then feel imposed upon or used when your sacrifices are unappreciated. On your positive side you are capable of considerable self-denial; are meticulous and thorough; and are punctilious in discharging your obligations.

Moon parallel Venus makes for an aboveboard frankness and ease of manner: you make yourself right at home in any company, and are unabashedly yourself at all times. Where the Moon–Venus aspects make a strong effort to please and be pleasing, you Moon parallel Venus natives are less self-conscious, more accepting of your own and other people's limitations than the aspects, and therefore less dependent upon approval from others for your own sense of inner worth. You go your own way, do your own thing, and if others care to join in, they are welcome. You are more impersonal in your comaraderie than the Moon-Venus aspects, with a better sense of your own emotional space, and you don't permit other people to disturb your inner balance. On your negative side you can be infuriatingly smug, blasé, and self-satisfied, with a stiff dignity that is quick to take offense. But you know the art of compromising with others without compromising your own true feelings.

Moon contraparallel Venus is sociable and outgoing, yet rather more guarded or restrained than the exuberant aspects between these planets. You tend to take your personal relationships more seriously than the Moon–Venus aspects do: you have fewer expectations of people; and therefore you tend to suffer fewer disappointments. You don't measure yourself against others or play to the crowd: you need little input from other people for your own sense of self-assurance and self-esteem. Therefore, you tend to be more respectful of other people and their private space (and zealously protective of your own). Your disinclination to become involved in other people's issues can strike intimates as stubborn intransigence rather than steadfast immovability. But like the Moon parallel Venus, you don't care a fig about what other people think of you; you are more circumspect and diplomatic than the unvarnished and indelicate parallels, while being every bit as forthright and true to yourself.

Moon–Venus Mutual Reception is vivacious and playful. The Moon-Venus aspects are primarily concerned with appreciation and harmony; thus, whether or not their earnest endeavors are rewarded by life they are quite willing to go out of their way for other people, and are extremely punctilious and attentive to details in their search for an ideal relationship and an agreeable environment. You MRs enjoy others' appreciation as much as the aspects do, and you are equally meticulous in your dealings with other people and the world around you. But you are gutsier and livlier than the aspects, more impulsive and free-wheeling, and less dependent on outside input to to reflect how you're doing. Your doughty optimism and cheerfulness are ironic and knowing rather than expectant: you do your own thing; tip other people a wink; and invite them to join with you in the fun if they care to. On the negative side your free-spiritedness and tendency to go your own way come what may often sends you off on your own tangents. You take joy in your creativity and the diligence of your efforts, rather than in the rewards or recognition you receive from them.

Moon–Mars Aspects and Mutual Reception

Moon-Mars has to do with holding firm and staying one's course. This combination is humorous and playful, with a childlike sense of mischief (though they do tend to come on pretty strong). At the same time, they embody an indomitability which commands the respect of other people. Moon–Mars aspects are simpleminded – not in the sense of being unintelligent, but in the sense of being naïve and trusting (hence easily hurt and disappointed). There's not much subtlety or feeling for nuance here – these natives are unvarnished and rough around the edges. They are true to their principles and unswerving in their determination, though they also have a prima donna streak, and are ornery and peevish. Afflictions of Moon and Mars (including the conjunction) can indicate conflictive or disillusioning relations with the mother, who may be pugnacious, rejecting, or mentally ill – so the children are forced to emotionally fend for themselves.

Moon conjunct Mars gives you a willingness to go all out and push the envelope. You are not so much rebellious per se as highly individualistic: you don't conform to the herd, but have to follow your own star wherever it leads you (and in spite of what anyone thinks of you). You are truly an original: experimentative and fancy-free; with a love for travel, seeing new sights, and seeking new adventures. You are animated by a great curiosity about the world and constantly seek opportunities to improve your competence and understanding. You know that you are any man's equal, and you don't back down from (nay – even relish) eyeball-to-eyeball confrontation. This is not a good position for marriage because you are something of a loner, so it is difficult for you to compromise (or, conversely, you attract uncompromising partners). You always know your own mind, and hold fast and stand your ground; which on the negative side can make you extremely bullheaded, critical, and sassy. But your blithe, devil-may-care intrepidity, singleness of purpose, and can-do spirit demonstrate the courage of your convictions.

Moon sextile Mars makes for a happy-go-lucky alacrity and willingness to fly with your impulses. You are perky, peppy, and unselfconscious in the extreme, and are inimitably yourself in any company or circumstances. You are rather enthralled with your own perspicacity and cleverness, and take mischievous delight in being the bad boy or girl. You unabashedly do your own thing; let it all hang out; and let the chips fall where they may. You keep yourself loose, untroubled and carefree – your ironic sense of humor, flip insouciance, and the knowing twinkle in your eye, keep everything on a light, lively plane (which can be very annoying to others when serious difficulties need to be dealt with seriously). On the negative side, your utter lack of diplomacy and social niceties, together with your insistence on calling a spade a spade, can often ruffle other people's feathers. But in their proper moment your pizzazz and panache – and unwillingness to let anyone bring you down – enlivens any group of which you are a part.

Moon square Mars makes for unfulfilled expectations and dashed hopes. You have an abstracted, preoccupied air, as if bearing up under a burden or onus – of being embattled. You never really feel a sense of stability or reliance in your life: the people you trust let you down (especially your mother); dreams turn into mirages which recede as you approach them; the simplest walkovers turn into baffling embranglements. You are rather naïve about the way the world works, and you tend to look at things in black-and-white terms. You are blunt and tactless, with little gift for guile or subtlety (or dealing with same in other people). You almost seem to take pride in dignifying the lost cause; in holding the abandoned fort; in making a last stand. Depending upon what is happening in the rest of your horoscope, either you, yourself, are abrasive, easily affronted, and quick on the trigger; or else you tend to draw situations of limitation and frustration – of being used, abused, taken for granted – which leave you seething. But your insistence on punctiliously fulfilling your obligations and doing more than your share enable you to invariably acquit yourself with honor.

Moon trine Mars makes you gutsy, frank, and forthright, looking people squarely in the eye with little need for pretense or whitewashing. You don't have it in you to dissemble or employ guile to get what you want: you're a straight-shooter who speaks your mind and damn the consequences. You believe in fair play and giving other people a fair shake; and you take umbrage (and can be quite vocal) at any injustice meted out to yourself or to anyone else. Since you make a fetish of doing your best and acquitting yourself honorably in everything you do, you tend to expect the best from other people as well, which can make you impatient and peremptory, given to steamrolling right ahead (and over other people's sensibilities). On the negative side, you can become supercilious and huffy when blocked, especially when you know unequivocally that you are in the right (which is most of the time). Your strong sense of honor makes you a bastion of righteousness which others look up to and admire.

Moon opposition Mars makes you truly an original: a person who is oblivious to what the people around you are thinking or doing, and who goes your own way without a fare-thee-well. You have no interest in impressing anyone, nor in scoring little points for yourself; and while you don't lack ambition per se, you are more inclined to live in the moment and go with the flow, with whatever presents itself, than you are in planning a future or dedicating yourself wholeheartedly to a set direction in life. Nor do you find it easy to commit yourself to relationships, perhaps because your mother wasn't there for you at the beginning, and as a result you've had to learn to fend for yourself and disdain emotional entanglements. There may be a condescending or snooty tendency on your part, looking askance at people whom you see as not as independent and staunch as you are. But your clarity of vision and constancy to your own unique view of life keeps you on a steady course in your wanderings. You are at your best when your staunch independence and courage of conviction lead you to stand alone.

Moon parallel Mars makes for a quixotic vivacity and verve. You parallels have the same spunk and cockiness as the aspects between Moon and Mars, but you are more aloof and impersonal, and therefore less intense. You are more impassive than the aspects, who are always taking a stand or proving a point. You parallels feel little need to win (or bowl) other people over to bolster your own sense of prowess because your self-confidence is more of an inner glow than an outer flash. You have your own, sui generis logic and lofty ideals which guide you and let you act with certainty. You are usually off on your own tangent, hearkening to the rumble of a distant drum. You are not so much daring or reckless as oblivious to everything but your own enthusiasms of the moment. When you get a bee in your bonnet there is no stopping or deflecting you; and other people tend to get out of your way rather than attempt to block or reason with you. They may complain that it's difficult to reach you and pull you down to earth from your cloud when earthly matters need attention.

But your serene self-certainty and unimpeachable adherence to principle lend you an endearing charm.

Moon contraparallel Mars indicates a person whose spur to action lies not in the rewards or approbation of other people, but rather in your sense of duty to yourself – in fulfilling your highest expectations of yourself. You are as emotionally detached as the opposition between these two planets; and you are quite as proud of your independence of spirit and refusal to go along to get along. But you have some overriding plan for your life, or labor under an incumbency to somehow make a difference or uphold some abstract principle in your everyday behavior and choices. You are not necessarily intellectual, or philosophical per se; but rather are thorough, meticulous, and proud of your competence and mastery. Your fearless willingness to follow your own heart wherever it leads you arises from your great faith in your own native ability to deal with whatever situations and difficulties might arise. Like the Moon – Mars opposition, you may tend to look down on other people who (you feel) are not as dedicated or responsible as you are. You pride yourself on your fitness and willingness to go that extra mile in order to acquit yourself with honor.

Moon–Mars Mutual Reception is the sign of a person who is both cheeky and staunch. Moon-Mars aspects are spunky, self-assured, and audacious: they manifest an ingenuous solipsism which acts on impulse (for better or worse). These natives barge ahead with little forethought or awareness of possible consequences, relying upon a fierce single-mindedness which overrides any confusion or contradiction. Although not combative per se, they are adamant about relinquishing a plan or idea once they've set their minds on it, and they have little facility for compromise or adjustment. You MRs have the same plucky resolution and intentness as the aspects, but you are less inclined to fasten yourself down to defending a particular aim or point of view. You know the value of a strategic retreat, and you also have the patience to wait for a favorable turn of events. You are as much an objective observer as you are a mover and shaker. You have a strong sense of personal style (self-dramatizing; play to the audience); and a shrewd feeling for the politics of everyday society. You can – by turns – be charming, diplomatic, finagling, or obdurately stonewalling, as required by circumstances. Thus, because you are so flexible in your inflexibility, you are able inspire other people rather than dominate or cow them;

and you thus obtain their willing cooperation in realizing your dreams with a minimum of fussing and fuming.

Moon – Jupiter Aspects and Mutual Reception

Moon-Jupiter has to do with clear discernment and a common-sense, down-to-earth practicality. These natives are sociable, clever, and glib; and they possess a facility for eliciting and enlisting the cooperation of other people. They take an objective, philosophical approach to life; have a wry sense of humor; and they possess a benign good-will towards everyone they meet.

Moon conjunct Jupiter is bright, perceptive, and cocky as can be. You are not so much an intellectual as you are thoughtful, reasonable, and not easily fooled by superficial appearances. You take a long-term, overarching view of things, and possess an ironic sense of humor. You greet life with great gusto and daring – you love adventure and are animated by an insatiable curiosity about life and people. You strike out on your own; push the envelope; and invent a life for yourself tailored to your exact desires. You are fond of change, travel, moving around and learning new skills. You have a unique personality (you're quite an original), and possess a winning personal flair, self-possession, and sense of noblesse – you are inimitably and unabashedly yourself in any company. You are as stubborn as they come: not in the Saturnine sense of being perversely obdurate; but rather in that you take your time to make up your mind, and then once it's made up you hold your ground through thick and thin. At your worst your idées fixes can evince an insufferable smugness with your own perspicacity. But you impress other people with your impeccable integrity and nobility of purpose, and win them over with your good cheer.

Moon sextile Jupiter makes you outgoing and idealistic, bursting with friendly interest and the desire to please and be pleasing. You are unvarnished, forthright, and candid: you are not afraid to speak your mind, particularly when you see injustice being done and when you know you are morally in the right. You are fair, positive, and practical-minded – you seek solutions and modus vivendi which take everyone's views into account rather than try to prove a point of your own. You try to look for the best in people and the positive side of any situation, and you refuse to allow yourself to be bogged down – you just turn aside and go your own way. You are principally attuned to whatsoever things are lovely and of good report; but you also can shut your eyes and turn away from anything you don't want to have to deal with – your easy-going manner can disguise a noncommittal vagueness or laxity. But your unflagging optimism and good cheer, even in the face of uncertainty, win you the allegiance of all who know you.

Moon square Jupiter makes for disgruntlement and disappointed efforts. You have a tendency to endure, to go along, to try to ameliorate, to play the victim; rather than stand up and speak out on your own behalf. As a result you are easily taken advantage of; and in any case often wind up feeling used and unappreciated. It's not so much that you are meek (that's definitely not your problem) but rather that you have a misplaced sense of honorable acquittal: you don't want to be seen as not having done your all and pulled your fair share of the load, even when (especially when) it means that you get shafted. As a result, this isn't such a good position for marriage or business partnerships, since you tend to attract people who will impose on you or abuse your good will. Although you at times can indulge a huffy poutiness or a tendency to play the role of the put-upon martyr, you always do give unstintingly of yourself and willingly sacrrifice in the service of others.

Moon trine Jupiter makes you judicious, fair-minded, and disinterested – the sort of person who makes a good arbitrator or ombudsman. You play by the rules and try to uphold the highest moral standards in your own thinking and comportment. You have a good sense of humor and an appreciation of the ironies of life; you don't allow yourself to get bogged down in other people's issues, but usually are able to come up with solutions or compromises that are in the best interests of all concerned. Your idealism sometimes fails you when forced to deal with bad faith or duplicity; and as a result other people can easily take advantage of you and leave you standing high and dry. But you are able to shake off bad vibes with your own upstanding ingenuousness and detachment rather than allowing yourself to be bent out of shape. You are a model of right thinking and behavior to all who know you.

Moon opposition Jupiter indicates a person who is guarded, shrewd and manipulative. You are quick-witted, canny, and calculating – a smooth talker who is able to insinuate yourself into any group, and who knows how to play to an audience. Albeit possessing the hail-fellow-well-met gregariousness and bonhomie of the other Moon-Jupiter aspects, you are never truly at ease in a group, and you never lose sight of your own goals and purposes. You are constantly aware of the impression you are making – cool, aloof, in charge – and you tend to distance yourself from people with an above-it-all vagueness or superiority. Because you can clearly see your own motives and machinations, you are also suspicious of those of others: you don't allow yourself to trust or depend on anyone else too much if you can help it. At your worst you can be smug, overweening, and coldly dismissive of people. Your considerable personal charm is the product of an acute resourcefulness on your part, which is able to make the best of things and turn any situation to account.

Moon parallel Jupiter shows a person who is straightforward, artless, and forthright: you say whatever is on your mind with no shame or desire to make some sort of impression. The Moon-Jupiter aspects are astute, genial, and relaxing to be around. You parallels are like the aspects in your positive and constructive attitude and your good-natured and amiable disposition, but you are more naïve and unaffected than the knowing aspects; and as a result you are more revealing of yourself. You are simple and natural – what people see is what they get – and you possess a puppy-like enthusiasm and inquisitiveness. Your simple and plainspoken manner disarms people and puts them at their ease; and your spritely twinkle and mischievous spirit of fun are genuinely infectious. Like the Moon-Jupiter aspects you are outgoing and positive, with a good sense of humor, but you don't rely upon others' approval to endorse your actions, and you don't indulge yourself in the aspects' smug self-satisfaction. Your ingenuous outspokenness and complete lack of finesse or tact tend to arouse people's protective instincts rather than antagonize them; and your principled quixotism and fearless willingness to follow your own star make you a natural-born leader.

Moon contraparallel Jupiter is artless, glib, and forthright, with an ironic sense of humor and a good eye for the foibles and frailties of human nature. Like the Moon – Jupiter aspects, you are enthusiastic and vivacious – everybody knows it when you walk into the room because of your inimitable sense of style and flair. Your outspoken frankness is inviting rather than grating because your (somewhat naïve) motives are harmless in their intent rather than designed to elicit some response from other people. Where the opposition between Moon and Jupiter uses its good-natured camaraderie to plan and scheme and look out for angles, with you it's a true joy in sharing good company and appreciating the people you interact with. You always put your best foot forward, and try to act in good faith and to address others with a smile and a detached good will. Therefore you win people over naturally, just by being yourself at all times.

Moon–Jupiter Mutual Reception makes you ruminative, judicious, and self-contained. The Moon-Jupiter aspects come on with an avuncular benevolence – an openness which accepts other people at face value, with all their little weaknesses and idiosyncrasies; and at the same time begs their indulgence. You MRs have the same non-judgmental approach to other people as do the aspects, but you are more private and less effusive, and hence are not so blithely overreaching and self-delighted. Your sociality is heartfelt rather than breezy, and you think things through and weigh your words and actions in terms of their possible impact on the people around you. Your bonhomie and optimism reflect high moral and spiritual values (rather than merely promote your own viewpoint). You are serious of purpose and feel a deep need to serve and to be useful. You do have a hardheaded, judgmental tendency; and your constant introspective scrutinizing can make for a stiffness at the expense of spontaneity. Your sagacity and insistence on upholding what you know is right makes you the conscience of any group.

Moon – Saturn Aspects and Mutual Reception

Moon-Saturn has to do with competence and self-dedication; self-limitation and sense of superiority. These natives are fundamentally solitaries who must do their own thing in their own time, and cannot be prodded or hurried. They are highly self-disciplined and independent, with little patience for strictures or direction by others (distrustful). Astute, ambitious, and self-aggrandizing, they cannot be stopped or deflected once they have decided on a goal or course of action. In the unfavorable aspects (which includes the conjunction) there may be issues of abandonment or rejection by the mother, which forced the native at a young age to be the responsible one, who had to assume obligations for other people.

Moon conjunct Saturn makes you diligent, persevering, never-say-die. You are serious-minded (grim), self-disciplined, and assiduous in carrying out your assigned tasks and discharging your obligations. You possess a down-to-earth pragmatism which is quick to see and to seize opportunities as they arise. Your great powers of concentration and focus are the source of your self-possession and steadfastness; and your analysis is eminently realistic and sensible. You are dogged and are most difficult to deflect: you hold to your own course, are resolute under pressure, and are cool-headed and collected in emergencies (albeit as stubborn as they come). You are very idealistic – or at least you strive to uphold high standards of moral conduct – and you can be overly trusting or naïve about the motives of other people. You have a solitary tendency, and are reserved and maintain your distance even with friends and family (especially your mother). You can be rather hard and critical: since you are very hardworking yourself, you have little sympathy or patience for those who are not, or whom you see as being slack or irresponsible. Your absolutism and bluntness in speaking your mind – and complete indifference to the consequences – can be quite bruising. But your conscientiousness, dedication, and strength of purpose are something the people around you can unfailingly rely on.

Moon sextile Saturn indicates a person who is exceedingly alert, astute, serious-minded, and practical. You cultivate some area of expertise in which your own prowess and superiority are undisputed; and your adroitness and proficiency make you rather unique – a person to be reckoned with and respected. You are shrewd, cagey, and ironic, with a somewhat jaundiced view of your fellow bipeds and their machinations; and you are not seduced by the prevailing social buzzwords and shibboleths. Rather, you always hold to your own orbit. You are rather taken with your own perspicacity, and possess an inimitable personal flair and panache. You have little patience for nonsense and you have a gift for the master stroke – for cutting across all platitudinous poppycock with some brusque, dismissive remark or coup de main which leaves everyone in an admiring daze. Although you can be unbearably smug and self-satisfied, and completely deaf to any sort of criticism or contradiction, your opinions are pithy and apropos, and your arch humor and flip commentary leaven any group of which you are a part.

Moon square Saturn is ornery, contentious, and easily frustrated. You are extremely autocratic and must do things in your own way, in your own time. There is little in the way of self-examination here, but beaucoup bullheadedness and outspoken contrariety. You make a fetish of wrongheaded individualism, so that your point of view is invariably at odds with that of your society. You are opinionated, critical, brusque, and unhesitating in expressing yourself with little regard for the consequences. You are basically a loner who cannot trust or depend on anyone

– or feel secure in the reliances or contrivances of your social milieu – which gives you a fearless willingness to take complete responsibility for yourself. You possess a pioneering spirit of adventure which leads you to strike out on your own, and to create a unique lifestyle very different from that of the people around you. You are courageous and willing to stand up and fight for your beliefs; and while you are super-self-serious and suspicious-minded, you nonetheless have a sardonic take on life and human motivation which – in its proper moment – can be quite insightful and droll.

Moon trine Saturn makes you shrewd, perspicacious, and judicious in your speech and behavior. It's not so much a matter of your thinking things through as it is an assiduity and fidelity to your own personal code of honor and dignity, and your sense of what is right and true. Your dependability and stalwart integrity are an assurance to other people that they can always rely upon your word and disinterested judgment come what may. Like the other Moon – Saturn aspects you don't go along with the crowd but follow your own intuition and weigh the consequences of your actions against your own high ideals. As a result, you can be a bit inhibited and stuffy, and people may consider you up on your high horse much of the time and too remote and self-absorbed to talk to. But when push comes to shove, you are a rock – you always know where you stand and what you stand for.

Moon opposition Saturn makes you uninvolved and standoffish. You are sensitive, touchy, and thin-skinned – quick to take offense and to resent any semblance of a slight. Pernickety and hard to please, you are exacting and adamant in your relationships (as, most likely, was your mother as well). Unlike the scrappy square types you disdain conflict, preferring to withdraw into your ivory tower with an above-it-all fastidiousness rather than soil your hands with other people's "issues". You rely upon a constant inner rumination to justify your actions rather than feedback from others. Your supercilious and condescending manner, and your rather brazen self-righteousness, can rankle people's sensibilities; but your blasé indifference also ensures you untrammeled freedom of action, since you don't particularly seek nor need other people's approval before making your decisions. You go your own way and do your own thing without a fare-thee-well, and you rely upon fait accompli to make your point. Your tenacity and staying power result from an admirable willingness to follow your own path without caring what other people say or think about you.

Moon parallel Saturn makes you reserved, composed, and thoughtful. The Moon-Saturn aspects greet experience with a grim, ready-for-anything stance. They are cautious and reserved, and they are quite canny and contriving. They always stop or step back for a moment to calmly weigh the pros and cons; they are meticulous, logical, and argumentative. They are not so much inhibited as girded for action, and prepared in advance for any conceivable contingency. You parallels are as discriminating as the aspects, and you have the same hesitancy: when a decision is required you also retreat for a moment to ponder. However, here the reach is towards a deeper understanding rather than for immediate personal advantage. You are ruminative and judicious rather than shrewd, and conscientious rather than contentious. You seek to comprehend a situation or relationship rather than try to dominate it through elaborate preparations and defenses. You are not so much self-disciplined as self-restrained and contemplative – measuring yourself and refining your capacities in the situations you encounter rather than descrying other people's weaknesses or evaluating possibilities for gain and control.

Moon contraparallel Saturn is introspective, deliberative and self-cloistering. You don't quite fit in or belong anywhere; and you don't particularly care; you are simple and guileless yourself, and are rather nonplussed by the machinations and gamesmanship of everyday society. Thus you are able to fit in anywhere, in any group, without particularly trying to. Like the opposition between these planets you tend to hold yourself apart from your immediate circle and look within (rather than to the other people around you) for clues as to how to act and react. But you lack the supercilious disdain of the opposition; you are humble, self-effacing, not given to pushing yourself or your own point of view forward. You are as reflective as the opposition, but by no means as intense and unyielding – you are emotionally detached rather than intellectually above-it-all. You seek peacefulness, non-involvement, spreading oil on troubled waters – immoveable as the Buddha while tempests rage all around you.

Moon–Saturn Mutual Reception is scrupulous and humane. The Moon-Saturn aspects order their lives through sheer determination, by hunkering down and digging in. They usually have a great capacity for self-sacrifice and self-limitation, and indeed they take satisfaction in making their own way in life with no help from anyone else. You MRs are as staid and sober-minded as the aspects; and you are as punctilious in discharging your obligations; but you are more relaxed, not as tightly strung and defensive; and hence you are not averse to showing your human qualities (such as weakness or self-doubt). You are not at such pains to make your point and dominate the proceedings as the aspects are, and therefore you are better able to take life as it comes and go with the flow rather than to make things as difficult for yourself as possible. You are a rock within yourself, but not an island: you possess an ease of manner and a friendly concern for others which is inviting, sympathetic, and nonjudgmental; and your sense of honor is ingenuous and sincere rather than the result of adherance to abstract standards of duty and propriety.

Moon–Uranus Aspects

Moon–Uranus is revelatory of the native's spontaneity – how he or she responds to the unexpected. Moon–Uranus aspect natives are extremely intelligent and fearlessly outspoken, with a jaunty, devil-may-care élan and an indifference to social niceties and consequences.

Moon conjunct Uranus is sharp and alert, with an amused, ironic point of view and an optimistic and hopeful attitude (albeit with a tendency to see the world through rose-colored glasses). Audacious and nimble, you quickly adjust to unforeseen circumstances, taking things in stride without undue pother or personal involvement. You are intellectually curious and always eager to learn new skills and to show off your stuff. You are brash and experimentative, and may come to embrace belief systems and lifestyles quite different from those of your parents or childhood social milieu. You must always figure things out for yourself: you take no one's word for anything and can be most difficult to influence or move when once you have made up your mind. You are forceful in your opinions and can be quite cavalier and dismissive: the flip side of your free-spiritedness is a high-handed contumely and authoritarianism which can ruffle other people's sensibilities. Your fearless willingness to strike out on your own is an inspiring model of irrepressible faith in oneself.

Moon sextile Uranus is unaffected, unvarnished, and out front. You are a simple person – artless, unassuming, and natural. Albeit a bit rough around the edges, lacking social grace and the concomitant ability to dissemble, your frank and guileless simplicity of manner wins people over rather than puts them off. You are adaptable and light on your feet, and quick to pick up and address feelings in the air. You are a glib straight-shooter who readily shares what is on your mind and lets the chips fall where they may. You are solicitous of others and genuinely desire to be helpful and serve in whatever capacity you can without particular expectation of recognition or reward. Like the Don of La Mancha, you are a defender of the weak and helpless and your incisive and penetrating intellect is good at solving problems and coming up with solutions that benefit all concerned. Your cool detachment can at times become an annoying vagueness and indifference, especially when you are off chasing your own windmills; and you are hard to reach in your ivory tower when you don't feel like being bothered. But your head-in-the-clouds optimism and nobility of purpose endow you with a winning joie de vivre.

Moon square Uranus is rather easily annoyed or put out. Exigent and exacting, you fiddle with this and fiddle with that, and must always have everything perfect; thus you miss out on a lot of life's serendipity, and you are easily discombobulated or knocked off your stride. You are fastidious and picky, fussing about your daily business with impatient discontent. Finical, unappreciative, and huffy, you are quick to take offense or affront. You are critical of other people and chafe at any sort of stricture: you must always be the boss or the one calling all the shots. You meet any disagreement with an overweening smugness and a mulish intransigence which simply ignores or steamrolls over any contradiction. Your brusque, dismissive bluntness and utter disregard for common civility can be quite bruising and off-putting, and tend to create opposition where none theretofore existed. On your positive side you are scrupulous and thorough, paying great attention to minute detail and technicalities; and there's not much that eludes your rigorous scrutiny, nor errancy which escapes your sharp tongue.

Moon trine Uranus is free-thinking and fearless in your convictions. You cut a swath through life based upon your own highly individualistic world-view (which differs markedly from that of the people around you and those you grew up with); and nothing can deflect you from your chosen path. You are beyond being merely idealistic in that you are willing to put your life on the line with every decision you make; there is a seriousness of purpose and sense of a higher calling in everything you do which reveals an untrammeled stateliness and rare nobility of character.

Consequently, you are most difficult to deflect (pigheaded to an extreme), which can disconcert other people as well as make you blind to anything not in your narrow compass of attention. But your strong sense of fidelity to what you know in your heart is right, together with your clarity of vision (usually) and courageous willingness to go wherever your destiny leads you, makes you the sort of person others look up to and admire.

Moon opposition Uranus makes you irascible and adamant. You are not so much contentious (going out of your way looking for trouble) as you are congenitally ornery and contrary. You possess a reflexive feistiness and a nasty temper, and you are continually on the lookout for someone trying to take advantage or put one over on you. The shameless gadfly in any milieu, you gleefully hurl down your gauntlet at the slightest provocation – nay, not even provocation – any old occasion will do. Argumentative as for sport, you must always have the last word or final coup de grâce. You are master of the stonewall; and when thwarted you withdraw into yourself with a sulky, injured innocence. Although extremely opinionated and scornful of social sanction, you do possess considerable insight and a highly original of point of view; and your boldness in action and readiness to seize and dominate the moment (particular when others are confused or indecisive) makes you a natural-born leader.

Moon parallel Uranus is shrewd and penetrating. The Moon-Uranus aspects are gregarious (albeit dogmatic), and are restless and intense. They can be coldly analytical – verging on cynical – and often manifest a caustic superiority or absolutism. You parallels take the same pride in your competence and fitness as the aspects do; and are equally free-thinking; but you are more mindful, lower-key, less overbearing. You possess the same uncompromising fidelity to your own hopes and dreams as do the aspects, but you don't just go off half-cocked and shoot from the hip since you are keenly aware of the impact your decisions might have on other people. You are cagey and politic, gingerly threading your way around or trouble-shooting obstacles rather than just blundering on ahead and damn the torpedos. You have the same dogged self-certainty as the aspects, and are as inflexible in refusing to kowtow to anyone; but you are cool-headed, and observant: your reach is towards ways and means of achieving your goals rather than merely asserting your own bullheaded self-sufficiency.

Moon contraparallel Uranus is determined to carve out your own niche in life wherein your fancies reign free and you can make your own decisions for yourself. But unlike the contentious opposition between these two planets, you are sensitive to nuances and prefer to feel your way along rather than just push forward on impulse and cast all restraint aside. You have a keen sense of the politic – or at least of how much you can get away with without stirring up undue antagonism – and you usually manage to find a modus vivendi by seemingly acceding to societal fiat, or the demands of other people, without compromising your own dreams and schemes. You are very idealistic – perhaps a bit too naïve for your own good – and thus can easily fall into other people's webs of intrigue and exploitation, which can make intimate relationship problematical. Although outwardly friendly and agreeable, you are basically a loner who goes your own way and keeps your own counsel; and you always maintain your gaze on the distant horizon.

Moon–Neptune Aspects

The Moon-Neptune combination symbolizes simplicity, innocence, lack of guile; not so much naïvete as an inability to cope with muddle or chicanery, hence a desire to bring things out into the open and deal with them in a straightforward, aboveboard manner. These natives have an impish glint in their eyes, as if relishing their own secret joke. They gaze past the things of this world with a look of yearning for some idealized universe. At times you can speak directly to them, looking them right in the eye as they smile and nod back to you, and they won't even hear a word you're saying. They may have psychic ability and tend to be religious, or at least are aware of the spiritual side of things: the ability to look beyond momentary hindrances to behold a vaster horizon.

Moon conjunct Neptune makes for an inspired hopefulness. You are abstracted and otherworldly – not altogether centered in this reality – always marching to the beat of a distant drum and following your own private guidance. Your decisions and actions are informed by an inner surety which is not dependent upon what other people or society think (but on the negative side this can be a negligence or obliviousness). You are soft and gentle, and prefer to withdraw from turmoil and contention rather than lock horns with other people; or – if that isn't possible – you acquiesce in your fate in dispirited silence with the hope that "this, too, shall pass away". Because you are highly attuned to vibrations and unspoken undercurrents, you have a brooding, dark side; and your moodiness and preoccupation can make you noncommittal and hard to pin down when bold decision is called for. You don't share your thoughts or feelings, but try to be aloof and unaffected and not make waves, so other people may complain of your vagueness and unreachability when definiteness and straightforwardness are what is required. On the other hand, you possess a creative, imaginative simplicity – a true touch with the divine and the ability to make do and to find good in whatever is at hand.

Moon sextile Neptune makes you perky and vivacious. You possess a spirited ebullience and a jaunty zest for life, and you are always on the go. You are artless and out front; are unselfconsciously chatty; and you readily share what's on your mind. You have a philosophical bent, and gladly hold forth on the Purpose of Life or the meaning of Ultimate Truth to anyone who is willing to listen. You harbor grand dreams, and are usually buzzing with enthusiasm and optimism for your pet project or cause of the moment. Spontaneous and willing to fly with your hunches, you are fearless in giving free reign to your impulses. Fervent in your beliefs, you have a facility for galvanizing yourself to action and pouring yourself body and soul into whatever strikes your fancy; and you endow everything you do with your own sui generis touch. Your free-wheeling brass can incline you to go off half-cocked, so at times you may overreach yourself or trample on the sensibilities of other people in your devil-may-care insouciance. But your cocky panache and the mischievous gleam in your eye win you the indulgence of everyone around you.

Moon square Neptune shows a misaligned idealism. You are rather credulous and trusting, hence are easily imposed upon or deceived. Because you are so susceptible to being duped and victimized, you have a paranoid tendency: you are guarded and suspicious in your outlook, cynical of other people's motives, ever on the alert for the catch or hook (which you nonetheless usually seem to miss). Although you believe you have everything figured out intellectually, for the most part your life is a disappointment to you, consisting largely of unfulfilled expectations, smashed hopes and dreams, an emptiness at the end of the day. Your seeking some ideal solution just beyond the horizon may lead you into religious cults or get-rich-quick schemes; or you may withdraw into yourself and seek your solace in drink or drugs. You may be a bit unbalanced mentally; or at least given to dark moods of brooding or disgruntlement. On the other hand, your simplicity, hopefulness, and artless (if grossly naïve) willingness to deal always in a straightforward and aboveboard manner, makes you the sort of person whom other people can instinctively trust.

Moon trine Neptune is thoughtful and judicious, with a clearly-defined sense of purpose in life which guides you and provides you with a feeling of assurance that everything will work out okay in the end. It's not that you are free of doubt per se; but rather that you are confident in your own intuition and the goodness of your own primary impulses, so you are willing to follow your star wherever it may lead you with little hesitation or fear of the repercussions or consequences. As a result, others find it difficult to pull you down off of your cloud when things get involved or sticky: while you are most responsible and meticulous at fulfilling what you conceive to be your duty, and pulling your share of the weight, you nonetheless tend to duck or shrug off other people's issues, or anything which doesn't resonate with your own sanguine vision or sense of what is right and appropriate. In their proper moment, your hopefulness and unflagging belief in yourself are an inspiration for everyone around you.

Moon opposition Neptune makes you insightful and brisk. You are not taken in by superficial appearances but possess a clear insight into the real rationales and underlying impulsions behind other people's behavior. You have high ideals and a strong sense of proper personal integrity and comportment. You have little patience for equivocation and are not afraid to speak out and articulate exactly what's on your mind: you are trenchant and contemptuous of hypocrisy, and quite deliberately bluff and brusque – even peppery and cantankerous. You have a lively sense of humor and irony, together with a rather jaundiced view of human motivation; so you can be something of the wiseacre or kidder. On your negative side you can be overly patronizing, holding yourself at arm's length with a trifling daintiness or condescending sanctimoniousness, and refusing to listen to or take other people's feelings seriously. But your acute discrimination endows you with a gift for cutting across obfuscation and cant and addressing the real issues at hand.

Moon parallel Neptune makes you insightful and knowing. The Moon-Neptune aspects are soft and vulnerable, and have a wistful, abstracted air about them, as if they were tuned into their own personal wavelength. They rely less upon societal fiat and approval to direct their actions than most other people do; they are simple, natural, salt-of-the-earth types in their naïve optimism and harmlessness. You parallels are as private as the aspects, and you have the same spritely and winsome manner and ability to tune in to underlying emotional vibrations; but you are nowhere near as woolly. In fact you can be quite shrewd and calculating in employing your pixie-like mischievousness to charm and wheedle other people; and your intuitive insight into human motivation and your ability to pick up on and exploit other people's hesitation and weaknesses can have a decidedly Machiavellian tinge. You are sharp and quick, and able to use your remoteness from everyday concerns to manipulate things your way (rather than to wring your hands and brood helplessly). You're never so far off in the stratosphere that you miss an opportunity down here on earth.

Moon contraparallel Neptune is shrewd and judicious, with a rather unique and oblique point of view. You are not easily fooled by appearances, but rather try to get to the bottom of things to broaden your own understanding and competence. Like the opposition between these two planets, you are very clear-sighted and possess a great depth of perception of human motivation and the machinations of everyday society; but you are far less lofty and supercilious than the opposition – not exactly humble per se, but with a keener awareness of your own limitations and an appreciation for those of others. You are unpretentious (in contrast to the know-it-all opposition); tolerant and sympathetic; and willing to grant other people the right to their own foibles and follies, as long as they grant you yours in return. You are a good listener, and excel as a teacher, advisor, or counselor since you are able to combine intuitive insight with detached, objective analysis.

Moon–Pluto Aspects

The emotional assurance of the Moon combining with the clarity of mind of Pluto can make for a driving self-certainty. These natives are most difficult to halt, deflect, or even to influence (much less convince). They are neither open nor amenable to suggestions: if an idea did not originate within themselves, then it holds little interest for them. They are not so much pigheaded as obsessively focused upon their own plans and ploys and indifferent to anything else; and it takes complete emotional wipe-outs (which occur periodically during the life) to force them to release their clinging.

Moon conjunct Pluto makes for a shrewd practicality. You are impassive, commanding, always in control of yourself and the situation. It's not that you have any more of a clue as to what you're about than anyone else does; rather you just act out a role model of the stiff upper lip (intently watch everything that everyone around you is doing, and don't let on how you are reacting to it all, or what you're really feeling inside). Albeit superficially pleasant and even sympathetic, this is just a façade you use to disarm people and keep them at a distance. Actually you are extremely private and guarded, masking your intentions by enveloping yourself in a fog of busyness or flightiness or distractedness or vagueness that no one can ever penetrate or see through. You are always weighing and numbering, with particular attention as to how you, personally, could possibly benefit or capitalize on the proceedings; and you can be rather cold-blooded in your analytical detachment and strategic maneuvering. Your cool-headedness under pressure, willingness to stand your ground, and ability to keep your head while everyone else is losing theirs, makes you a rock of stability in times of doubt and confusion.

Moon sextile Pluto indicates a person who is fresh and saucy. You are direct, unvarnished, and plainspoken, with little in the way of mannered social artifice (brusque and jarring). You're not afraid to speak out and say what's on your mind and let the chips fall where they may, and your remarks are usually apropos and right on the mark. You are truly an original. You possess an ironic, irreverent, self-deprecating sense of humor which doesn't take anyone (even yourself) too seriously. Like all Moon-Pluto aspect types, you have a penetrating intellect and a good head for problem-solving and trouble-shooting. You step back a moment for assessment and calculation rather than blunder ahead on impulse; and as a result you may be lacking in true spontaneity and warmth in spite of your outward good cheer. You seek ways and means of avoiding or getting around obstacles, and prefer to cast oil on troubled waters and to ameliorate or sidestep direct confrontation whenever possible. Your objective impartiality makes you a good arbiter or ombudsman, and a voice of sobriety and reason in the midst of discord.

Moon square Pluto tends to be ornery and pernickety. You possess a keen and penetrating intellect and considerable insight into the motivations of everyone around you (suspicious and distrustful). Unfortunately, however, you take your own point of view and rationales so completely for granted that you lose all objectivity and any possibility of gleaning advantage from your otherwise incisive analysis and attunement to subtleties. You are unreachable except upon your own terms, and are adamantly dismissive of anyone who doesn't acknowledge and respect your quixotic logic and fastidious sensibilities. You are not so much abstracted as completely focused upon your own ends: you are trapped in an ideal world in which you have everything worked out to perfection, but which has no bearing upon reality. Everything must be *just so*, and you are easily put out or stressed when things aren't. At times you almost seem to invite out-putting, stressful situations and relationships just to frazzle yourself. Thus you tend to run around in circles pursuing your dreams without actually accomplishing very much to achieve them; and you stew in a perpetual state of disgruntlement. On your positive side your nobility of purpose and willingness to go your own way without needing the support or approval of anyone is an admirable model of staunch individualism.

Moon trine Pluto shows a person who is astute and perspicacious. There isn't much that escapes your keen analytical mind; and you have a broad, tolerant, and generous take on human nature and the follies and foibles of your fellow bipeds. You are not so much philosophical as practical and *real*, with the ability to cut across obfuscatory blather and get down to the true business at hand with little wasted motion, posturing, or scoring little points for yourself. Like all Moon–Pluto aspects you tend to isolate / insulate yourself in your own ivory tower idealism, but you lack the emotional intensity and guardedness of the other aspects. Rather, you hold to your own orbit and keep a positive attitude no matter what confusion is going on around you (which others can see as a frustrating, noncommittal aloofness). You are able to dominate the proceedings by virtue of your impartial benevolence and trustworthiness, which are a reliance for everyone who knows you.

Moon opposition Pluto is canny, knowing, and suspicious of other people's motives and easy solutions. You are cagey, skeptical and acute; and you possess an inquisitive mentality which is not easily fooled by superficial appearances or bound by the taken-for-granted conventions of your cultural milieu. You have a feisty, can-do spirit and a sharp-tongued imperiousness which is not afraid to speak its mind and let the consequences be damned. Your tactlessness and disdain for social niceties give you a rough-hewn, bumptious bravado which is not without its charm in its proper moment. You are not rebellious or combative per se, but rather possess a smug, superior contumely which believes that it sees through everyone and has got everything all figured out. You act on the assumption that other people will simply get out of your way; and you prevail with an above-it-all obstinacy which you take to be a form of invulnerability (or at least an exemption from the rules which behoove the common herd). Your fearless willingness to take a stand and your adamant fidelity to your own personal vision can be an inspiration to all in times of doubt and confusion.

Moon parallel Pluto is discerning and authoritative. The Moon-Pluto aspects are detached, examining, intent, and manipulative: gritty, tenacious, and indomitable in carrying out their own designs. You parallels are as fully wrapped up in your own expectations and schemes as are the aspects; and you act with the same decisiveness and finality. But you are more flexible and willing to modify your plans as a situation dictates, instead of always insisting on your own preconceived notions. You are capable of executing a strategic retreat if need be, or of simply waiting patiently until things turn your way and you can then make a strike for what you want. You are more forthright and willing to explain your thinking and motives to other people (rather than holding yourself above or away from them); and you always seek a modus vivendi (if not a compromise of your principles – which is as unacceptable to you as to the Moon-Pluto aspect types). You always keep your sense of humor and proportion, and you use the perspicacity and discrimination of Moon-Pluto to slither around obstacles rather than to just butt blindly through them.

Moon contraparallel Pluto is clear-sighted and utterly realistic. Albeit as fixated on your own designs as the Moon–Pluto aspects, you are able to take a considered overview and thus trouble-shoot how best to arrive at your goals without stepping on toes on the one hand, nor unduly compromising your own sense of integrity on the other. You choose a life / lifestyle which tends to be outside the mainstream or norms of your society and upbringing; and because you are basically a private person who doesn't much share what you are about, you are able to steer a course through the shoals of everyday life by simply going quietly and diligently about your work and not drawing especial attention to yourself. This is not to say that you are incapable of making a stand or bullying your way through when faced with unreasoning opposition – quite the contrary! But your tact and elegant economy of action – which eschews wasted motion and attitudinizing – usually are sufficient to enable you to get what you want with little pother on your part.

Mercury–Venus Aspects and Mutual Reception

Mercury-Venus aspect natives are original and imaginative. When the Sun (parent) is not involved there is an economy to these natives' actions – a straightforwardness which eschews wasted motion or attitudinizing, and cuts right to the heart of any matter. Albeit aloof, they can relax and just be themselves in any company, with no excuses or need for self-deprecation.

Mercury conjunct Venus (sans Sun) makes for an unvarnished frankness and conviviality. You are smooth and sociable: chatty, good-natured, and optimistic. You make good eye contact and carry yourself with ease and self-confidence – a sense of rightful place and belonging no matter whom you are with. You are a good listener – interested in other people and respectful of their ideas and points of view – so you are adept at teaching, sales, and other occupations which rely upon one-on-one communications. You are a glib, animated conversationalist with an upbeat sense of humor. You have a simplicity which sees through pretense, and a knack for seeing the inherent irony, so you can laugh things off rather than become huffy or offended. You are light and breezy; and on the negative side can be overly detached, non-committal, and trifling. Intimates may complain that you are vague and unreachable, just shrugging off anything which you find distasteful or simply don't want to have to face. But your pleasant manners and winning affability deflect opposition and keep everyone around you on an even keel.

Mercury sextile Venus is discerning and judicious. You are an original thinker, possess an insatiable intellectual curiosity, and are willing to experiment and play with new ideas and philosophies. You are positive and forthright, with a good-humored bonhomie which gets right to the point without preliminaries or pother. In contrast to the emotional repression of the Mercury-Venus conjunction types (which is an automatic response based upon fear), you have a conscious governor on your impulses which holds back and watches the proceedings dispassionately. Your reserve does not invite ready familiarity: there may be a huffiness, or exaggerated sense of personal dignity which is easily ruffled; and a sharp tongue which lashes out unrestrainedly at indelicacy or Pharisaism. You see clearly through hypocrisy, are intolerant of pretense, and are not afraid to speak your mind. You are objective and clever at problem-solving, and possess an astute and discriminating mind; thus you make a good facilitator, arbiter, advisor and communicator. Your sense of fair play and justice makes you a natural champion and defender of the dispossessed and helpless.

Quintile aspects (of 72° separation – thus dividing the zodiacal circle into fifths) are not usually taken into consideration (although Kepler thought well of them). But since the Mercury-Venus aspect repertoire is otherwise rather paltry, we shall discuss them briefly here. In *Pythagorean Astrology* Dr. Jones stated, "The quintiles ... represent the definite talents of the native and show in what manner he may succeed in linking together his inner and outer being. Every man is an artist in some realm of expression, and only through his artistry is any analysis of his activity of pure soul to be gained. ... The quintiles ... reveal the special privileges of each native and tell him in what way he may demand co-operation and spiritual assistance from the cosmos as a whole." I would put it that quintile aspects indicate resourcefulness: the ability to land on one's feet; to look around at the potentialities; and to capitalize on or make use of whatever is at hand with no apologies or second thoughts.

Normally minor aspects (when they are considered at all) are not taken with orbs greater than 1°; but since the quintile aspects of Mercury-Venus are so very rare – occurring only when Mercury is near its maximum Greatest Western Elongation at the same time that Venus is near Greatest Eastern Elongation, or vice versa – we shall allow here a 2° orb (i.e. an angular separation between 70° and 74° between the two inner planets).

Mercury quintile Venus makes for a detached efficiency. You are poised and aloof, taking people in your stride and letting nothing get under your skin. Albeit outgoing and gregarious, you don't play to the gallery or call especial attention to yourself, but rather move freely through any social milieu without making waves. Very low-key and unobtrusive, you have a genius for blending into any group in which you might find yourself without in any way compromising your independence or dignity as an individual. You are by no means secretive, but you play your cards close to your chest, don't blab what you are about, and rely on others as little as possible. Thus you are able to go your own way and accomplish your goals with a minimum of fuss or friction. Your unassuming naturalness wins immediate acceptance, not because you try to impress anyone, but rather because you don't – thus you make an excellent teacher or public speaker. People instinctively trust you because of your impeccable personal integrity; and and they look up to and respect you because of your self-adequacy which neither seeks nor needs approval or sanction.

Mercury parallel Venus: The Mercury-Venus aspects are easy-going and self-possessed. They have a realistic view of other people and their motives, and they have a gift for persiflage which enables them to communicate without unduly compromising or involving themselves emotionally. You parallels have the same bantering irreverence as the aspects; and with your lively and droll take on the passing scene you are equally blithe and unaffected. In fact, you have great personal flair and panache; and possess a facility for dominating your social milieu with showmanship and flamboyant originality of self-expression (everyone knows the minute that you arrive on the scene). Your personal manner is more sincere and inviting than that of the cool, impersonal aspects. You evince a genuine concern for other people and are always ready to make a meaningful commitment of your personal time and energy to help them – to go out of your way to do whatever you can. Your dedication and seriousness of purpose convince other people and command their respect (assuring that your views prevail). Your levity does not preclude sympathy, nor is your detachment standoffish. Your cheerfulness is heartfelt rather than casual and offhanded.

Mercury contraparallel Venus is rather more humble and self-effacing than the showy aspects (and parallel) between these two planets. You possess the same outgoing alacrity and gregariousness, and you are as glib and off-the-cuff; however you possess a conscientiousness which reaches out to people – you truly concern yourself with their well-being and points of view. You are something of the outsider looking in – participating fully in your social milieu, but not needing to assert your sense of place or status (needing neither recognition nor approval). You are less interested in demonstrating your own intellectual prowess and sagacity than you are in understanding people and making heart contact with them.

Mercury–Venus Mutual Reception makes for a reliance on reason and consideration. The Mercury-Venus aspects are charming, outgoing, and friendly. There is a childlike optimism and harmlessness about them. Since they are rather vulnerable emotionally, they may try to keep their relationships relatively superficial so as to avoid the possibility of being hurt. Hence they may have many acquaintances but few real friends with whom they can just open up and be themselves. You MRs have the same outgoing amiability and goodheartedness as the Mercury-Venus aspect types, but you are not as vulnerable because you are able to take things impersonally, in stride, as they come. Like the aspects you are a highly social butterfly and enjoy camaraderie; you are glib and love to lecture and teach; and you bring a thorough interest and eye-to-eye attention to the give-and-take relationships of everyday society. But there is a gentility and delicacy of feeling here often missing in the mannered and self-conscious aspects – a warmth and personal touch which reaches out to people with a heartfelt genuineness. You focus on others rather than on your own self-images (preserving your dignity or exhibiting your dexterity); and so you feel little need to dominate or control the proceedings. You have a genius for rolling with punches; for detachedly trouble-shooting the possible; and for influencing other people with an unassuming civility. Your conviction, stability, and hopefulness are beacons for everyone in times of confusion and doubt.

Mercury–Mars Aspects and Mutual Reception

Mercury-Mars aspect natives are shrewd, analytical, outspoken, and firm, with little time or energy to waste on such nonessentials as tact or propriety. These natives are clever and practical, ever trying to get on the inside track of things; and they may fancy themselves quite the wheeler-dealers. They fearlessly speak up and speak out; are at pains to make their own views prevail; and have a tendency towards one-upmanship.

Mercury conjunct Mars gives you an incisive, questioning intellect. You take pride in your proficiency and excel at investigation, research, problem-solving, and improvising. You pick up on things quickly, are an assiduous student, and are an eager learner and teacher. You are not content with the pat, socially-approved credos which most people accept unquestioningly, but have to think things through and come up with answers for yourself. You have an intellectual or religious bent, and diligently search for an overarching system of thought to make sense out of your life and get an objective handle on its ultimate meaning. In everyday society you are candid, forthright, and trenchant; doughtily expressing what's on your mind and standing up for the principles of fairness and justice. You have a tendency towards criticism and discontent with the status quo, and in speaking your mind you can be extremely mordant and sharp-tongued, ruffling people's sensibilities needlessly (gauche). But your originality, leadership and stick-to-your-guns tenacity are an inspiration to everyone.

Mercury sextile Mars endows you with a positive attitude of Panglossian cheerfulness: "all's for the best in this best of all possible worlds". You are always in fine mettle, with a radiant and buoyant alacrity that enlivens any group of which you are a part. You don't let things get you down, but possess a facility for just shaking off disappointments rather than letting them fester or get under your skin, and just moving on to something more upbeat. You try to keep light, loose, and flexible; not allowing yourself to be pinned down; always keeping your options open. Because you don't take things to heart, there is a noncommittal perfunctoriness – a refusal to accept ownership or take responsibility for other people's feelings – which makes you annoyingly vague, abstracted, and unreachable precisely when you are most needed. But your pleasant, inviting manner and unflagging optimism when the going gets tough keep any situation on an even keel.

Mercury square Mars gives an impatient fastidiousness. You are easily frustrated, ooze disgruntlement, have a skeptical and suspicious view of other people's motives; and you take any sort of disagreement as a personal affront. You possess an overbearing, pugnacious manner which girds its loins and butts its way through; and you are ready to hurl down the gauntlet at the slightest provocation. Utterly lacking in any sort of diplomacy or discretion, you pride yourself on your brass and bullheaded self-assurance: you can always muster an overwhelming array of indisputable arguments – Talmudic in their intricacy and irrefutability – to bolster and justify your highly opinionated *Weltansicht*. And when that doesn't work, you just walk right over people without a fare-thee-well. Because you stick to your guns and hold unswervingly to your own course through thick and thin, you become the hero of the hour when the cause you champion happens to be well-founded (although you are as contemptuous of other people's applause as you are of their dissent). Your willingness to take a stand and stand alone lends a certain nobility to your character in spite of your contumacious bravado.

Mercury trine Mars is benevolent, sagacious, and interested in other people and their points of view. Although you possess strong opinions of your own, you tend to hold back on expressing yourself until you have analyzed all the available facts and taken everyone else's thinking into account. You generally don't rush into things on impulse, but rather carefully consider and weigh all possible choices and their consequences before making your decisions. As a result, when you do act it is with a calm assurance born of thorough premeditation and diligence. On the other hand, once you have made up your mind it can be extremely difficult for you to be influenced by what you may regard as other people's bothersome vagaries and trivial objections, which renders you deaf to entreaty and reveals a blind spot in your careful planning and thinking. But you are always able to maintain an unruffled exterior no matter what doubt and confusion others around you are experiencing, which makes you a stolid rock of composure upon which others instinctively rely.

Mercury opposition Mars makes for a subtle and supple rumination. You are abstracted and curt, preoccupied with your own plans and schemes, unfathomable and unstoppable. You possess a calculating, chess-playing view of human interaction – not so much secretive or devious as subtle, canny, close-mouthed, and intent upon your own designs. You need very little in the way of feedback or approval from anyone before acting, and you rely upon the fait accompli rather than on rationales and explanations to get your own way. Unlike the brash and brazen square types, you prefer to sidestep or slither around opposition; and you have the patience to outwait or outwit (as the case may be) rather than waste your energy in ineffectual expostulation. Your narrow-mindedness and pigheaded tenacity incline you to brush right past people and give them the cold shoulder, which makes you infuriatingly unreasonable and unreachable except on your own terms and in your own time. But your singlemindedness, perseverance, and unwavering earnestness are a model of staunch resolution and decisiveness

Mercury parallel Mars makes for an aware and knowing judiciousness. The Mercury-Mars aspects are forceful and direct, possessing the no-nonsense, take-charge air of born commanders. They are fair and just, fearless advocates of the moral right, who will bear no quibbling (read: difference of opinion). You parallels are as positive and cocksure as the aspects; and you are quite as indomitable. However, you have a far more ingratiating manner and an appreciation for the rights and sensibilities of other people. You are as blunt and plainspoken as the aspects, but not as argumentative: you are capable of listening to differing points of view and finding a middle way without feeling that you are thereby compromising your own position. You try not to take sides in other people's disputes, but maintain your integrity with an impartial reserve. You are calm and discriminating rather than insistent and pushy and your views are reasoned and considered rather than categorical and dogmatic. You clearly grasp that the essence of effective leadership is patient persuasion rather than peremptoriness.

Mercury contraparallel Mars is similar to the opposition in your insistence on going your own way and doing your own thing come what may; and you can be equally quixotic and capricious in choosing a course of action. But you possess a greater alacrity and delight in your own perspicacity and readiness to be your own inimitable self under any circumstances, thereby winning people over with your considerable flair and panache. You convince others with a tongue-in-cheek brazenness (rather than rudely ignoring them or pushing them aside); and your thinking is indeed original and offbeat enough so that others are intrigued by your ideas and rationales and willing to go along with your idealistic (or pie-in-the-sky) schemes. On the negative side you may be more of a dreamer than a doer; contenting yourself with grandiose visions rather than taking responsibility for making them come true. But your unfailing optimism and buoyancy are a delight to everyone who knows you.

Mercury–Mars Mutual Reception is sober and self-possessed. The Mercury-Mars aspects are engaging and cocksure. They need to feel that they're on top of their milieu, and they hate to be left out. They constantly try to command the respect of others, and they take offense easily at any hint of criticism. You MRs are also self-assured and authoritative, but you are more tolerant and forbearing than the aspects, and more supportive of the efforts of other people. This is why you make a good teacher – you explain rather than declaim; and are more inclusive rather than exclusive in your viewpoint (while still holding yourself and your own intellection apart and above). You are more wary and circumspect than the assertive aspects with their knee-jerk reactions and judgments; and you are thoughtful and conscious of consequences rather than demonstrative or pontifical. Because you arrive at your convictions by thinking things through rather than jumping to conclusions, you radiate a sense of quiet dignity and self-possession, and you are determined without being overbearing. Like the aspects you are inclined to worry about whether or not you measure up, but you are more concerned with your competence and the soundness of your thinking and conclusions than with the impression you are making.

Mercury–Jupiter Aspects and Mutual Reception

Mercury-Jupiter aspect natives are logical, analytical, and discerning. These natives must examine the evidence, think things through, and rely upon reason to make their decisions. They base their actions on intellectualized precepts and they seek ultimate meanings in the passing parade of events. They are facile at interpretation and explanation, and they regale in mental pursuits as careers and pastimes.

Mercury conjunct Jupiter makes you composed and astute. You are disinterested, forthright, possess an inquisitive spirit; and you love to lecture and teach. You possess a broad, avuncular bonhomie and a good-humored altruism which enables you to spread oil on any troubled waters and to dominate any proceedings with your calm self-possession. Albeit a simple person with simple tastes (not in the least ostentatious or affected), you nonetheless appreciate the good things of life – whatever you conceive these to be: good fellowship, good cheer, good food, good times. Your impartiality makes you a natural arbitrator or go-between; and you possess a tolerance and generosity which makes light of the follies and foibles of others, always making allowances for human frailty. You put all your cards on the table – favoring open covenants openly arrived at – which encourages others to do the same. Your above-it-all loftiness can be a vexation when people need a firm commitment from you – taking definite sides rather than offering well-meant but vague assurances. But your no-nonsense professionalism and humanitarian benevolence win you the allegiance of everyone who knows you.

Mercury sextile Jupiter makes you a good teacher since you are forthcoming and glib, and never nonplussed or at a loss for words. Moreover, you love to hold forth and show your stuff and glow in the approbation of an appreciative audience. You are pragmatic and brisk – quick to pick up on nuances, and quick to respond – usually with some flippant or ironic retort that cuts right to the heart of the matter. You're smart – you know it, and you want everyone else to know it too. You have no patience for fiddle-faddle, nor for the usually accepted canons of yak-yak which comprise most casual, everyday conversation. You need to be the center of attention (whilst feigning disinterested modesty), dominating the proceedings with a humorous and self-mocking bravado and an acerbic view of human nature which is engaging, entertaining, and absolutely apropos. On the negative side, your absolute self-certainty and dismissive attitude towards anything which contradicts your carefully constructed world-view can be irritating to people who are sufficiently intimate with you not to buy it. But you possess the élan and chutzpah to bring it off no matter what.

Mercury square Jupiter tends to a pernickety perversity. You are organized, orderly, and fastidious: everything has to be perfect; and you feel intolerably ruffled and put out when it isn't. Unabashedly finicky and zealously protective of your personal prerogatives, you are huffy, touchy, and easily offended – taking umbrage at any perceived slight, and quick to return a snappy rejoinder. You are perspicacious and critical, with a rather unique take on everyday society that places you above the hoi polloi; and you are not afraid to stand alone in your opinions (or to vigorously voice them). Whimsical and willful to the point of wrong-headedness, you incline to get one obsessive idea in your head – usually couched in terms of defending some Higher Truth or the Moral Right – and then you go off half-cocked and devil take the hindmost. Albeit crotchety and pigheaded, nonetheless you do possess a certain genius for being absolutely in the right now and then – for spotting subtle errors or possibilities which everyone around you is overlooking – which confirms you in the infallibility of your insight and wins you loyal adherents amongst the hoi polloi.

Mercury trine Jupiter: Your thinking is investigative and logical (as opposed to intuitive), and cuts right to the heart of any matter. You are plainspoken and blunt without being forward or impudent, perhaps due to your ameliorating irony and brass-tacks realism. You have a facility for efficient problem-solving: you roll up your sleeves and get down to whatever must be done with little wasted motion or pother. Your impersonal, impassive sang-froid betrays little of what is really on your mind: albeit pleasantly loquacious and a good listener, you don't really say anything of substance or react to anyone with genuine sympathy. You don't reveal what you are really up to so as not to engender opposition or reproach; and you don't go much out of your way for anybody. Your smooth manner, amiable diffidence, and distaste for direct confrontation enable you to pursue your own ends without making waves or attracting notice. On the negative side your utilitarian practicality can be cold-bloodedly dismissive; and it's often difficult for you to make a response from the heart (no matter how much you would like to). Your cleverness and cool-headedness under pressure make you a stabilizing influence in any environment.

Mercury opposition Jupiter indicates that you are thoughtful, considered, and imaginative. You are wary, deliberative, and observant – a watcher and waiter rather than a mover and shaker. In contrast to Mercury conjunct Jupiter, there is a craftiness here, or at least a reticence about being too revealing and a preference for behind-the-scenes tergiversation rather than overt disclosure of intent. As with all Mercury-Jupiter aspects there is an insatiable intellectual curiosity and fondness for learning, which here is expressed as a desire to explore new frontiers of knowledge or to look at common things in a highly original way; and you are quite willing to go to any extreme necessary to test your theories in practice. You are highly ingenious and follow your own ideals and eccentric point of view wherever they may lead you. Although you are often up on your own cloud or marching to the beat of some distant drum, you possess an inventiveness and facility for improvisation which rises to any occasion.

Mercury parallel Jupiter makes you patient and reflective. The Mercury-Jupiter aspects take a positive, optimistic attitude towards life, and they approach other people in a spirit of goodwill as they eagerly proffer their advice and opinions. Although they endeavor to be convincing (and indeed they have themselves thoroughly convinced), they do have their unacknowledged blind spots which become apparent when they exhaust their stock of pat answers and cut-and-dried solutions. You parallels are as sanguine and forward-looking as the aspects, and you take the same constructive interest in other people. But you are animated by a more penetrating and thoughtful introspection than the outward-directed aspects are: you are artless and straightforward rather than pedantic; natural and unaffected rather than categorical. You carry the air of the outsider looking in – the sojourner who never quite fits in or belongs – with an intellectual integrity which sets you apart and isolates you in your musings. There is a sense here of appreciating and learning from others rather than trying to impress them; of savoring ideas rather than flaunting them. The incessant rumination of Mercury-Jupiter here becomes a reach for wisdom rather than mere collecting and displaying knowledge.

Mercury contraparallel Jupiter is as clear-thinking and original as the aspects between these two planets, with the same ironic or sardonic take on life. But you are far lighter and more spontaneous than the ponderous opposition – you possess a bouncy, saucy joie de vivre and a willingness to fly with your gut-level instincts and throw caution to the winds. You care not a fig for what impression you are making on other people, so long as you are free to do your own thing in your own way. You possess a quixotic (or capricious) freedom of thought and action unfettered by societal norms: you bluntly speak your mind, or rely upon the good old fait accompli to achieve your aims, without too much concern over where the chips may fall or what the consequences might be. Where the aspects love to teach and preach, your influence is more a matter of just being unabashedly yourself at all times and in any company, which inspires others to cede you the lead (or at least get out of your way).

Mercury–Jupiter Mutual Reception makes you highly aware and knowing. The aspects between these two planets are gregarious and sociable, and appear (at least outwardly) to be cheerful and happy-go-lucky. They usually don't care to admit when they are confused or hurt, but try to take life in stride and maintain a pleasant equanimity no matter how much they are boiling inside. You MRs also take an amiable, hail-fellow-well-met role among your fellows, but you are not as sensitive to the agreement or approbation of other people for your sense of self-esteem. You are more capable than the aspects of applying firmness and resolve when the situation requires it since you are humbler and less concerned with upholding an image of cleverness and savoir-faire with everyone you meet. You always maintain your distance and reserve: you possess a shrewd, incisive objectivity which sees right to the heart of matters and enables you to rise above petty partisanship and dominate the proceedings with a detached sagacity and authoritativeness. On your negative side your amused, know-it-all superiority can resemble smug stone-walling; and your equanimity and blasé indifference can at times seem overdone. But your dispassionate allegiance to truth as you conceive it and your calm moderation in any circumstances are a steadying influence in your social group.

Mercury–Saturn Aspects and Mutual Reception

Mercury-Saturn reveals something of people's attitude in the face of trial and travail: how they gird their loins and hunker down with concentration and dedication. These natives are serious-minded, no-nonsense; and are thorough and meticulous in discharging their obligations. They also tend to be rather hard and harsh, with an air of world-weariness, of being put-upon, of long-suffering and patient forbearance.

Mercury conjunct Saturn is stolid and reticent. Albeit outwardly friendly and sociable, you always maintain your own personal space with aloofness and reserve, and you carry yourself with a quiet dignity which commands respect. You are a broad and considered thinker, but are undemonstrative and rarely share what you are really thinking and feeling with anyone. You have firm lines which are not to be crossed, and are quick to take offense at the least slight. You turn a cold shoulder and withdraw into yourself (rather than reach out or compromise) in the face of opposition or misunderstanding; and you prefer to go off own your own rather than rely upon supporters. Although you are pensive and are quite capable of listening to calm reason, you nonetheless have a somewhat absolutist streak which steams ahead and rolls over any obstacle (or other people's sensibilities) once you have decided upon a course of action. You show your best in moments of doubt and confusion, when you are able to calmly hold your own while everything is flying apart or dissolving into turmoil. Your ability to fearlessly take a stand endows you with a nobility of character which others look up to.

Mercury sextile Saturn is the mark of a staunch self-certainty. You are realistic and efficient, with a good sense of the art of the possible and how it can be achieved with the least wasted motion and pother. You possess a positive outlook which takes misfortune in stride and is able to optimistically persevere in the face of adversity, with no regrets or self-reproach because you always do your best. You are feisty and brusque, possessing a hard, direct manner which cuts across other people's ego games and machinations, and gets right down to brass tacks with little subtlety or need for excuses. You tend to regard diplomacy and social niceties as being bothersome mummery; and you can turn stone-cold in a trice and slam down the portcullis when you run out of patience with someone. On your negative side, you can be quite hard-nosed and contemptuous (rather than sympathetic) when a bit more gentleness might ameliorate and spread oil on troubled waters. But your refusal to take setbacks to heart and your facility for shrugging off disappointments and hurling yourself back into battle lend you an admirable decisiveness and conviction.

Mercury square Saturn is disgruntled and pessimistic, with something of a chip on your shoulder. Bluff and blunt, gruff and grunt, you are easily frustrated and tend to let things get to you and fester inside. You are dubious and distrustful – your perspicacity can always find the catch, the hitch, the fly in the ointment. You look at the Eeyore side of life and sigh with weary resignation. In fact, you victimize yourself with your assumed and affected indifference, which puts you out of synch with the course of events and out of step with the people with whom you must deal. You are not so much deliberately tactless and bruising as you are timid and clueless with regard to convincing other people and winning them over: you prefer to close up into yourself and salve your wounds rather than take command of affairs. You combine indelicacy and insensitivity to faux pas with a huffy umbrage and bullheadedness. You mistake self-exculpation for honor: you'd "rather be right than president". On your positive side you are punctilious and conscientious, so it can never be said of you that you didn't fulfill your obligations and pull your fair share of the load.

Mercury trine Saturn shows a single-mindedness and seriousness of purpose which is based upon high ideals and stern self-discipline. You are determined to carve out your own niche in life, and you follow your own star without needing or expecting much support or encouragement from other people, but rather depending upon your own inner resources and pluck. The path you follow in life is unique and very different from that of your family and most other people in your ambient society; and you keep your eyes unwaveringly on the horizon. You are truly an original. You are very clear-sighted, are not fooled by superficial appearances, and take very little for granted. Since you are off on your own tangent most of the time it can be very difficult for others to pull you down off your cloud to deal with their issues and what you may regard as hum-drum, mundane exigencies not worthy of your notice. But your high-minded earnestness and nobility is truly an inspiration to everyone who knows you.

Mercury opposition Saturn makes for a superior remoteness. You are focused on your own personal designs and hold yourself at arm's length from the common masses with their plebian concerns. Solitary, secretive, and self-contained, you are a perennial outsider looking in who stiffly resists and resents any prying into your affairs. You are politically minded: always second-guessing the angles, plotting all the ins and outs, believing that you're one up on everyone else. You are disputatious and fond of quibbling: it's difficult for people to get on firm ground with you because you are evasive and patronizing, and disappear behind a Cheshire Cat smile. You can be maddeningly aloof and supercilious – as if you had your own private joke going – which makes other people feel as though they are being humored rather than taken seriously. On your positive side you are more than competent intellectually; and you *do* have a great deal of insight into human motivation and a skeptical eye for the cant and hypocrisy which most people accept unquestioningly.

Mercury parallel Saturn is dogged and hopeful. The aspects between these two planets can be overly serious-minded and easily become bogged down in drudgery, as if resigned to accepting whatever new load life might care to pile on top of their already overburdened shoulders. You parallels have the same perseverance and sense of long endurance, but you are more positive than the aspects. You also slog through life, but with the idea of looking forward to some bright future (rather than gazing sullenly down at the trodden earth below). You take self-limitation and self-denial as a matter of course, as a necessary rule of the game; therefore you are able to take joy and consolation in your heavy responsibilities rather than view them as an onerous burden. As Don Juan said, "The basic difference between an ordinary man and a warrior is that a warrior takes everything as a challenge, while an ordinary man takes everything either as a blessing or as a curse." Where Mercury-Saturn aspects detach themselves from other people, you are capable of detaching from yourself, viewing your life with objectivity, dispassion, and a self-effacing good humor. Your equanimity under pressure and your willingness to accept and deal with your circumstances as they come demonstrate that it's possible to be both realistic and upbeat – that you can't keep a good man down.

Mercury contraparallel Saturn makes you positive and cheerful even in adversity. Where the aspects between Mercury and Saturn keep their distance from people, isolating themselves with an impersonal reserve and reticence, you are quite sociable, open, and forthcoming about what is on your mind, while being no less individualistic and determined to follow your own star. You have high ideals to which you submit yourself which take precedence over your own personal comfort and convenience, and you are quite happy (rather than resigned) to make whatever sacrifices are needed to attain your objectives. When confronted with obstacles you don't moan and groan, or try to butt your way through, but rather have the patience to wait, finesse, explain – i.e. take a step back to reexamine your thinking objectively to find a reasonable solution. You understand quite well that the goal does not lie at the end of the road, but is the road itself.

Mercury-Saturn Mutual Reception is broadminded, intellectually curious and non-judgmental. The Mercury-Saturn aspects are tense, guarded, on edge and also rather curt and dismissive in their personal manner. They tend to be fixed and authoritarian in their thinking, so they often find themselves defending the same old threadbare rationalizations and lines of thought. You MRs possess the same diligence and scrupulosity as do the Mercury-Saturn aspects, and you prefer the same sort of grooved existence. But where the aspects' interest in other people is largely limited to protecting their position or prerogatives from encroachment, you MRs are prompted to be more gregarious and sympathetic to the suffering of others. You are straightforward, artless, and plainspoken, possessing a pleasant amicability (rather than a sullen prickliness) which treats other people as your equals and thus encourages them to open up, relax, and just be themselves. You are a good listener and are genuinely interested in other people's stories, with the idea of learning from them and encouraging their collaboration or winning their acquiescence. You do well in the helping professions and in the role of teacher / advisor. On your negative side you have a tendency to permit others to impose their ideas on you rather than make a definite stand on your own; but your desire to seek meaning and make sense of things endows you with the ability to keep on keeping on in times of stress.

Mercury–Uranus Aspects

Mercury-Uranus natives are reserved and insular, and work best in solitude. They are lone wolves – part visionary and part crank – with a hard-headed realism and down-to-earth practicality. These types think outside-the-box with an unshakeable self-certainty born of high ideals and a powerful sense of justice. They are very alert, perceptive, and mentally clear; and they are capable of acting with lightning speed and total self-assurance. They are by no means rebellious – their noncomfority is merely the natural byproduct of an unconcern with other people's belief systems, or for playing other people's games. Mercury-Uranus natives hold unswervingly to their own personal code of honor, which guides all their actions and against which they measure their sense of personal fitness.

Mercury conjunct Uranus is inquisitive, free-thinking, and ready and willing to seek the truth wherever it may be found. You are serious-minded, sober, and possess a strong sense of personal dignity with which you hold yourself at arm's length from everyday society. Not much escapes your scrutiny; and you must always figure things out for yourself and arrive at your own conclusions in your own time. You are not so much a misfit as on your own wavelength and engrossed in your own speculations; you possess a highly original point of view, and you are largely indifferent to (or oblivious of) other people's opinions. Nonetheless, you are highly articulate when you feel like sharing your thoughts, and you speak out fearlessly with little concern for the consequences. You go your own way and do your own thing without needing or asking anyone's permission, and you have an adventurous and trail-blazing spirit of enterprise. You possess a somewhat cynical cast of mind and an abrupt, cavalier manner which cuts across pretense and obfuscation; and on your negative side you can be maddeningly wrong-headed, obtuse, and unstoppable – incapable of any sort of compromise or accomodation. Your probity and inimitable individualism win you the respect of everyone who knows you.

Mercury sextile Uranus makes for a playful impetuosity. The harmonious aspects of Mercury-Uranus are similar to the conjunction, but far more outgoing and gregarious (not as individualistic and self-contained). You are fresh and lively, daring and optimistic, with an eager, ready-for-anything audacity. You are excitable and impatient – you want it all *now* – and your infectious alacrity and enthusiasm for your own ideas and schemes garners willing cohorts. You are also encouraging of other people's efforts to take chances and fly with their impulses. Bold and brash, you possess a sassy (albeit humorously ironic) tongue and a blunt outspokenness. Your willingness to shoot from the hip with little regard for decorum or other people's sensibilities can at times be brusque and bruising; and you have no qualms about steamrolling over anyone who gets in your way. At your worst there is more than a tinge of headstrong and contumelious Great-I-Am to your makeup. Your unvarnished intrepidity and upbeat ebullience enliven any group of which you are a part.

Mercury square Uranus makes for a guarded intensity. Albeit outwardly sociable and tractable, you are something of a loner even in the midst of company – at least you never feel a secure sense of belonging or of being part of the proceedings. You dislike making waves unnecessarily, or attracting undo attention to yourself. Although you are rather judgmental, you hold your tongue and let many things pass. You are wary and secretive; and you go your own way with an impassive self-control which belies an inner simmering or seething. There may be an unexpressed anger or frustration which animates your singluar isolation and obsessive focus on your own ends. You hunker down with a grim seriousness and dig in your heels with a dogged, ready-for-anything tenacity. Your obstinacy and one-pointed concentration make you a formidable force to be reckoned with when thwarted: you simply bulldoze your way through obstacles and steamroll over anyone who gets in your way with no need for explanations or apologies. Your willingness to hold to your own course through thick and thin endows you with an admirable staunchness.

Mercury trine Uranus shows a person with a highly original viewpoint and philosophy of life, together with the will and willingness to put your theories and ideas into practice in everyday life. You choose a lifestyle quite different from that of your family, or most of the people in your social environment; and you use your freedom of thought and action to advance abstract (rather than merely personal) goals which are to the benefit of all. You need to have a staff and banner – a consciously articulated purpose and plan – to justify your decisions and keep you marching onward and upward; and you are able to overcome disappointments and avoid bogging down by keeping your eyes on the ultimate prize. On your negative side you can be a trifle stuffy or haughty, particularly when others don't seem to appreciate your noble motives or try to involve you in their tiresome issues. But your originality and high ideals are an inspiration to all.

Mercury opposition Uranus is utopian and elusive. You are usually off on your own tangent, pursuing your own sui generis agendas. There may be a pleasure-loving tendency; or a dominating fascination which rules your life. In spite of being very outgoing and gregarious, you are a perennial outsider who delights in your free-spirited eccentricity. You are artless, unaffected, and candid, possessing a childlike playfulness and a winning simplicity of manner. You create a world of your own in the midst of this one – or better said, you have a knack for getting the world to rearrange itself around you – and you are blissfully indifferent to any intrusion of stark reality. On your negative side your blithe and mercurial insouciance renders you completely impassive and unreachable when something doesn't particularly strike your fancy; and and you can display a lofty disdain for the common weal. Your steadiness in the midst of confusion and your irrepressible optimism even in the face of disappointment are a beacon for those who know you.

Mercury parallel Uranus is staunch, intent, and perspicacious. The Mercury-Uranus aspects hold themselves apart from the throng with their oblique points of view and readiness to fly wherever their impulses may lead them. You parallels possess the same freethinking mentality; and are just as individualistic and aloof; but without the self-satisfied swagger and bravado of the aspects. You are more conscientious and restrained, seeking in your life a sense of meaning and understanding rather than mere license. There is a constant sifting and analyzing going on here, refining your thinking and testing it against actual experience. You maintain your independence of thought and action with a strong moral sensibility and an unerring, intuitive inspiration which guides you (as opposed to an intellectualized system of belief or need to feel in the moral right). You measure yourself in terms of worth and effectiveness rather than success.

Mercury contraparallel Uranus is considerably more low-key and laid-back than the intense and bullheaded aspects between these two planets. You are softspoken, undemonstrative, and matter-of-fact, yet you possess a keen perspicacity which cuts right to the heart of matters. You can be equally firm and unyielding in your absolutism, but without the ostentatious contumely and the need to register an impression on other people which characterize the aspects. It's not that you have a consciously articulated point of view or philosophical stance to defend, so much as a keen understanding of human nature and frailty which makes you empathic and always willing to make allowances for good faith; and a firm grasp on who you really are at root that you will never surrender under any circumstances. You are eminently reasonable and pragmatic – searching for solutions and modus vivendi rather than trying to make your own point. Your unhurried detachment, objectivity, and disinterestedness make you the cynosure to whom others naturally look for a clue in times of turmoil or perplexity.

Mercury–Neptune Aspects

Mercury-Neptune aspect natives are positive and idealistic, with strong convictions. These natives rely upon a surety that is based upon instinctive, gut-level feeling, which is always more convincing than logic or reason. They always want to believe the best, which on the negative side can make for tunnel vision – blind to anything they don't want to see. They are unsophisticated and unselfconscious, like playful puppies wagging their tails, with a surplus of enthusiasm and good intentions.

Mercury conjunct Neptune is the sign of a naïve (credulous) self-certainty. You are earnest, wholehearted, and live in a world of your own making in which things are black and white, and everything has its proper place. There may be considerable artistic ability, or at least a highly creative approach to everyday living: everything you do must have your own personal touch. Gentle and softspoken, you possess a strong conscience and are nonplussed by conflict and confusion (become easily flustered or discombobulated). You are inclined towards psychic and / or spiritual matters, and are subject to the intrusion of spirit forces in your life (for better or worse). More than most people, you rely upon your intuition to make decisions, and you may seek some religious – or at least highly idealistic – orientation to undergird your thinking. You possess a strong faith, and as a result can be overly credulous, given to wishful thinking, or gullible in your choice of associates. On the negative side there may be a tendency to wring your hands helplessly or wallow in self-pity rather than stand up for yourself to right matters. Your childlike trust in essential goodness and reliance upon what is right does tend to bring out the more indulgent impulses of others.

Mercury sextile Neptune makes you impulsive and headstrong. You are pert and spontaneous – possessing a bouncy spirit of adventure and an unadorned loquacity which up and speaks its mind in any company (and your remarks are usually quite pithy and apropos). You have an amusingly ironic view of the passing scene and an infectious gusto for life which endears you to other people, and you love to perform and show your stuff. You are actually something of a character, whose sui generis point of view and ideas are novel and original: you are improvisational, inventing yourself as you go along. You are willing to trust your hunches and fly with your spur-of-the-moment fancies, and not worry too much about where you land. You are undaunted by second thoughts or much concerned about other people's opinions. On your negative side you can be overly vague, trifling, and noncommittal. Your refusal to "get serious" or to go much out of your way for anyone; and your willful whimsy and insistence on getting your own way; can wear thin for the people who depend on you. But in its proper moment your cheerful breeziness is a welcome gust of fresh air.

Mercury square Neptune tends to be insightful but dogmatic. You are a keen observer of the passing scene, and must figure things out for yourself rather than accept other people's opinions. You are animated by a great intellectual curiosity which reaches out to embrace the recondite and obscure (and is usually at variance with the ideas and beliefs of your society or milieu). There is a tendency towards extemism or zealotry in one form or another, and you can be quite doctrinaire and intolerant of disagreement with your own ideas and values. You (correctly) see yourself as endowed with considerable clarity of mind, and are able to pick up on subtleties and complexities which other people overlook. You have a fondness for intricate, Talmudic argument; and on your negative side can be a bit of a sophist – the peerless pundit registering supercilious disdain for intellectual inferiors. Impatient and gruff, you are easily annoyed and irritated, and can be touchy, huffy, and quick to take offense: people have to tiptoe around you, especially when you have one of your "moods" on. On your positive side there is no doubt but that you are indeed brilliant, and that you possess a unique slant on things which – in its proper moment – can be most illuminating.

Mercury trine Neptune endows you with a self-certainty based upon an intuitive understanding of what is right and true. Like all Mercury-Neptune aspects you rely on your own intuition (rather than common sense or conventional wisdom) in making your decisions; but you carefully weigh all the consequences and ramifications before acting. It's not so much that you must think things through first; on the contrary, you can be quite spontaneous in word and deed, particularly in the face of confusion, when others around you are in doubt. But there is a considered heedfulness, or sense of a higher imperative than momentary advantage or expedience which you must needs obey, in all that you do. As a result you can sometimes strike other people as being mulish, intransigent, immoveable; particularly when they are all in a tizzy. But your strong moral sensibility is always a rock of surety for others.

Mercury opposition Neptune makes you both both capricious and uncompromising. You are a head-in-the-clouds dreamer – something of a knight with a plume – a romantic with the single-mindedness and élan to follow your vision wherever it might lead you. You must always be the leader, never the follower; and your positive, can-do attitude sneers at obstacles and defeatism. When you have a bee in your bonnet there's no stopping you, nor dissuading you from your rose-colored-glasses optimism. You are somewhat formal and reserved in manner (stiff), and you possess a lofty superiority (but also a philanthropic – if somewhat condescending – sense of noblesse oblige). You are extremely dignified, punctilious, and disciplined, both in your own comportment and in your expectations of other people: meticulous, scrupulous, and particular. On your negative side you can be most impatient, finical, and demanding; and outspoken to the point of rudeness. Your blithe and breezy disposition and staunch courage of your convictions lend you a true nobility of character.

Mercury parallel Neptune makes for a reflective conscientiousness. The Mercury-Neptune aspects are dreamy and visionary, and have a highly utopian outlook on life and human nature. Albeit rough and blustery on the surface, underneath they are soft-hearted and a bit soft-headed, which makes them easy to impose upon or deceive. You parallels evince the same naïve trust in people as the aspects, but you are more cautious and wary – more *attuned* (rather than trying to uphold some idealized image). You parallels have more personal warmth and magnetism than the know-it-all aspects. You are less fixed within yourself, and thus are able to pick up on other people's feelings and the undercurrents of the moment, which allows you to see and sympathize with the points of view of the people you meet; and also to seize opportunities as they arise. You are adept at slithering around obstacles rather than confronting directly or obliviously shirking. You have a governor on your impulses (which the aspects totally lack) that lets you intellectually examine a situation before committing yourself to it. You temper the emotional vulnerability of the aspects with a modicum of common sense and self-appraisal.

Mercury contraparallel Neptune has all the intuitive self-certainty of the aspects between these two planets, but you are less assertive, more respectful of other people's beliefs and opinions, and more interested in learning from them than in holding forth to them. You do not seek to uphold some idealistic world-view and fit everything that happens in life into it; rather you seek understanding and a way of appreciating the way things actually are. You possess the Mercury-Neptune recognition that there is more to life than meets the eye – that what's really going on is swirling about beneath the surface – but you are less interested in feeling yourself to be on top of things than in just going with the flow. You possess a nobility of character and purety of impulse which guides you (rather than other-worldly concepts). The assurance which animates all your doings is grounded in a deep sense of conviction rather than an intellectual construct.

Mercury–Pluto Aspects

Mercury-Pluto natives are scrupulous, picky, and highly aware. Aboveboard and direct, they are not afraid to call a spade a spade. They know their own minds and they are always on their way to achieving their goals; and it's hard to knock them off their pins because they are so single-minded and intent. If blocked or hindered, they are adept at trouble-shooting a way around any obstacle – they are subtle, wily, and willful.

Mercury conjunct Pluto indicates a person who is thoughtful and meticulous – a deep thinker and analyzer, with considered judgment and a penetrating insight into other people's character and motives. Albeit cagey and a bit cynical, you make a point of keeping your own dealings as open and straightforward as possible; and you are quick to react to any sign of equivocation or insincerity. Articulate and disputatious, you possess a sharp, cutting tongue, a fiery temper, and very fixed opinions. You are not so much rebellious per se as highly imaginative, original, and impatient with convention: you prefer to try new ideas (go off half-cocked) rather than idly accept the canons of established orthodoxy. On your negative side you can be a petty dictator – believing that you've got everything figured out, and that you're one up on everyone else – and then there's just no reasoning with you at all. Your utter faith in your own convictions and fearless willingness to follow your own star wherever it may lead you endow you with an admirable uprightness.

Mercury sextile Pluto makes you self-assured and headstrong, with a good humored bravado and panache. You are bold and optimistic, ready to follow your impulses wherever they may lead you with the certainty that wherever you wind up will be just fine. You are not so much uninhibited as intellectually curious and daring, ever ready to push the envelope, to reach out to people and to new experiences with gusto. You trust yourself, and are usually willing to give other people the benefit of the doubt as well. You have strong convictions to which you hold firm through thick and thin; but you are quite democratic and tolerant of other people's points of view. You encourage others by your example and by your willingness to go out of your way, to do a bit more than is absolutely necessary, to be thorough, meticulous, and leave nothing undone. Your positive, upbeat attitude and friendly, outgoing disposition are an invitation to others to join in the fun.

Mercury square Pluto tends to be finicky and irascible. Constantly buzzing about in a never-ending hurry, you are short, exacting, and blunt to the point of rudeness. You live in a state of busyness, preoccupation, and distraction: you give the impression of not favoring people with your full attention because your mind is always on other matters. Suspicious and dubious, you always attempt to anticipate any possible eventuality; keep all your bases covered; and watch in every direction so that you won't be taken unprepared. Since you are easily irritated by any disruption to your wonted routines, you appear to be perpetually annoyed with everything and everybody – you are testy, peevish, and huffy, which serves to keep other people and their bothersome demands on you at bay. You are inclined to sacrifice even common courtesy to your own convenience, and at your worst run roughshod over people and their sensibilities. On your positive side you are diligent and painstaking, and pay careful attention to details – dotting all the i's and crossing all the t's – which makes you a conscientious and tireless worker and organizer.

Mercury trine Pluto is reasonable and just. You are a simple, uncomplicated person: what people see is what they get. Albeit as headstrong as the other Mercury-Pluto aspects, you are more low-key and politic: you rely upon patience and forbearance to achieve your ends rather than dazzling intellect or the bold stroke. Relaxed and unaffected, you make good eye contact and your conversation is right to the point (which sometimes disconcerts people). You have a strong sense of fair play, and you are judicious and discriminating in your handling of others. You think things through objectively and thoroughly before arriving at your opinions and decisions; and you convince people by soberly appealing to their rationality and logic. You do have a tendency to get up on your high horse and identify your own viewpoint with the Moral Right – which at times can make for a cocksure smugness and complacency. Most of the time, however, when your sentiments are in the right place, your steadiness and composure have a calming effect on any group.

Mercury opposition Pluto makes you discerning and ironic. You are forthcoming and glib, and quite chatty about what's on your mind. Alert and acute, you are quick to pick up on nuances, and quick to react to them. You are calm and cool-headed, and cannot and will not be rushed or goaded. Cheerful and positive, you possess a wry sense of humor and the ability to see both sides of any issue. Your detachment and impartiality, as well as your patient and considered judgment, make you an ideal arbiter and a sagacious counselor. Your down-to-earth practicality and cleverness, and your willingness to put all your cards on the table, disarm people and win their trust and loyalty. On your negative side – when your disinterestedness turns to indifference – your chintzy humoring of people and your blasé disinclination to bother yourself can smack of rank self-indulgence. At your best your blithe and devil-may-care cockiness enlivens any group of which you are a part.

Mercury parallel Pluto makes you prudent and inquisitive. The Mercury-Pluto aspects are keen and sharp: ever on the qui vive for nuances, with a diplomat's attunement to the subtle shades of meaning in the words and gestures of others. They clearly perceive hidden motives, and they are fond of making cynical remarks about the covert rationale underlying other people's behavior. You parallels exhibit the same wariness and stealth as the aspects, and you have the same dubiety about other people and their intentions; but you don't have the strong competitive urge that characterizes the aspects—the need to make comparisons with other people. You too like to feel that you're on the inside track of things, that you're smart and nobody's fool; but you are more willing to accept your own limitations and those of others, rather than indulge in a game of sneering one-upmanship. You are more of a listener than a talker – curious to learn other people's thoughts and ideas – since your reach is for understanding to fortify your own thinking, rather than to try to impose your viewpoint and beliefs. Your reliance is common sense rather than intellectual tour de force

Mercury contraparallel Pluto is considered and thoughtful. You are as mentally agile and penetrating as the aspects between these two planets, but are less quick to act and react. Rather, you must take your time and thoroughly ruminate and digest information before you arrive at your own conclusions. You also tend to be less judgmental than the aspects, with something of a "live and let live" philosophy which keeps you on an even emotional keel even in the face of confusion, opposition, or bad faith. This is not to say that you are a patsy or pushover; merely that you decline to take things personally or draw undo attention to yourself until / unless you find you are forced to make a stand, at which time you become an immovable force and formidable opponent bolstered by the knowledge that you have the moral right on your side. Where the Mercury–Pluto aspects are calculating and shrewd, you see things from the point of view of what is best for everyone involved.

Venus–Mars Aspects and Mutual Reception

Venus-Mars aspects symbolize – naturally – interpersonal relationships; particularly those with the opposite sex. These aspects describe how natives make a place for themselves within their social milieu. Albeit highly sociable on the surface, they nonetheless maintain a cool reserve: they are quite adept at securing the validation they seek from the social whirl without in any sense compromising their own integrity or betraying their true feelings. Dr. Jones says of natives without a major aspect between Venus and Mars that there is "a lack of real ordering of man's superficial opportunities ... a tendency to neglect his ramifying day-by-day interests. This neglect may be deliberate and a cheerful insulation from petty worries ... it also may be the result of an inability to stir to any immediate or pressing need without exceptional stimulus, either at the hands of other people or of some compelling course of events. ... The ability to function without any especially sharpened concern over little things can be an asset or a handicap."

Venus conjunct Mars makes you genial and positive. You possess a sunny disposition, a mischievous glint in your eye, and a winning alacrity which pleases and delights. Your youthful, puckish, coquettish good humor has a definite sexual basis, and your seductive charm is very attractive to the opposite sex. There is often a sense of androgyny here: Venus conjunct Mars women are a trifle butch; and the men are a trifle effeminate, or else exaggeratedly macho. It's not that you Venus conjunct Mars natives are any more bisexual than anyone else, but rather that you act this role out openly for everyone (instead of repressing it). You are not afraid of your sexuality; and indeed you tend to flaunt it, or turn it to your best advantage. You possess an emotional self-sufficiency within yourself; love peace and concord; and are nonplussed by conflict or entangling yourself in other people's issues. Therefore, you are liable to adopt denial / avoidance tactics to turn your attention to pleasanter things when (intimate) relationships become too onerous and demanding. Your ease of manner, utter absence of pretense, and blithe self-acceptance make it easy for other people to accept you on your own terms as well.

Venus sextile Mars makes for a spirited joie de vivre. You are unabashedly yourself and completely self-possessed in any company or situation. You are very much the social butterfly; and you are an animated conversationalist and accomplished raconteur, so you excel at teaching and sales. You immediately make yourself at home in any group, and you assume the role of cynosure or focus with your idiosyncratic personal style and panache. You have a great sense of humor and a droll outlook on life so you don't take yourself too seriously; nor do you permit other people to bring you down. Your childlike exuberance and ebullient optimism carry you forward with little concern for niceties, propriety, or consequences; which can lead you at times to blindly brush past people or make light of their concerns in your headlong pursuit of the good life. Your facility for not taking setbacks or rejection to heart but keeping your cool under the most trying circumstances is a model of unshakeable intrepidity and enlivens any milieu.

Venus square Mars is socially awkward and bluff; with something of a disconnect from the people around you (particularly those of the opposite sex). You are plainspoken, crusty, and brusque, with little native delicacy or diplomacy. Like the other Venus-Mars aspects you are out front and unaffected, but you lack their social grace and charm due to your acute self-consciousness and Willy Loman-esque neediness: "It's not enough to be liked – you have to be *well-liked*" (or at least to make a good impression). Your outreach often misses the mark because you are at pains to fit in; thus you can be unsociably bumptious or presumptuous in your attempts to command respect from people; or play-act a role rather than just feel relaxed and at home with them. It is difficult for you to see yourself as others do; thus you can be unreasonably demanding of yourself and exacting of other people. You have definite lines which are not to be crossed, and you react with an overweening huffiness when they are – as though yours were the only feelings that mattered. On your positive side you possess an unvarnished frankness and a scrupulous attention to discharging your responsibilities and obligations.

Venus trine Mars is poised, self-possessed, and comfortable in any milieu, while nonetheless holding yourself a bit aloof and above the proceedings. While you are friendly and gregarious by nature, you are definitely on your own wavelength most of the time. You possess a quiet dignity which neither asserts itself nor bids for attention overtly, yet you manage to assume a leadership role or at least make your opinions known through the power of your presence and the seriousness of your demeanor. Your natural reserve and distaste for effusive display, as well as your strong sense of personal space – your own and other people's – may at times incline you to brush past people rather than engage them directly, which can cause frustration and bruised feelings where a bit more empathy might have ameliorated discord. But holding to your own orbit through thick and thin, and not allowing yourself to be swayed by the convolutions or brouhaha of the moment, make you a calming, pacifying influence.

Venus opposition Mars makes for a proud self-sufficiency. You are a loner / misfit; but unlike the Venus-Mars square you don't force the issue of trying to belong. Albeit as outgoing as the other Venus-Mars aspects, you content yourself with sitting alone on the edge of things and watching the proceedings, rather than barging in with your own pizzazz. Likely this is the role you assumed within your family constellation while growing up, and you continued it into adulthood: the detached observer, who holds yourself apart and goes along rather than instigates. "I do my thing and you do your thing. I am not in this world to live up to your expectations, and you are not in this world to live up to mine. You are you, and I am I, and if by chance we find each other, it's beautiful. If not, it can't be helped." – Fritz Perls. You are the proverbial leader without followers – but that suits you fine. On your negative side you can be sullen and peevish; easily take umbrage; or feel put out and close up into yourself when not accorded the proper consideration – you become coldly obstinate and deaf to entreaty. In their proper moment, your stateliness, independence, and disinterestedness command respect.

Venus parallel Mars is gregarious, ingenuous and wholehearted. The Venus-Mars aspects are gracious and engaging, with an easy manner and a breezy disposition. They use their considerable charm to win and to woo, enabling them to get what they want from others without the necessity of entangling commitments. You parallels are also cheerful and saucy— in fact you are far more brazen and forthcoming about what you're really thinking than are the aspects (who usually gloss over their real intentions). Albeit as aloof as the aspects, you are far more straightforward and natural because your friendliness is genuine – not a tactic to wheedle favor or indulgence. There is a warm, plaintive quality about you which disarms people because they sense that you are for real: you are always true to yourself. Your utter simplicity and artlessness makes it easy for people to relax with you – you are at ease within yourself, which puts others at their ease in your presence. On your negative side there can be a solipsistic, self-coddling tendency. But your complete sincerity and earnestness win you the appreciation of everyone who knows you.

Venus contraparallel Mars, like the opposition between these two planets, is friendly and outgoing, but with a sense of the outsider looking in. You are able to fit yourself into any group situation precisely because you are not out to prove anything or impress anyone, but are able to just be yourself at all times. You are soft-spoken and low-key, possessing a quiet dignity which commands respect: you don't rely on others or seek approval or emotional support from them, but rather go your own way and neither expect (nor particularly want) followers or admirers. There's something of a gruff, rough-around-the-edges aspect to your disposition; you don't put on airs, or disguise annoyance in the name of diplomacy or expedience, but say exactly what you think and do exactly what you will. You manifest a true nobility of spirit on which other people can always rely.

Venus–Mars Mutual Reception is companionable, spirited and game. The Mars-Venus aspects possess a youthful charm and sparkle with which they ingratiate and insinuate themselves. They are spontaneous and impulsive, and move quickly to dominate situations and relationships. You MRs have the same bon vivant amiability as the aspects, but without the varnish of naïve innocence. You are open and unapologetic about your little machinations, and you have a wry and knowing zest for all the petty intrigues of everyday life. Hence you find more genuine enjoyment in your dealings with others than do the aspects, who are often too intent upon scoring little points for themselves to pay much attention to the game. Your roguish, conspiratorial pluckiness seduces the connivance of others; and when it doesn't, you're quite content to plunge ahead on your own. Your chutzpah and hubris at times get you overboard, and your rough-hewn peremptoriness can border on the gauche. You live your life with gusto and abandon, and let the chips fall where they may.

Venus – Jupiter Aspects and Mutual Reception

Venus-Jupiter aspects reveal natives' adaptation to their social milieu, particularly the need to be heard and appreciated. They make for popularity: these natives possess pleasant personalities and are good listeners and congenial companions. They have a touch of gallows humor, as if to acknowledge the fact that we're all in the same leaky boat. They are blithe and optimistic, but a trifle cool and standoffish. These natives assume an avuncular, hail-fellow-well-met role in their group, so they are sought out as trusted confidants, advisors, and adjudicators.

Venus conjunct Jupiter makes for a low-key manner and the ability to take things in stride. You are poised, relaxed, and unhurried, with an optimistic attitude and a practical sense of proportion. Gregarious, convivial, and companionable, you don't let things get to you but have a facility for focusing on the present moment rather than resenting the past or worrying about the future. You are judicious, considered, and soberminded rather than effusive: yours is the voice of calm reason in your social circle, and your avuncular bonhomie invites the confidence and confidences of others. You possess a sense of fitness and rightful belonging in any milieu: you easily assume your place with dignity and aplomb (and are generally accepted on your own terms). Your lofty pride can at times verge on haughtiness and condescension; and you refuse to bother yourself much with anything which is not in line with your own personal aims and concerns. Your positive, accepting attitude buoys up any group of which you are a part and gives people hope in the midst of hard times.

Venus sextile Jupiter makes you charming but politic. Like the conjunction between these two planets you have a prepossessing affability; but you are less disinterested and philosophical, more opportunistic and expedient. There is a smoothness and economy to your actions; a polish and panache; a conspiratorial gleam in your eye which induces acquiescence. You are a bit of a showman, with an ironic good humor and a mischievous sense of fun. Artful and clever, you are adept at handling yourself in any circumstances, and are deft at managing people and situations to your ultimate advantage. In a spirit of cheerful camaraderie, you quickly move to dominate the proceedings, or at least keep the focus of attention on yourself and your intentions. You avoid indelicacy and conflict wherever possible since you are usually able to wheedle or insinuate your point of view in a cordial manner; but you can also be quite brusque and gruff, and turn the cold shoulder when someone doesn't buy your act. Your devilmay-care joie de vivre and genuine enthusiasm enliven any group.

Venus square Jupiter is socially awkward and self-conscious. You have few or no close friends because your outreach often misses the mark

– either because you are too timid or else too blatant. Usually Venus-Jupiter squares are soft-spoken and hesitant; but there's another type which is pushy, strident, and jarring. In any case, you are discomfited in a social setting and are at pains to win acceptance. There is something plaintive and a bit pathetic about you – you mean well, but find it difficult to just be yourself since you feel as though all eyes are on you. A sense of misunderstanding or lack of appreciation (perhaps originating in your relationship with your parents) creates an incumbency to try hard to fit in – too hard. Nor do you know how to stand up for yourself – you either back down in an effort to appease (or at least not make waves); or else you go overboard with righteous indignation. Naturally you take rejection very much to heart; and you close up into yourself and sulk at the slightest provocation. On your positive side you are – like the other Venus-Jupiter types – cordial and attentive to other people's feelings.

Venus trine Jupiter is a highly favorable combination for leadership, facilitation, and counseling. You thoroughly immerse youself in any group of which you are a part with your democratic outlook and your contagious verve and enthusiasm. Nonetheless you possess a quiet dignity and self-sufficiency which both commands and proffers respect. You are somehow able to balance being warm, intimate and empathic, while nonetheless maintaining your own space and not intruding on that of others. You have a sense of personal style and flair which is not particularly intended to impress anyone, and for that reason is all the more impressive. You are unselfconscious, with an ease of manner that invites the trust and confidence of others. Like everyone else you have your issues (shown by other aspects no doubt), but you don't permit them to infect your relationships or dampen your sunny disposition. Your optimism, poise and complete confidence in yourself make admirers and supporters of everyone who knows you.

Venus opposition Jupiter makes for a good-natured impassivity. You possess an aloof, imperturbable manner which remains unfazed and unaffected even in the face of turmoil and confusion (especially in the face of turmoil and confusion). You don't break a sweat but remain in possession of yourself under all circumstances. You may cultivate some specialty (of which you are the undisputed master) which attracts the admiration and plaudits of those in your circle; and you show your stuff with unabashed alacrity and glee. You are intellectually curious and experimentative, and are always on the lookout for new adventures and acquaintances to demonstrate your skill and augment your repertoire. On the negative side, your irreverently droll cynicism and patronizing smugness can be overdone at times, and are especially unappreciated when push really comes to shove and something more earnest than above-it-all chintziness is called for. But your spry resiliency and ability to keep your cool under pressure are a rock for the people who depend on you.

Venus parallel Jupiter is spunky, plucky, and doughty. The Venus-Jupiter aspects maintain their positions in social situations through their winning charm and aloofness. They are basically jovial people; but they also have a political sense which knows how best to manipulate people to obtain their own ends. You parallels are as genial and gregarious as the aspects, but you are more down-to-earth and less cocky and pretentious. You have a deeper insight into yourself than the aspects do, and are more comfortable within yourself (not needing feedback from others to bolster your self-esteem). Where the aspects strive for some form of acceptance or appreciation, you are accepting and appreciative of others. You are truly interested in people – in learning from them (rather than impressing them) – and your manner is welcoming rather than lofty. You are not so much fearless as indifferent to fear – animated by a great intellectual curiosity, the desire to learn and to know everything you can about life, other people, and yourself. Although your unadorned exuberance can at times verge on the gauche, your irrepressible good humor is the product of an inner delight rather than a calculated pose.

Venus contraparallel Jupiter gives you a rather romantic or visionary take on life and other people, and a wistful idealism which always strives to uphold the highest moral standards in your thinking and comportment. You possess a freshness and vivacity which enlivens any group of which you are a part; and your ironic viewpoint and your perceptive commentary on the passing scene makes you popular in any circle. You delight in other people, listening to their stories and appreciating their thoughts and ideas; and you are a delightful conversationalist yourself. You are cool, calm, and collected even when everyone else is in a tizzy; and you are the voice of reason and common sense in the face of confusion or conflict. You always seem to be gazing past the horizon, or looking at everyday society from your own unique and oblique standpoint which sees details and subtleties which everyone else seems to miss. You are balanced emotionally within yourself and therefore require little in the way of stimulation or feedback from others.

Venus–Jupiter Mutual Reception is spontaneous and sympathetic. The Venus-Jupiter aspects possess a vaguely supercilious (albeit humorous) detachment. However, they are not so amused by any suggestion of their own weaknesses, or by any affront to their stiff dignity. You MRs are like the aspects in your wry humor and your air of being on top of any situation and focus of any group, but you are far more homespun and earthy. You can view even your own foibles with benign amusement; and you have considerably more self-insight, less of a psychological blind spot with regard to your own motives. Thus you are genuinely benevolent and caring in your impulses – willing to go out of your way for other people and stand up for what you know is right (rather than hedge or temporize to maintain a façade of equanimity). You're not afraid to speak your mind, and you delight in your candor and willingness to let the chips fall where they may. Your brash cockiness and tendency to strut occasionally miss the mark; but you are accepted because you are inimitably yourself at all times.

Venus–Saturn Aspects and Mutual Reception

Venus-Saturn is not a felicitous combination: at best it implies that enjoyment is taken in responsibility; at worst it implies that enjoyment is subservient to responsibility. These natives are not warm-hearted, kindly souls; nor do they expect gentleness or indulgence from others. Quite aware of their own little ploys, they are equally dubious about the motives of others. These aspects are not good for intimacy: they tend to delay or prohibit marriage, or create problems therein; and they make for dutiful (albeit demanding) partners.

Venus conjunct Saturn is cold, brusque, thorny, and inhibited. You are stiff, proper, and highly suspicious of other people's motives. You keep your emotional distance and don't let anyone in. Perhaps due to unfortunate childhood experiences you tend to view relationships in terms of power and control (rather than nurturance); and you won't permit anyone ever again to exercise ascendance over you. You set up minefields which any would-be intimate must thread their way through in order to reach you. You are very defensive, closing up like a clam and stonewalling anyone who has the temerity to approach you with an offer of love (you tend to view this as prying). Intimates must handle you with exteme patience and tact; in terms of lovers this means an older – or at least mature – partner: one who doesn't take your testing personally, who loves you in spite of your apparent rejection. On your positive side you are steadfast and punctilious in observing the formalities of relationship – no one can ever accuse you of not fulfilling your obligations. Your willingness to sacrifice spontaneity and to set aside your personal happiness in the name of obeisance to an abstract sense of honor wins the respect of those who know you.

Venus sextile Saturn is cool, brisk, and always in command. You try to keep things (particularly relationships) on an even keel by not breaking stride and not permitting yourself to get too involved emotionally. You paper over conflicts and difficulties with a smiling savoir faire or abstracted obliviousness so as to get past dealing with current problems and other people's issues with a minimum of fuss on your part. As a result, you have a high tolerance for being bent out of shape inwardly while maintaining an outward pleasantness and equanimity; or else just walking over people and their feelings without a fare-thee-well. It's important to you that other people see you as always being in control of yourself (and your relationships); that your image isn't tarnished by the peccadilloes of those close to you which might reflect back on your competence as a spouse, parent, or friend. On the other hand, your ability to keep the peace by not reacting or flying off the handle is – in its proper moment – a steadying influence on others.

Venus square Saturn makes you finicky, exacting and touchy. Albeit outgoing and sociable, you are nonetheless rather self-sufficient and aloof. You have a need for considerable private space, and hotly resist any encroachment thereon by others. You demand respect, but don't always respect other people's feelings or points of view in return because it is difficult for you to put yourself in their place. You are idealistic rather than realistic, living out your own vision of how things ought to be and how other people ought to comport themselves. You tend to withdraw with adamant self-righteousness (which you regard as "being honest") rather than reach out for conciliation or seek a modus vivendi. You stand on your pride and dignity, and prefer going it alone to compromising your own aims and aspirations one whit. You tend to make conflictive or unsatisfying relationships because you need to have everything *just so*: you are exigent, severe, and dismissive in dealing with people. On your positive side you are hardworking and dedicated, and make a fetish of dutifulness, so that other people know that your word is your bond and can be relied upon unequivocally.

Venus trine Saturn is smooth – smooth talking, smooth acting, taking everything in stride smoothely without missing a beat. You maintain your equilibrium and generally positive, forward-looking attitude by focusing completely on your own ends and not letting yourself be bothered much by other people's issues or demands – you just don't let things or people get to you. You possess a no-nonsense, down-to-earth practicality which takes charge in the face of doubt or distress, and is usually successful in spreading oil on troubled waters and bringing people to an accord. Therefore you make a good arbiter and negotiator, standing above disputation (and thus able to give events a tangential shove this way or that to your own benefit). Staunch and philosophical in the face of setbacks, you are able to exercise patience with people and their foibles because you don't let them knock you for a loop; and you are quite capable of turning a cold shoulder when diplomacy fails. Your cool-headed sang-froid militates against your being too committal, which can become an annoyance when people need a true heart response from you, or anything beyond best wishes and superficial good cheer. Your straightforwardness and ability to put matters on a basis of good faith leads others to hear you out and cede you the lead.

Venus opposition Saturn makes you restless and single-minded. You are extremely self-willed and driven: always in motion and on your way to somewhere, you never relax for a moment. Nor do you have patience for anyone else, or for dealing with people's "issues"; but unlike the conflicted squares you have few expectations of others (for better or ill), but prefer to go it alone. Therefore marriage and other intimate relationships are successful only to the extent to which the people involved are willing to forgo their own dreams to serve or assist you in realizing yours (e.g. Jupiter in your 7th house). Whether you sacrifice everything to your career or ambition; or whether you just live day-to-day with no particular plan; you are not above using people for your own ends and cold-bloodedly discarding them when their usefulness has ended. On your positive side you are an unstoppable engine: when you have a bee in your bonnet you are dynamic, indomitable, disciplined, and willing to sacrifice all personal comfort and convenience to achieve your goals.

Venus parallel Saturn makes for a judicious disinterestedness. The Venus-Saturn aspects tend to be wary, reserved, and calculating. They play their cards close to their chest, and they have a real zest for all the power politicking and artfulness which underlie everyday society. They are forever scoring little points for themselves and trying to be one up on everyone else. You parallels are as cautious and cynical as the aspects, but you have a highly developed sense of irony, and you take benign amusement in the passing scene. You are detached and aloof rather than intensely involved in strategies of control or avoidance. You don't lack ambition, but rather refuse to permit your moods to go up and down depending upon your current status vis à vis your fellows. You are stable and centered within yourself, and it takes quite a lot to pull you down from your lofty eminence. On your negative side, your noncommittal Cheshire Cat smile can leave people feeling frustrated and disgruntled. Like the aspects you are basically a loner, but you are generally more interested in keeping yourself emotionally disentangled from other people than with trying to outfox or best them.

Venus contraparallel Saturn is deft at handling people by respecting their space and not permitting them to intrude on yours. Albeit outgoing and friendly, you are on your own wavelength most of the time; and in spite of your ironic view of human nature and your apparent bonhomie you are not really much of a people-person at heart. You need very little in the way of support or appreciation; you go your own way in an economical, businesslike fashion with little wasted motion or need for explanations and justifications. You are able to avoid much conflict by evasion and sidestepping (rather than by coming to grips with problems directly), and as a result people sometimes feel pushed aside or run over by your single-minded insistence on doing your own thing in your own way. You win people over with your earnestness and sincerity rather than trying to manipulate matters one way or another.

Venus Mutual Reception Saturn makes you expedient and brisk. Venus-Saturn aspect natives are often fearful of being tied down emotionally, or of being abandoned; and they therefore maintain a tight grip over their feelings (and relationships) at all times, tending to be shrewd and manipulative rather than relaxed and spontaneous. By contrast, you MRs appraise possibilities and advantages realistically rather than in terms of your hopes and fears. You don't invest as heavily in your expectations of other people, but rather keep your personal commitments loose and convenient. You have a far lighter touch than the aspects do, without being any warmer or more intimate; hence you are able to maintain your inner equilibrium and remain optimistic and eager even in the face of rejection or defeat. Instead of seeking the approval or approbation from others for your sense of self-esteem, you concentrate your interest and energy upon some special competency in which your ability is manifest and in which you can take pride and satisfaction; and in this area you are serious-minded, meticulous, and self-validating. You go your own way and do your own thing, and therefore you are less prone to self-doubt or to pendulum swings between triumph and disappointment.

Venus–Uranus Aspects

Venus-Uranus is not that favorable for intimate relationships since it is uncompromising and shies from shackles. These natives psychologically distance themselves from any group (for example, family) in which they unavoidably find themselves, unless they are indisputably leading or dominating it. They are dogged, fearless, and unyielding; but also quite nimble and highly adaptable in new environments and milieus.

Venus conjunct Uranus is outspoken and audacious. You delight in expressing yourself and letting it all hang out. Because your repartee is both pert and pertinent, your saucy intrepidity is generally winning rather than abrasive. There may be some sexual promiscuity or adventurousness – pushing the envelope of what your society deems acceptable. You have a fresh, bold point of view and fearlessly (or quixotically) stand up for yourself and defend your principles even if you must stand alone. You are idealistic rather than practical; and your head-in-the-clouds optimism and can-do spirit thrive on challenge and derring-do. You possess a headstrong insistence on having your own way, and a penchant for endless quibbling to wear other people down to acquiescence. You simply ignore anyone who disagrees with you; and you resort to fait accompli to achieve your ends rather than waste energy on explanation; which can lead you to bowl people over when they object or proffer a variant scenario – even when they have your own best long-term interests in mind. Your never-say-die cockiness and jolly good humor get you out of any scrapes, and usually land you on your feet and on top of any contretemps.

Venus sextile Uranus makes you hopeful and forward-looking. You are a positive thinker – always seeing the bright side and expecting the best both of other people and the situations you encounter. You decide for yourself where your responsibilities will lie, and you are punctilious in discharging them. You may cultivate some hobby or specialty (which you can do on your own) at which you are expert, and which brings you the pleasure and fulfillment which most people find in the approbation of others. Albeit gregarious and chatty, you are basically a free spirit who goes your own way and does your own thing with little need for support or encouragement from anyone. Indeed, you dislike being tied down or having to curtail your own pursuits and pleasures in the name of compromise or propriety. Therefore you can at times seem self-centered and oblivious to the needs of others, since you refuse to allow yourself to be bogged down in their issues and snares. Your irrepressible alacrity buoys up the mood of any group of which you are a part.

Venus square Uranus is resolute and bullheaded. You are self-willed, ornery, and have utmost faith in your abilities and native superiority. You generally eschew the well-traveled path in order to create a sui generis lifestyle in which your own intent holds sway and you are able to implement your vision and follow your dreams. If, on the contrary, you belong to an organization, you swiftly rise to the top, or at least to a position in which you are untrammeled and able to do as you will with little interference. You are as exacting with subordinates as you are with yourself, and you have little patience for shilly-shallying or foolishness (i.e., disagreement with your point of view). Your indomitable mien and your propensity for stonewalling or just ignoring anything you don't want to hear obviate any need for concession, and usually suffice to ensure that other people defer to you, or at least stay out of your way. Your originality, daring, and utter indifference to the opinions of other people or the dictates of convention arouse the admiration of those who know you.

Venus trine Uranus is free-thinking, impetuous, and emotionally independent. You don't give a hang about expectations put on you by others (such as family, friends, or intimates), but are determined to go your own way in life and find congenial circumstances and relationships wherever they may lie. You have a great intellectual curiosity and love to experiment with new experiences, lifestyles, modes of thought and behavior – i.e. you let it all hang out, but not particularly to impress or scandalize – just to be inimitably yourself. You don't like being hedged in, and as a result may find intimate relationships become too demanding or limiting after a while; and you are able to up and transplant yourself or reinvent yourself as need be without breaking much of a sweat. In consequence, you may leave a trail of bruised sensibilities or disappointed expectations in your wake; but you don't see that as being your problem. Your buoyant optimism and never say die alacrity carry you through any imbroglio with a minimum of pother on your part.

Venus opposition Uranus tends to be prickly and irascible. Like all Venus-Uranus aspect natives you are a free-wheeling maverick with considerable perspicuity and panache. However, your usual state of mind is disgruntlement with the status quo, and you possess a snide or disparaging view of your fellow bipeds. You expect the worst from people and situations, and focus on their deficiencies and shortcomings rather than take a detached or sympathetic view. Your congenital impatience and hypercritical intolerance for any sort of stricture tend to bog you down and make you a target, so that your life becomes an unending struggle against limitation rather than a quest for transcendence: "I am a rock; I am an island." Your prissy perfectionism and callousness do serve to induce other people to leave you to your own devices, which suits you fine and also proves your point (their unreliability). On your positive side you are competent, hard-working, and courageous; and you are always willing to stand on your own two feet; take complete responsibility for yourself; and acquit yourself with honor.

Venus parallel Uranus makes for a blithe inimitability. Venus-Uranus aspect natives exhibit an extreme pigheadedness and intransigence. While they are gregarious and sociable creatures on a tête-à-tête level, they are staunchly individualistic and resist being lumped together with other people except in terms of supremacy. You parallels are as emotionally self-sufficient as the aspects – in fact you're even more off-beat and unconventional – but you are far more companionable and collaborative. Like the aspects, you parallels don't permit other people to get to you or bring you down, but your presence is relaxing and inviting. You have a knack for maintaining your distance and keeping the spotlight on yourself while nonetheless reaching out to people so that they feel included in your privileged circle. You give your attention wholeheartedly (rather than cursorily); and you bring a spirit of mischievous fun to any group undertaking. You are playful rather than lofty and forbidding, so people quite naturally gravitate to your orbit and willingly lend themselves to your projects and schemes. Your aloof breeziness and unwillingness to deviate from the beat of your own distant drum can at times leave others in the lurch. But your cheerful camaraderie lightens the mood of any group.

Venus contraparallel Uranus is cool, collected, and breezy. You generally don't take things personally or involve yourself unduly with other people's convolutions, but go your own way and do your own thing making as few waves as possible. While not self-effacing per se, you are undemonstrative and not out to prove anything to anyone (except yourself), so you don't really care what sort of image you are projecting. You are emotionally self-sufficient and democratic, able to relate to people as equals, and are generally more interested in interacting with them and learning from them than in impressing them. When you give people your attention you do so whole-heartedly, and truly concern yourself with their feelings and points of view. You are a good group organizer and leader precisely because you are able to keep your *self* in the background; and your unselfconscious enthusiasm enlivens any group of which you are a part.

Venus–Neptune Aspects

Venus-Neptune natives are inclined to live with their heads in the clouds and to see the world through rose-colored glasses. Because they are so fixated on their own private wavelengths, they possess little sensitivity to nuances or subtleties, or tolerance for ambiguity. They are open and candid about their feelings, and they are naïve and trusting in their dealings with others. They are simple (although they feel things deeply), and they adhere to high standards of comportment.

Venus conjunct Neptune is gentle, sensitive, and empathic. You are kindly, soft, and vulnerable (defensive or inclined to worry unduly). You are artless and out front – always true to your word and faithful to your principles. You are a good listener because you are truly interested in understanding other people and their concerns; and you cheerfully go out of your way to do whatever you can to ameliorate their woes or intercede in their behalf. You are something of a crusader who holds unswervingly to a strict ethical and moral code, and who is genuinely seeking to make the world a better place. Even if you are not especially religious you are attuned to the spiritual side of life, and you uphold the highest standards of honor and honesty in your personal affairs and transactions. On your negative side you incline to idealize the people and situations you are involved with; thus you can be overly trusting, and hence easily victimized or deceived.

Your cleanliness and purity of motive are a model of true righteousness for everyone who knows you.

Venus sextile Neptune is spontaneous and at ease in any company. You are natural, informal, and are always willing to go with the flow and follow your inclinations wherever they may lead you. There is nothing subdued or restrained about you: you freely say whatever you are thinking with no concern for the consequences; and your wry, sassy, uninhibited observations are usually quite apropos (if at times jarring). You flit like a hummingbird from here to there, and prefer acting on spur-of-the-moment impulse rather than planning ahead and bogging yourself down in intricacies. You rely more upon feel than upon reasoning things out; thus on your negative side you can be quite unreasonable (and irresponsible) in your extemporization, and you are inclined to let unpleasant things slide rather than confront and deal with them directly. Thus you sometimes land in dire straits which could easily have been averted with a little foresight and sensitivity on your part. But your ability to recoup your aplomb and to bounce right back from any predicament is part of your vivacity and charm.

Venus square Neptune is blissfully optimistic and visionary. You possess a fresh, youthful innocence and a romantic, chivalrous, and devil-may-care enthusiasm. Your jaunty obliviousness recalls the spirit of the don; and your inclination to go off half-cocked and tilt at windmills can lead you into like imbroglios. Your starry-eyed innocence and credulity make you easy prey to the unscrupulous; and your inability to see stark realities right before your eyes and anticipate complexities is an annoyance to those who depend on you. Your unrealistic expectations and innocent perplexity when these go awry; your seeming inability to learn from painful experience and guard against future eventualities; your adamant insistence on holding out for your pie-in-the-sky daydreams; and your zealous excitation when you are off on one of your tangents (combined with your shutting-your-eyes and keeping-your-fingers-crossed inertia when timely action is called for), make it difficult for other people to take you seriously or include you in group decision-making. Your noble and unimpeachable forthrightness is nonetheless a model of steadfast rectitude.

Venus trine Neptune is sensitive and knowing. You have a deep intuitive understanding of people and their motives, and are quick to pick up on vibrations in the air. You are straightforward, ingenuous, and aboveboard – incapable of insincerity or subtlety, with a strong distaste for the petty politics and machinations of everyday society. You freely speak your mind – particularly in defense of the weak and helpless – and let the chips fall where they may. You are self-effacing without being the least bit timid; and you are a sympathetic listener without pushing yourself or your own agendas forward. You are just there for people. Even if not overtly religious you uphold high spiritual aspirations in your own behavior, and you feel a strong need to consciously live your life as model of right comportment for others. You have high ideals and a positive, optimistic outlook on life which is able to see past current disappoinments and always looks forward to a bright future.

Venus opposition Neptune tends to be secretive and temporizing. You are rather insecure with other people and try to keep your relations with them as pleasant and non-confrontational as possible. Soft-spoken and wary, you go way out of your way to pacify and placate, even if this means putting up with uncomfortable intrusions into your own space. You try to look at the bright side of any issue and see the ultimate good in adverse circumstances and in other people. You realize that everyone's just trying to do the best they can; and you try to do yours as well. Because you find everyday society rather harsh and merciless, you may seek or create some safe niche or escape for yourself well out of the mainstream. Unless other horoscopic elements bolster your self-assertiveness, you tend to be vague and noncommittal when push comes to shove, and therefore not as dependable in a pinch as those who rely on you might prefer. Your conscientiousness and meticulous attention to fulfilling expectations and discharging your obligations makes you a good and loyal citizen.

Venus parallel Neptune is unaffected and forward-looking. The Venus-Neptune aspects have to do with reconciling one's own images of people (and oneself) with the realities of everyday society. You parallels are similarly off on your own lively wavelength most of the time, and pursuing your imaginative dreams come what may; but you are more relaxed within yourself (and with other people) because you are basically out to enjoy yourself rather than to prove anything. You look people straight in the eye, and you address them with an unabashed frankness which thoroughly disarms them and effortlessly wins them over. Although you can be difficult to detain or influence when you have a bee in your bonnet and are buzzing off in some oblique direction, your naturalness, simplicity of manner, and refreshing artlessness call forth a similar candidness from others; and your infectious enthusiasm carries people along with your visionary ideas and plans.

Venus contraparallel Neptune is as natural and outspoken as the aspects between these two planets, but you are not as supersensitive and abstracted. You're a real toughie and nobody's fool, so you don't need to appeal to or rely upon other people's indulgence for protection. You have a blunt, rough-and-ready manner (in contrast to the shrinking-violet aspects), and you have little patience for hypocrisy or double-talk. You possess a childlike vulnerability and attunement to emotional undercurrents, but are able to address them openly and capitalize on them rather than escape into avoidance or denial. You are sanguine and positive, with a hopefulness based upon a realistic appraisal of the realities, and your confidence in your own prowess at dealing with whatever may come. You are a dreamer, but a thoroughly practical one, who is able to thread your way through confusion, stand your ground, and resist being blown hither and thither by the winds of circumstance.

Venus–Pluto Aspects

Venus-Pluto symbolizes a rather self-centered and utilitarian approach to personal involvements, which often makes for fervid and stormy relationships, and ardent, Gatsby-esque, romantic obsessions which terminate in devastating betrayals and breakups. These natives are like fire and ice: furiously passionate when smitten and coldly dismissive when repulsed. There is always an element of craftiness and calculation in these aspects which preempts much in the way of natural compassion. They need to have the power in any group or relationship.

Venus conjunct Pluto is intense and demanding. You possess considerable personal charisma and flair, and you give the impression of being on top of any development and in charge in any situation – unmoved and unmoving even in the face of catastrophe. Albeit saucy and brash, your flippant cockiness may cover a deeper sense of insecurity. In intimate relationships there can be a self-centeredness which is impatient and exacting, requiring unstinting allegiance and subservience (which you also offer in return). At times it may seem as though you are more in love with an image that you have – a Beatrice, Dulcinea, or Daisy Buchanan – rather than a real, live person, since your attentions can become unduly smothering or devouring; or else you lose your own center and willingly become a submissive slave to the object of your affection. You grab on hard; and it's hard for you to let go. In any case your relationships tend to become struggles for supremacy rather than relaxed and easy-going give-and-takes – with you it tends to be either all give, or all take. Your zealous loyalty and unstinting allegiance to people is your finest hallmark.

Venus sextile Pluto is spirited and impetuous. You are energetic and self-assured, unhesitatingly reaching out for and taking whatever you fancy with no apologies or self-deprecation. There is nothing subtle about you or what you're after: you are bold, self-aggrandizing, and incisive. You get right to the point with no hemming or hawing, and your outspoken assertiveness takes people by storm. Your brass and bumptiousness are tolerated and even indulged because of your idosyncratic cheekiness and panache: you don't bowl people over so much as wheedle and cajole them with a conspiratorial twinkle; and you can exert considerable charm to seduce acquiesence. You are able to fabricate intricate arguments and justifications to convince and convert; but when these fail you rely upon the good old fait accompli to obtain what you want. On your negative side you are callous and obtuse – steamrolling right over people in blind pursuit of your own objectives. You don't take setbacks to heart, but have a resiliency (or hubris) which bounces right back from any rejection or defeat.

Venus square Pluto makes for a suspicious and closed-up attitude. You are stern and hardheaded, and are self-conscious and unrelaxed in intimacy. You are detached and aloof rather than spontaneous and sympathetic, and you feel a need to take the upper hand to maintain a semblance of stability and control in any relationship. You possess a shrewd intuitive grasp of other people's ulterior motives and weaknesses (and have a horror of anyone possibly prying into yours). You view others in terms of what they can do for you or how they can best serve you, and you maintain a mental tally of benefits vs. deficiencies, gains vs. losses, points won and lost. Although you usually only enter into relationships which you can dominate, you nonetheless may tend to see yourself as the victim of any disagreement, or exculpate yourself from responsibility when others confront you with demands for warmth and tenderness. You operate on a mental rather than heart level; but you are ever at pains to make sure that no one can say you didn't give your all and pull your share of the load.

Venus trine Pluto is shrewd and judicious, maneuvering your way around people to get what you want from them rather than overtly revealing your cards. You keep your eyes on the prize, and by turns can charm, or wheedle, or cajole; but prefer to avoid direct confrontation whenever possible. When you are flummoxed or defeated, you pause to regroup yourself rather than take it personally; and if forced to abandon a goal you do so with a philosophical, sour-grapes "Who cares anyway?" attitude. It's almost as if you enjoy the chess game aspects of everyday social machinations – the cut and thrust – more than whether or not you actually obtain what you desire. Intimates may complain that you are non-committal when serious matters must be dealt with: you tend to slither away rather than allow yourself to be pinned down, which can exacerbate problems which, with a bit more attentiveness on your part, could easily be obviated or resolved. But your tremendous staying power and patience, in their proper moment, are a secure reliance for others.

Venus opposition Pluto is brisk, impassive, and business-like. Albeit outgoing and gregarious on the surface, you are fundamentally a loner who is emotionally self-contained and self-sufficient. You are perspicacious and critical, with a rather jaundiced view of other people and little patience for their follies or foibles. You go your own way and do your own thing with little care for the opinions or sentiments of others; and you insist upon your own space and your own life even in partnership. You hold yourself above the multitude with a lofty noblesse oblige which tends to look down upon any sort of effusiveness or demonstrativeness. You freely manipulate people for your own ends with little sensitivity or compunction, as if by divine right; and then coolly discard them when they have outlived their usefulness. You are not unkind so much as oblivious to the sensibilities of others in your sedulous devotion to your own purposes. Your single-minded intent and high-wire energy make you the cynosure of attention for everyone around you.

Venus parallel Pluto is alert, observant, and canny. The Venus-Pluto aspects possess an acute perception of human nature, with a penetrating grasp of emotional undercurrents, and the ability to sense and react to extremely fine shades of nuance. They feel a driving need to maintain a tight grip on their relationships. They have a skeptical turn of mind, and can be very exigent and irascible with other people. You parallels are as perceptive and incisive as the aspects, but you are far more tolerant of other people's shortcomings, and hence less inclined to patronize them or let their antics affect you. Like the aspects you like to be the center of things; but you are lighter, *gemütlicher*, than the aspects – you lack their dark self-obsession. You don't put a great deal of personal stake in your relationships, so you can be dispassionate and disinterested without being cold and distant. Your good-natured bonhomie belies your acute analytical discernment, but your nonjudgmental, live-and-let live disposition allows you to be skeptical – and nobody's fool – without succumbing to defensive maneuvering. You take a broad, gentle, humorous view of yourself and the people around you.

Venus contraparallel Pluto is friendly and outgoing, but without caring much how others see or react to you. In contrast to the aspects between these two planets, you don't weigh people in terms of gain vs. loss, or control vs. thrall – you possess the knack of being very perceptive and analytical without much need to score points for yourself or to manipulate things your way. You have your own unique, sui generis viewpoint and philosophy of life, and your articulate and insightful remarks fascinate the people you know. You boldly sally forth without looking around or ahead, which induces people to follow your lead since you always give the impression of being in command of yourself and of knowing what you are about, whether you do or not. You maintain your own integrity not through maneuvering but rather by cheerfully going your own way and accepting the support of others, or not, as they themselves choose.

Mars–Jupiter Aspects and Mutual Reception

Mars–Jupiter has to do with deft handling of people in order to fulfill one's desires and succeed in the game of life. These natives are outgoing and self-possessed, and they are able to mobilize their energy and resources smoothly and effectively. They are unbothered and unafraid; quite at ease in unfamiliar and confusing situations; comfortably themselves in any group; and always focused on what they expect to get.

Mars conjunct Jupiter makes for a controlled self-possession. You are poised and unruffled – never nonplussed or at a loss for words – at all times. People readily accede to your take-charge style because your commanding, no-nonsense presence radiates competence and self-certainty, which puts people at their ease and makes them feel secure under your auspices. You strive to be worthy of their trust, upholding the highest standards of correct comportment and honor in your own demeanor; and you feel a sense of obligation to look out for the weak and helpless. You are a good teacher and lecturer, and you love to hold forth and display your knowledge, keeping your audience absorbed and rapt. You possess a down-to-earth common sense which convinces with its unadorned simplicity; and your confident manner and positive attitude are especially looked up to in times of doubt and confusion. There may be something of the Great-I-Am about you; and you can be a stickler for principle when flexibility and compromise are the order of the day. However, your noble aspirations and diligent attention to your duty make your excesses forgivable rather than overweening.

Mars sextile Jupiter is ingenuous and genial. You have a relaxed, welcoming manner which is soothing and inviting. You make good eye contact, and your sparkling, playful mischievousness and brisk good cheer cut across all social boundaries and niceties to put everyone at their ease. You are bold and adventurous, filled to the brim with dreams and schemes, and eager to share your fancies with everyone you meet. You more or less have your way with people because they feel unthreatened by your candidness and openness; and your unflagging optimism disarms them and readily wins their trust and collaboration. Thus you are a natural-born leader and organizer, and your childlike sense of wonder and spirit of derring-do inspire people to follow your direction. On your negative side you can be unduly whimsical and capricious: contrary, rebellious, or simply off on your own tangent when onerous obligations are required of you. But your ability to bounce right back from any defeat and remain undaunted and hopeful endears you to all who know you.

Mars square Jupiter is headstrong and insistent. Albeit outgoing and gregarious, you are not quite at home amongst your fellows but feel a continual need to focus attention on yourself. You love to shine and strut your stuff, and you do have a characteristically cheeky bravado that is not without its charm. Your boldness and brass gloss over a restless little engine which is always playing to the gallery and finessing the approval and approbation of others – "Look, Ma! How'm I doing?" In intimate relationships you usually seek compliant partners who will unquestioningly cherish (if not adulate) you, and who will bow to your wishes and encourage your desiderata with little fault-finding or interposition of their own dreams. You are basically a rather headstrong person who – if you cannot find willing followers – will just charge ahead on your own account, cross your fingers, and hope for the best. You possess considerable courage of your convictions and will not be stopped or deflected from your goals come hell or high water: when you cannot enlist the support of other people you are perfectly content to go your way alone.

Mars trine Jupiter possesses a spirited enthusiasm which is both gracious and inviting. You make a good leader or teacher since you project an earnestness and nobility of purpose which others look up to; and you are thus able to win supporters and adherents without seemingly trying to. You rather enjoy being the center of attention, but there is nothing blatant or effusive about you. Rather, you possess an economy in your behavior and actions which keeps you focused on the goal at hand, which is to dominate matters through sheer force of personality. You are a master of the grand gesture or pithy remark which cuts right to the heart of the matter and sweeps everyone along with you. You have a sharp, critical mind (and tongue) and somehow are able to get away with voicing your opinions without unduly ruffling sensibilities (most of the time). Needless to say, humility is not one of your faults; but when you do overstep yourself you are able to quickly regain your composure and go on as before without skipping a beat.

Mars opposition Jupiter is bold and willful. You are cool, brisk, and business-like, with an abundance of can-do optimism and faith in your own native powers. Guarded and unrevealing, you play your cards close to your chest and do not rely upon anyone's sanction or sufferance. You are remote, on your own wavelength, and possess a quixotic and capricious exhilaration which believes it is capable of anything. You are determined to carve out your own niche in life in which your own fancies can reign supreme and you do not have to kowtow to anyone. You are quite deaf to entreaty or counsel, and prefer acting alone to depending upon the good graces of others. You are not so much pugnacious – indeed you avoid open confrontation if possible – as you are oblivious and heedless in pursuing your own ends: you merely close up into yourself with an enigmatic, non-committal shrug. You possess a fortress mentality which is not so much defensive as it is sullen and grim: your first recourse is to grit your teeth, gird your loins, dig in your heels, burn your bridges and make your stand.

Mars parallel Jupiter is realistic and practical in handling people. The Mars-Jupiter aspects are very stubborn and set in their ways, and quite impervious to other points of view. They can even be a bit thick at times when their ornery bullheadedness shows through the façade of well-intentioned impartiality and reasonableness. You parallels are amiable, like the aspects; but you are far more agile and diplomatic in your dealings with others. Like the aspects, you are good-natured and plain-spoken, but you are not as forceful and imperious in imposing your own point of view: you are centered without being self-centered. Although by no means irresolute or a shrinking violet, you much prefer frank discussion and consensus to merely enforcing your own will by hook or crook. You understand that your best strategy for the smooth realization of your own purposes is to seek concord – even if this necessitates some give and take on your part. You are at pains to watch out for the rights of others, and are usually willing to modify your own plans in the name of peaceful coexistence. You possess a true objectivity instead of merely benign detachment.

Mars contraparallel Jupiter is staunch and resolute, yet politic and capable of finesse and charm. You possess considerable swagger and cheek, and you quite consciously use your charisma to seduce other people's compliance, rather than bowl them over or take them by storm (as the aspects between these two planets tend to do). You have a magnetic personality which draws people into your orbit by your boldness, exuberance, and never-say-die optimism. At the same time, you are hard-working, dedicated, and serious of purpose – meticulous in dotting all the i's and crossing all the t's – and you are sedulous in discharging your responsibilities and fulfilling your duty. On the negative side there is a tendency to go off half-cocked and confuse idealism with caprice; and true self-esteem with smug self-satisfaction. But your self-certainty and utter confidence in your ability to handle any eventuality is an assurance to everyone who relies on you.

Mars–Jupiter Mutual Reception makes for an unpretentious enthusiasm. The Mars-Jupiter aspects are friendly and sociable, but with an ever-present undercurrent of calculation and cognizance of relative advantage. They like to be in positions of authority, and they can be quite magisterial or patronizing in dispensing their favors. You MRs possess the same good-natured amiability as the aspects; and you are as single-minded in following your own star; but your cordiality is free and undemanding. Instead of self-aggrandizing ambition you possess a sincere desire to share what you can and to be liked and respected for what you are able to contribute. Although you are firm as a rock in standing by your principles, you are not in the least bit vaunting or pushy. You have a humble, plaintive air since you feel with people rather than use them for your own ends. You are attuned to a higher level of achievement than social gamesmanship; and you are able convince others by putting all your cards on the table and encouraging them to do the same. Your hallmark is a straightforwardness which gives the best you can, and in turn brings out the best in other people. Your hopefulness acts like a glue which binds together any group you are in.

Mars–Saturn Aspects and Mutual Reception

Mars-Saturn symbolizes dominance and control, and tends to bring conflicts and oppressive situations. These natives are single-minded, determined to have their own way come hell or high water, and damn the torpedoes. Solitary even in the midst of company; and obsessively fixated on their own ends; they go their own way asking no one's sanction or succor – they hunker down and pull their wagons into a circle. Their only use for society is when they are looked up to and can assume their rightful positions of leadership.

Mars conjunct Saturn is feisty and pigheaded. You are self-willed and hard-charging, with an overbearing mien which does not shy from confrontation or conflict – "Outta my way, buddy!" You are not unsociable per se, but possess a callous, pitiless impatience when your desires are thwarted or opposed. Your individual adaptation of this planetary influence reflects the coping mechanism which you developed in childhood in response to harshness and lack of sympathy. You may possess a sharp tongue which lashes out like a striking snake with little concern for niceties or propriety, or else you silently and grimly bear up in the face of adversity, concealing your resentment beneath a mailed fist. But in any case you tend to regard any attempts at compromise or conciliation as a sign of contemptible moral weakness; and your fearsome aggressiveness steamrolls over anyone who has the temerity to stand in your way. Therefore, to deal with you requires an unflinching doggedness as resolute and ruthless as your own. On your positive side you are daring and adventuresome; honorable and scrupulous to a fault; and your courageous self-assurance and utter disregard for consequences and other people's opinions can, in their proper moment, provide a shining example of heroic intrepidity.

Mars sextile Saturn: makes for a shrewd practicality. The sextile between these planets has much the same meaning as the conjunction, but without the defensive combativeness. You are serious-minded yet approachable, possessing a self-effacing, "aw shucks" hominess and down-to-earth amicability which disarms people and inclines them to let you have your way with them. Albeit basically a loner, your low-key suavity and adherence to the basic Marquis of Queensbury rules of social intercourse facilitate your making a place for yourself (and taking a leadership position) in any group. You are unrelenting and indefatigable in pursuit of your goals, but you refer your actions to a high standard of moral conduct to which you owe unquestioning allegiance (and from which high perch you tend to view the foibles of your fellow bipeds with unconcealed distaste if not disdain). Rather than blunder your way ahead and sweep aside any obstacles in your path, you are able to defer to necessity or beat a strategic retreat temporarily as the situation requires, without feeling cowed or diminished thereby. You are not so much warm or compassionate as you are skilled in the art of the possible.

Mars square Saturn is plaintive and pessimistic. Like Eeyore, you go through life with an air of disgruntlement and expectation of the worst. You may have suffered parental rejection or neglect, or otherwise have been thrown on your own resources and forced to fend for yourself at an early age; and subsequent relationships are likely to be similarly frustrating and disappointing. The hallmark of your life is sincere and strenuous effort which is unrewarded; great sacrifices made with no acknowledgement or recompense; the sense of being on a never-ending treadmill of discouragement and discontent. You make a fetish of the nobility of suffering, hugging your *Weltschmerz* to your bosom and keeping a stiff upper lip. You prefer to seethe inwardly and bear up outwardly, making the best of things, and not revealing your inner ruminations or failed dreams to anyone. Your own malaise gives you considerable native compassion for the travails of the helpless and downtrodden, and you make a point of making yourself useful and going out of your way to assist others in any way you can.

Mars trine Saturn is serious-minded and purposeful, but without the grim intensity of the conjunction between these two planets. While not particularly laid-back per se, you are nonetheless content to relax and let matters run their course, guiding them with interested concern rather than embroil yourself in issues of control and dominance. You are diligent and attentive to details rather than relentless, taking pleasure in getting the job done well rather than in triumphing in the end. As a result, you are thoughtful and philosophical, and can regard setbacks and obstacles detachedly, as learning experiences, rather than taking them as an annoyance or affront. You tend to avoid direct confrontation whenever possible, which can be frustrating for those who demand more commitment than you feel comfortable giving. You are more interested in honing your skills and personal effectiveness than in proving a particular point; you excel at occupations wherein trouble-shooting, diplomatic facilitation, or patient development are required.

Mars opposition Saturn is bullheaded and sassy. You are a real character, who comes on strong and takes people by storm: "My way, or the highway!" Poised and self-assured, you possess considerable cheek and bravado, and you cut a wide swath through your social milieu. Even the more sedate Mars opposition Saturn types need to be at the center of things: in this case you call attention to yourself with an understated intensity and authoritativeness which commands acquiescence (if not subservience). In any case, you will not be deflected: in the face of obstruction you try to take another tack and go around when this is possible; but when push comes to shove you are quite capable of stormy wrath to force your opponent to back down. Albeit a bit theatrical and fond of swagger, you're essentially a cool customer who doesn't fume or wring your hands helplessly; rather you appraise the possibilities with Machiavellian realism and with imperturbable detachment. It takes quite a lot to knock you off your pins or put a crimp in the impassive aplomb which is your signature and ultimate refuge.

Mars parallel Saturn is cautious, painstaking, and intransigent. Unlike the aspects between these two planets, you don't take take much personal satisfaction in winning; nor much engage in self-pity when losing; but rather greet whatever happens with an impersonal, businesslike impassivity. You possess considerable self-will and gumption, and know that anything worth accomplishing requires considerable effort and discipline. Punctilious, uncompromising, and thorough, you are always ready to go the extra mile and undertake whatever responsibility or sacrifice is necessary to achieve your aims. You are also extremely difficult to influence or deflect once you have set your mind on something, and are not especially interested in, nor adept at, soothing the sensibilities of people whom you have pushed out of the way or trodden upon. You have little patience for diplomacy or like fiddle-faddle; but prefer to cut across obstacles or dissent with a bold stroke or fait accompli. Your calm, unruffled mien and ability to hunker down rather than stress out, or react precipitously, can be formidable deterrents in themselves; and your detached seriousness of purpose and cool staunchness under pressure are assurances upon which others can always rely.

Mars contraparallel Saturn is diligent and painstaking. The Mars-Saturn aspects have a serious, earnest demeanor, and a sense of beleaguerment – of strenuous exertion and unremitting struggle, with neither the time nor patience for frivolity or nonsense. They are disciplined and hard-working, but also intolerant and critical of others. You contraparallels are as intent and obstinate as the aspects between these two planets, and you possess the same fortitude, but you are not as grave and severe. You are more conscientious and meticulous than the self-absorbed aspects – more concerned with being thorough and competent and fulfilling your obligations than you are with the acknowledgment or approbation of other people. While by no means humble, you are not pushy or self-dramatizing, but are content to stay quietly in the background and do your job well. You possess an ironic sense of humor, and therefore you can laugh at yourself and the world around you, so you don't have the sense of being besieged or the fear of being hemmed in by circumstances which characterize the aspects. You have a knack for being cheerful and optimistic in times of trouble, and not taking setbacks personally.

Mars Mutual Reception Saturn is aloof and hopeful. The Mars-Saturn aspects are rather stubborn and opinionated, clinging fiercely to their own views and resisting all logic and argument. They deal with disagreement or restriction by trying to outflank or smash their way through it. You MRs can be just as persistent and willful as the aspects, and just as obdurate; but you have a more objective perspective – a wistful longing which looks past current imbroglios, or concerns about who is presently one up on whom, and focuses instead upon a sanguine anticipation: "You can't keep a good man down." You trust in yourself and your own powers to deal with whatever vicissitudes might present themselves, rather than relying on knee-jerk reactivity or trying to maintain an iron grip. Therefore you are better able to roll with life's punches; to keep light and uninvolved; and to bounce back and land on your feet. You are cheerfully resigned in adversity, and you have a resourcefulness and alacrity which make whatever use they can of any given circumstances.

Mars–Uranus Aspects

Mars-Uranus is fierce, determined, and purposeful, with a bullheaded unwillingness to accept any sort of restraint or restriction. These natives are impulsive and spontaneous, tending to shoot from the hip and ask questions later. They are courageous and pioneering; and unafraid to fight for what they believe in.

Mars conjunct Uranus is impetuous and indomitable. You possess a restless spirit which thrives on challenge and adventure. You dislike working in harness or being dictated to; and you fiercely reject any limitations on your freedom of action. You may strike out on your own in some new direction to blaze an original trail through life. You are blunt, sarcastic, and vociferously contemptuous of pretense, double talk, and fiddle-faddle. You are ardent, outspoken, and cut right to the chase, fearlessly standing up for yourself and tergiversating those who would have you fit and trim to conform to their mold. You are not necessarily an extremist, but do tend to eschew the middle ground and view things in terms of black and white, good and evil. Easily frustrated and provoked, you are ready to hurl down your gauntlet at the slightest provocation. There may be considerable stress and turmoil in your life, whether instigated by your own rash contumely or blundered into by your propensity to leap before you look (or look, and leap anyway). Your frank, aboveboard manner and utter lack of subtlety or stealth encourage plain dealing and plain speaking in any group of which you are a part.

Mars sextile Uranus is single-minded yet pragmatic. You are as insistent on your personal liberty as Mars conjunct Uranus, but are nowhere near as pugnacious. You quietly go your own way, slithering around obstacles and adapting to the necessities of circumstances as need be, without in any way compromising your own principles or losing sight of your ultimate goals. You possess a keen political instinct, detachedly and realistically evaluating all possible consequences and shrewdly gauging how best to exploit any opening; and you don't expose yourself (your thinking and opinions) needlessly, so as not to make yourself vulnerable to attack or reproach. When you finally do act it is with a master stroke: bold, daring, with finality and the utter self-assurance of one who has calculated the probabilities and bet all your chips on one throw of the dice. When off on one of your tangents you can be as deaf to argument or entreaty as the other Mars-Uranus types; but you bow out of the picture with a smiling, self-exculpatory vagueness rather than with a defiant scowl. Your democratic and even-handed approach to people is usually sufficient to induce them to let you have your way.

Mars square Uranus is ornery and domineering. You are impatient, irascible, critical, and easily irritated and put out. Imperious and dictatorial, you love being the center of attention with all eyes on you. You quite naturally assume (or seize) a position of leadership in your social milieu, from which podium you can hold forth and spout your unorthodox views and opinions to your heart's content. The fact is that you *do* possess a highly original insight and discrimination, a well-articulated philosophy of life, and a humorous (if jaundiced) take on human society; which is what saves you from being just another screwball crank. Your acuity and perspicacity are not easily taken in by superficial appearances or the current folderol of the hoi polloi. In fact, you possess an acute cunning and feel for the jugular, and are not above exploiting other people's weaknesses or hesitation to impose your own agendas. Your high-handed self-aggrandizement, withering disapprobation, and brusque dismissal of adversaries to oblivion, incline others to get the hell out of your way. But you are able to win people over with your earnestness and complete devotion to your own personal vision.

Mars trine Uranus possesses all the bullheaded stubbornness of the conjunction between these two planets, but is far more cautious and patient. You take a long-range view, and hence are in no particular hurry to achieve your goals, but rather are content to do what is possible in the moment, and allow the fruit of your endeavor to ripen and drop naturally. You cherish your independence as much as the other Mars–Uranus aspects do, and prefer acting alone and taking responsibility only for yourself. But you are no shirker – you are punctilious in fulfilling what you consider your duty to be no matter how onerous or thankless. You are good at keeping your cool, not allowing other people or the press of circumstances to bend you out of shape, because you take your principle satisfaction in the faithful adherence to your own high standards of conduct rather than in obtaining the approval or approbation from other people.

Mars opposition Uranus makes for a frustrated eccentricity. Albeit extremely strong-willed and concentrated, you are completely wedded to your own mindset and opinions, and seem to delight in wrong-headed perversity and contrariness. While by no means antisocial, you maintain your emotional distance from the throng with a supercilious hauteur and zealous devotion to your own personal vagaries. You may believe that you are on the inside track and one-up on others in the game of life; nonetheless, you tend to find yourself in a rut much of the time, running around in little circles rather than advancing towards your goals, because your know-it-all smugness and unquestioning obeisance to your own caprices do not heed counsel, or acknowledge the possibility of wishful thinking on your part. You uphold your fancies – your "honor" if you will – to the bitter end, no matter how threadbare or self-defeating it may become. You prefer to make your point or to get your lick in; to regale yourself with "I-told-you-so" self-satisfaction; even (especially!) at the expense of driving everyone around you crazy. On your positive side your integrity and quixotic faith in yourself enable you to surmount any repulse or rebuff with your whimsical optimism and good cheer intact.

Mars parallel Uranus makes for an unflappable maverick. The Mars-Uranus aspects exhibit a wild and abandoned streak. No matter how sedate they may appear in repose, they are in fact creatures of impulse who secretly harbor a melange of utopian visions and wild schemes. Self-willed and buoyantly optimistic about their prospects, they charge on ahead with little forethought or concern for the feelings of other people. You parallels are as frisky and hearty as the aspects; and you possess the same resolve and courage of your convictions. But you are more level-headed and judicious than the aspects: you know how and when to move warily and skillfully, and how to take other people's sensibilities into account without necessarily deferring to their will or curtailing your own designs. You are therefore more agreeable in your resoluteness, and less prone to histrionic bluster or stonewalling. You really don't much care about the impression you make on people; nor do you measure your effectiveness through their eyes; which is the true essence of freedom. You possess an irrepressible zest for life and boundless hope for the future, which get you through the night and which are a model of composed self-reliance for others.

Mars contraparallel Uranus is free-thinking and independent – like the aspects between these two planets – but you are far less blatant, demonstrative, or imperious. You make a point of being self-effacing and not pushing yourself forward, while quietly nurturing dreams and schemes quite as outlandish as those of the Mars–Uranus aspects. You don't particularly fit in or belong to your ambient social milieu (a fact of which you have been acutely aware all your life); and early on you stopped trying to force yourself to fit into their square holes. You are fundamentally a simple, straightforward person, artless and incapable of the guile and hypocrisy which everyday society demands as a matter of course. You find your own niche wherein you are the undisputed master, and try to live as independently of other people as you can, free of their onerous and distasteful clatter. You are well aware that true freedom lies in being unnoticed and hence prefer to be left alone to pursue your unique vision in peace.

Mars–Neptune Aspects

Mars-Neptune aspect natives are high-minded and visionary, and not altogether centered in everyday "reality". They live in an idealized world – an ivory tower – of their own devising, from which they sally out sword in hand to fight for the right. They are peppy and peppery, blunt and dogmatic; and when they find that they've overstepped themselves they cheerfully shrug their shoulders and muddle their way through.

Mars conjunct Neptune makes for an abstracted cantankerousness. You are grumpy, crotchety, and pessimistic. Completely focused on your own concerns, you go through life with a "can't be bothered – just go away" air. Irritable and short-tempered, your brusque, tactless deportment and acerbic, sharp-tongued outspokenness often leave other people feeling bruised, or afraid to approach you at all. You seem to look for the worst in people; and of course that's what you tend to find. Because your initial response is usually to withdraw and pull your wagons into a defensive circle, your outreach may miss its mark: you seem to prefer stewing in impotent frustration to making yourself heard and understood. Therefore you often feel unappreciated – as though the world is passing you by and nobody cares. You learn early on that you must do things for yourself and depend on no one; and indeed you tend to be self-effacing and retiring in group situations, and something of a solitary even in intimate relationships. On your positive side you are always true to yourself and make a point of maintaining unswerving allegiance to your high principles.

Mars sextile Neptune is canny and resourceful. You are very imaginative and have highly original ideas and points of view, together with the prodigious energy and inspiration needed to put your designs into actual practice. You are always buzzing about in pursuit of this scheme or the other; and your enthusiasm readily attracts willing supporters and allies. You most likely have well thought-out religious or spiritual aspirations which guide your actions; and your candid, aboveboard manner is refreshingly frank. You can see clearly into what motivates people, and you advance your own ends by catering to their hopes and desiderata. You are adept at maneuvering and manipulating, finagling and finessing; but these are done openly, in a spirit of good fun and gamesmanship, so other people usually defer to you and let you have your way. Although at times you can get carried away by your own imagination and lose touch with what is real and possible, nonetheless your blithe and free-spirited insouciance usually suffice to carry the day.

Mars square Neptune is suspicious and driven. You are overreaching and unstoppable – wholly preoccupied with your own agendas, glancing neither to the left or right in the single-minded pursuit of your objectives. You cannot relax or let up for a minute, but need to be perpetually "on". You possess a quick, nervous energy and must always be moving and shaking, constantly performing both for other people and yourself. There is a basic distrust here of both your own motives and those of others; a dubiety which is always on guard and wary of being too trustful (and hence betrayed). This tendency may stem from unfortunate experiences of perfidy in your childhood; and may lead to serial victimization, or to becoming a conscienceless victimizer yourself as an adult. Just as you constantly push yourself, you are pushy with people and are not averse to overwhelming or running roughshod over them if need be. It's not so much that you are unreasonable as that reason plays very little part in your makeup – you act on knee-jerk reactivity rather than thinking things through. On your positive side you are not afraid to speak up and stand up for what you believe in.

Mars trine Neptune is frank, candid, and convincing. You are friendly and outgoing, and look the people you are addressing right in the eye with no shame or hesitation. You have nothing in particular to hide, and your cordial bonhomie wins people over without your seemingly trying to. You are very idealistic and positive, always trying to see the best in other people and the situations you encounter in life. This is not to say that you are a weakling or patsy – you know what you stand for, and hence are able to stand your ground in the face of confusion and conflict. Your optimistic good cheer is able to overcome disharmony by spreading oil on troubled waters and resolving any disharmony amicably. You quite consciously use your simplicity of manner and disarming openness about your motives to enlist others in your own schemes, and therefore you make an excellent salesperson or teacher. Your excitement and enthusiasm for your own ideas is a delightful enticement to others to join in the fun.

Mars opposition Neptune makes you a sterling example. You have very high expectations of yourself and give your all to live up to (and even exceed) them. You may possess a touch of genius, or some extraordinary talent (at least you believe you do); in any event you devote your life to pursuing a highly individualistic lifestyle which you created for yourself, and which others may look up to and admire. There is no lack of self-esteem here; and there may be a tendency to overweening hubris or Great-I-Am grandiosity. You take pride in your self-reliance, in making your own way and depending on no one but yourself for sustenance or succor. You may tend to look down your nose and treat other people as chelas or mendicants; but you do not begrudge them your gracious deference and invaluable counsel. Indeed, you are as meticulous in meeting the expectations of others as you are in fulfilling your own. Your indomitable courage and emotional self-sufficiency are a beacon of assurance for all.

Mars parallel Neptune is sensitive and optimistic, but very much centered in what is possible and prudent. Where the aspects between these two planets tend to be very idealistic (or credulous), pursuing their own fanciful views of who they are and what life is all about, you hold fast to what you know feels right in your heart, and use that as a guide (rather than intellectualized concepts). Like the aspects you go your own way and do your own thing, and tend to feel yourself to be alone even in the midst of company; but you don't compare yourself to others, nor appeal to them for support, succor, or suffering (as the case may be). You are more or less content with your lot in life, and don't look to some fantasized future for happiness, but try to find it in the here and now. On your negative side you are truly oblivious – to censure, to danger, to any considerations except your own instinctive sense of what is fair and just. You are emotionally self-contained, and you find all the self-esteem you need by just being yourself and doing the best you can in any situation.

Mars contraparallel Neptune is staunch and true. The aspects between these two planets breeze through life with a cheeky and brazen obliviousness. They are not so much presumptuous as naïve and inclined to take a lot for granted. You contraparallels exhibit the same heartiness and gumption as the aspects, and the same chivalric idealism; but you are more humble and self-effacing. You are equally mischievous and irreverent, but have a greater sensitivity and attunement to feelings. Like the aspects you are not particularly swayed by the mores and demands of your society; but you do not measure yourself against others, nor look into their eyes for a reflection on how well you're doing. You scrupulously weigh your decisions (rather than blindly follow your impulses), always trying to live up to your highest expectations of yourself, which lends you a nobility of mien and demeanor. You do not impose yourself on people because you have a well-developed sense of your own private space, and you can respect the space of others in turn. You unerringly follow your own inner guidance to create a sheltered nook for yourself away from the swirling madness around you.

Mars–Pluto Aspects

Mars-Pluto aspect natives are obsessively focused on their own ends; and their lives tend to have more than average stress and strain. These natives are shrewd, tenacious, and insistent, and they don't take "no" for an answer. They are solitary, self-reliant, and pioneering – usually to be found in the forefront (or on the margins) of what is going on, but never in the midst. They glance neither to the right nor left, but are wholly concentrated on the path beneath their feet.

Mars conjunct Pluto is stern and judgmental. You are hard-nosed, sharp-tongued, and driven; and you must always have the last word or be the one who made your point. You tend to lack sensitivity to other people's opinions and feelings, but just steamroll right ahead over anyone in your way. You rely upon the fait accompli rather than waste your time with explanations or pleas. You are firm and cool under pressure, and are animated by a haughty (if at times overweening) self-certainty which bowls people right over. You see clearly into human motivation, possess an unerring sense of the jugular, and are quick to attack and exploit any opening or weakness. Your brusque, outspoken, and blatant criticisms can leave people feeling bruised and resentful; but you don't particularly give a damn – you come to life and thrive on conflict. When forced to retreat, you dig in your heels (rather than give an inch) and bide your time until you are ready to strike again. But your courage, audacity and pluck win the admiration of all who know you.

Mars sextile Pluto is intent and persuasive. The favorable Mars-Pluto aspects are as obstinate and immovable as the conjunction, but are far less highhanded and adamant. You are realistic and diplomatic, and are more concerned with accomplishing your ends than with merely getting a lick in. You are pragmatic rather than pugnacious, and you rely upon maneuvering and good-natured cajolery to get your way rather than upon combativeness or bluster. You prefer to see things carried out in an orderly manner, with a minimum of fuss, pother, or posturing; and are able to utilize your organizational skills to cut across quibbling and equivocation without stepping on toes or giving needless offense. Precisely because you are able to make allowances for other people's sensibilities, you are persuasive without being argumentative, and are reasonable without for a moment losing sight of your own goals and prerogatives. Albeit unwavering, you are also plucky and forthright, with nothing to hide; and you are not afraid for others to see where you stand and what you stand for.

Mars square Pluto makes for an ineffectual posturing. Here the intensity of Mars-Pluto is turned inward: you are grim and bear it, possessing an air of world-weariness and long-suffering martyrdom. You are quick to take umbrage at trivial peccadilloes, and as a result you are easily put upon or knocked off your stride. You prefer to suffer in silence – and seethe and simmer inwardly – rather than reveal your feelings and perhaps rock the boat, or put yourself in a disadvantageous position. You may mistake priggish attitudinizing and self-righteous huffiness for nobility of character and stoical forbearance. You have a horror of appearing vulnerable, and therefore must always maintain a stiff upper lip and the pretense that everything is just fine and dandy. As a result you are often victimized; or feel that your good faith and candor are being taken advantage of and exploited by the unscrupulous. On your positive side you are conscientious: careful to ensure that your own motives are above reproach (or at least cannot be construed otherwise), and you have done everything possible to acquit yourself honorably.

Mars trine Pluto makes for a judicious firmness. Like the conjunction between these two planets you possess a single-minded focus on your own goals, but you are more patient and willing to take other people's points of view into account in your planning and calculations. You are a master of the art of the possible. You project a self-certainty and sense of always being in command or control even when (especially when) you aren't, which induces other people to cede you the lead and give way to your wishes. You are quite aware of this facility, and try to be a model of responsibility and disinterested uprightness so as to deserve their trust. On the negative side you (like the conjunction) tend to blunder ahead on impulse whenever you get a bee in your bonnet; but your delicacy of feeling and sense of duty is a strong governor which keeps you on the straight and narrow in times of confusion or doubt.

Mars opposition Pluto is sedulous and knowing. Although you are canny and perspicacious (not much escapes your notice), you are nonetheless somewhat otherworldly, or at least not wholly committed to this one. You are a lone wolf who does not suffer people getting too close or too clamorous. Albeit assiduous and headstrong, you are the least personally ambitious of the Mars-Pluto types – you live your life by feel rather than by plan and you prefer to take the road less traveled and carve out a personal niche for yourself rather than do what is expected of you by your family and society. Perhaps due to early family influences you keep your head down and try not to make waves, or attract undue attention to yourself: you keep a close mouth and do not reveal what you are really thinking or feeling to anyone, which on the negative side, can become an ornery contrariety. When you do act it is with finality: you cross the Rubicon and burn your bridges behind you, so there is no question of going back (even if there is nowhere in particular that you are going to).

Mars parallel Pluto is sober and calculating. The Mars-Pluto aspects are brash, self-certain, and pig-headed. They are unyielding and inflexible, with a decisiveness about their acts and proclamations which leaves no margin for misunderstanding their intentions or point of view. You parallels are as stubborn and persistent as the aspects, and every bit as committed to following your own star; but you are wilier, more reflective, and therefore less intense. You thread your way around people and obstacles instead of battering your way through. Facing doubt or confusion you pause for a moment and weigh the probabilities; you trouble-shoot obstacles or finesse around opposition rather than impulsively blundering ahead irregardless of consequences just to prove a point. You have an overarching philosophy or set of principles which guides your behavior, and you seek to uphold high moral standards in your own comportment. This is not so much conscience as it is common sense: recognition of what is possible, and the most straightforward way of obtaining it. While you can at times evince something of a supercilious self-certainty or holier-than-thou attitude in your makeup, you always endeavor to do your best and give your all

Mars contraparallel Pluto is sedulous and intent but abstracted. You possess the obsessive single-mindedness of the aspects between these two planets, but you are far less intense and abrasive – you are subdued rather than effusive or demonstrative. You are hard-working and dedicated, always keeping your eyes on the path beneath your feet rather than pushing other people out of your way. You are meticulous, thorough, responsible, and possess great powers of concentration. To others you may seem preoccupied, woolly, not altogether here; which is not so much a strategy of avoidance as it is indifference to anything which doesn't fall within your own narrow focus of attention. Where the Mars–Pluto aspects tend to be malcontents, you are largely satisfied with your lot. You are not unambitious per se, but are more concerned with doing your job as best you are able rather than with advancing yourself or proving anything to anyone.

Jupiter–Saturn Aspects and Mutual Reception

Jupiter-Saturn knows where it stands. These natives are honorable, upright, and emotionally stable: they are well-centered within themselves, like those dolls which are weighted at the bottom so they bounce right back up when knocked down. These natives are gregarious but have little stake in belonging – they separate themselves from the dictates of their society and cling fiercely to their own inner sense of what is good and true. Dr. Jones says of natives without a major aspect between Jupiter and Saturn that there is "a lack of real ordering of life's fundamental motives ... a tendency to underrate the value of any genuine discipline of the character, and thus to permit too great a dominance of the personal life by intimates or associates ... at times there is a surrender to conformity for the sake of peace, and so a betrayal of all spontaneity or ultimate discrimination."

Jupiter conjunct Saturn is thoughtful and dedicated. You are sober-minded and stern, with a unique perspective on life and a willingness to commit yourself all the way. You possess keen judgment and clear-sighted perception of human motivation. You are painfully aware that life is a serious business and demands serious consideration; thus you do not rush into action but rather take your time and weigh all factors and possibilities before making your decisions. You are fearlessly individualistic and solitary even in the midst of people. You don't so much reject or rebel against your upbringing or milieu as invent some new personage – some "you" – whose dreams and goals have little in common with what you were taught or what is expected of you by the people around you. Bullheaded doesn't begin to describe you: you are largely indifferent to what others think or seek; nor do you measure your success or failure according to their lights. Thus – much of the time – you can be arbitrary, dictatorial, and impossible to deal with. Your salvation is your great inner strength, faith in your own original slant on life, and your utter fidelity to the guidance of your inner voice.

Jupiter sextile Saturn is earnest and sincere, with something of a noblesse oblige or ethical ideal that you are striving to live up to. You make good eye contact and reach out to people with an inviting, open manner; blunt, straightforward speech; and the overriding imperative to be just and impartial, concerned that everyone gets a fair shake. You are not unambitious per se, but you will never betray your deeply-held principles for petty advantage or personal gain. Therefore your words are convincing without being argumentative, and your patient resolve appeals to the reasonable side in other people. Since you always hold fast to what you know (or believe) in your heart to be right, you may fall back on supercilious self-righteousness as a justification when you are clearly in the wrong. But your very presence is a calming influence in any company; and your earnest and aboveboard comportment induces other people to automatically cede you the moral high ground.

Jupiter square Saturn can be broody and ineffectually conscientious. Albeit upright and well-meaning, your feelings and initiatives don't seem to count for much. You often find your circumstances overwhelming, and feel yourself to be hemmed in or embattled – pushed around or shoved aside by other people. You try to be a straight-shooter and play the game by the rules, but somehow the rules keep changing on you. You possess a plaintive tentativeness or servility which is easily exploited by others who are more assertive and sure of what they are after than you are. You wring your hands helplessly in the face of injustice, soothing yourself with the meager consolation of believing that at least you were the one who was honest and trusting and acting in good faith. Thus you tend to victimize yourself by trying too hard to be the nice guy and win approval – taking refuge in your sense of rectitude instead of acting on what you know to be true inside yourself. Your humility and sincerity, on the other hand, make you the sort of person whom others instinctively trust and rely upon.

Jupiter trine Saturn is imperturbable and immovable. You are simple and natural, plainspoken and plain dealing, with a pensive, abstracted air. While not exactly otherworldly or spaced-out per se, you tend to find some intellectual niche for yourself wherein your idealistic worldview – whatsoever things are honest, just, pure, lovely, and of good report – holds sway; and people who wish to approach you must do so on your own terms (and you can be stubborn as an old boot otherwise). You are mild-mannered and correct (without being a patsy by any means) and you put all matters on a basis of good common sense. You possess a basic decency and faith in yourself which is not affected by the acceptance or rejection of others; thus you are not as subject to the emotional ups and downs which plague most of your fellows, and you are able to remain the calm, impassive eye in any hurricane.

Jupiter opposition Saturn is impersonal and businesslike. Albeit outgoing and amiable, you are self-contained, dignified, and restrained. You are forthcoming about what's on your mind – even loquacious. Nonetheless you possess a stately bearing and a stiffness of manner which is sociable without inviting intimacy: you always keep your distance. You are intellectually inquisitive, particularly regarding what makes people tick; and your detached and nonjudgmental interlocution encourages honesty and forthrightness from others as well. You tend to find wheeling and dealing distasteful, and prefer open discussion and decision to maneuvering and manipulation. You make no excuses for yourself, but take action with the certainty that you have taken all factors into account and that your own motives are pure (whether they are or not). Your above-it-all condescension and paternalistic humoring of others can at times be overdone; and your self-assured insouciance is not always as free of self-interest as you are inclined to believe. Your evenhanded and commonsensical approach to problems – particularly in times of confusion – is the basis of your effective and sought-after leadership.

Jupiter parallel Saturn is voluble, ironic, and forthcoming. The aspects between these two planets are careful, reflective, and deliberate. They aren't interested in the latest styles, trends, and buzzwords but hold to a high moral orbit. You parallels are just as staunch and conscientious as the aspects, and have as strong a sense of honor and integrity; but you are far lighter in spirit, with a mischievous twinkle in your eye and a tongue-in-cheek repertoire. You have a grand sense of personal style and flair, and your daring and pithy remarks impress people with your insightful and forthright take on the passing scene. Although you are democratic and are a good listener, with a sincere interest in other people's ideas and points of view, you rather enjoy being in the limelight and holding forth with your own entertaining, sui generis sentiments which hold other people in rapt attention and animate them to think for themselves.

Jupiter contraparallel Saturn makes for a considered diligence. The aspects between these two planets have high standards of conduct to which they scrupulously adhere, and a moral courage which is the source of their deep inner pride. They are not old-fashioned so much as lofty and uninvolved – they are like sojourners even in their own families and social group. You contraparallels have the same strong sense of personal probity as the aspects; and you are equally removed from the prevailing cultural mores. But you are less self-conscious, more easy-going, down-to-earth, and *real* than the stuffy aspects. Although you also distance yourself from your milieu, what sets you apart from the opposition between Jupiter and Saturn type is your conscientiousness and ruminative self-examination instead of a mannered noblesse oblige. You are more of a watcher than an actor – someone who is more interested in learning than in demonstrating your prowess and compelling admiration or deference. You go your own way rather than hold court; and your artlessness and integrity are inviting rather than commanding. You don't warrant yourself better than the common herd, but rather have a true policy of live and let live.

Jupiter Mutual Reception Saturn is realistic, earthy, and skilled in the art of the possible. The aspects between these two planets are characterized by an exalted wistfulness – a longing for some sort of utopian situation in life. They are not wholehearted participants in this world, but seem to look beyond it. Usually they seek some life-style or career outside of the cultural mainstream, wherein they can dream their ivory tower dreams and minimize the intrusion of harsh reality into their lives. You MRs are fully as idealistic as the aspects, and possess the same staying power, but you have your feet firmly planted on the ground. You are not as suspicious of the "system", but rather use your detachment from it to better seize opportunities and avoid pitfalls (rather than elevate yourself). You feel little need to project an image of stalwart rectitude, but possess a willingness to trust in other people and in your own ability to handle the situations you encounter rather than to dominate them through a ponderous or pontifical prerogative. You possess a sassiness and spunk usually absent from the weighty self-possession of the Jupiter-Saturn aspects; and you don't need to assume the role of psychological hermit in order to maintain your own sense of psychological uniqueness.

Jupiter–Uranus Aspects

Jupiter-Uranus is acutely intelligent and observant, with a highly original viewpoint. These natives are candid and aboveboard, and do not shrink from speaking their mind. They possess a strong need for considerable personal freedom and scope; and they are predominant within their own sphere (snooty, sniffy).

Jupiter conjunct Uranus is impersonal and businesslike. You are short, curt, and laconic, with no tolerance for excuses or explanations – your own or anyone else's. You possess a forbidding mien, an impatient, absolutist manner, and a single-minded concentration on the path beneath your feet which looks neither to the right nor left but just steams full speed ahead. You go your own way asking no one's leave or sanction, and try to stay as unfettered and unencumbered as possible. Where most people depend upon the encouragement and approval of others, your reliance is on your own competence and acuity. You cultivate some area of expertise in which your own superiority is indisputable and don't give much of a damn about anything else – certainly not human relationships (unless other horoscopic factors contraindicate). Therefore dealing with your pigheaded obduracy and unsympathetic impassivity can be a bruising exercise; although your impartial and disinterested leadership wins you ready followers and disciples (even though you don't particularly seek them, and indeed tend to find such involvements messy).

Jupiter sextile Uranus is plain-spoken and convincing. You possess the same deftness and self-sufficiency as the conjunctions between these two planets, but you are far more outgoing and courteous. It is important to you that you be taken seriously; and indeed you possess a unique way of thinking and an idiosyncratic slant on human relations, and you have a persuasive repertoire. Although you keep your own counsel regarding your personal affairs and do not burden others with your inner ruminations and feelings, you are most forthcoming and loquacious on abstract, philosophical topics and matters of common concern. You strive to be the leader – or at least consigliere – of any group of which you are a part: the voice of calm reason and logic. You don't much care for effusiveness or demonstrativeness, but put your faith in dispassionate discourse and a meeting of minds (with yours dominant, of course). On the negative side your chi-chi self-delight can wear a bit thin for the people who have to deal with you intimately; and your smug self-satisfaction often renders you deaf to their emotional plaints. Your cool self-possession and sang-froid are an anodyne in times of turmoil.

Jupiter square Uranus is idealistic to a fault. You have high expectations for yourself and the people around and under you, but it seems that these rarely bear fruit or work out the way you had hoped. You never seem to fit in or belong anywhere no matter how hard you try (and you certainly do). You apparently give your all; go the extra mile and dot all the i's and cross all the t's; nonetheless your outreach always seems to somehow miss the mark. Your antsy, restless energy never sits still but is always humming and on the go; but it's like you always find yourself back on the same old treadmill of unfulfillment. On your positive side you are quite clever and adept at problem-solving, possessing good ideas and intentions; and your comportment is always meticulously correct. Your feisty enthusiasm and courageous outspokenness – in the proper moment – can be an engine for positive change and a dynamo that gets everyone moving in unison.

Jupiter trine Uranus makes you forthright and enthusiastic, with unconventional ideas and an earnestness which makes you a most convincing sales- or spokes-person. You have an eccentric (some would say oddball) take on people and the way the world works; and you are more than ready to put your theories to the test in your own life. You tend to follow the path less traveled, seeking your fulfillment in the new and experimental rather than in the common goals or ambitions of the people around you. Your thinking may be undergirded by a particular philosophical or religious point of view; but even if not consciously articulated in such terms, your perspective tends to the abstract or wistful rather than mundane or practical. Consequently, you can be difficult to influence or deflect once you set your mind to something; but your persistence and optimistic good cheer are an inspiration for all who know you

Jupiter opposition Uranus makes for a penetrating intellect and upstanding character. You are eccentric, abstracted, off in your own little world and somewhat nonplussed or faintly repelled by this one. You have very high ideals and are a straight-shooter; and your openness and frankness are fresh and inviting. You are more of a thinker and observer than a doer: people are attracted by your moral rectitude and profound insights, and they delight in your pithy bon mots and wry observations on the passing scene. You have an elfin mischievousness which others find endearing; and your ironic and witty sense of humor enables them to forgive your not taking them (or anything) seriously. Your mannered superciliousness and overweening self-congratulations can be exasperating when real commitment is called for; and your refusal to deviate one iota from your own pursuits and prerogatives can isolate you in your above-it-all hauteur. Your unswerving devotion to your principles and your willingness to uphold your honor in the face of pressure, provocation, or profit make you the sort of person others can trust and depend on through thick and thin.

Jupiter parallel Uranus is conscientiously free-spirited. While the Jupiter-Uranus aspects are gregarious and cheerful, they are not truly warm or sympathetic. Their zealous individualism and intolerance for any stricture keep them at a distance from even their boon companions. There are times when they can become callous in their determination to pursue their own ends and enjoy life come what may. You parallels are as perky and irrepressible as the aspects, and you have the same maverick streak. However, you are far more democratic in your outreach than the lofty, lordly aspects; and you have a greater awareness that there is more to life than just what you want this minute. You have a well-developed sense of purpose or mission, and your intellectual strivings are directed towards understanding what this is and how you can best implement it as your life unfolds, rather than to demonstrate or prove anything to anyone but yourself. Your free-wheeling independence of spirit is informed by a deep sense of service and obligation.

Jupiter contraparallel Uranus is as intellectually inquisitive and philosophical as the aspects between these two planets; and quite as ready to follow your own star wherever it may lead you. But you are more self-contained and ruminative, less exuberant and demonstrative than the aspects tend to be. Your search is for a way of understanding yourself and the world around you (rather than to impress or influence anyone). You punctiliously observe other people's space as the best means of demarcating your own; and you feel no especial need to lord it over them or vaunt your free-wheeling prowess. You are as scrupulous in preserving other people's right to life, liberty, and the pursuit of happiness as you are in guarding your own. While you are as aloof as the aspects, you have a greater sense of perspective and long-range consequences; and hence tend to be more respectful and gentler in your handling of people.

Jupiter–Neptune Aspects

Jupiter–Neptune is sensitive, susceptible, and kind-hearted. These natives are artless and highly moral, with a capacity for self-abnegation and a desire to live up to the highest ideals and principles. They are convivial and hopeful, and are often endowed with psychic ability (or at the least an attunement to nuances) which redounds to their benefit.

Jupiter conjunct Neptune is naïvely hopeful and aboveboard. You are gentle and genteel, a fundamentally decent person, with a strong sense of justice and fair play. You possess delicate sensibilities and a dislike for any sort of conflict or unpleasantness. You wear your heart on your sleeve and are rather vulnerable and easily moved. Because you are incapable of subtlety or guile yourself, you possess a naïve hopefulness regarding the motives of other people which at times permits the unscrupulous to take advantage of you. For better or worse you have an idealized image of how things ought to be which doesn't always correspond to how things actually are. Unless other (more aggressive) tendencies are indicated in your horoscope, you tend to wring your hands helplessly rather than take decisive action, preferring to suffer the slings and arrows of outrageous fortune rather than take arms against a sea of troubles, and by opposing end them (and like the Prince, indulge your self-pity at your own lameness). Your forte is your ability to patiently work through difficulties without losing your cool or your sense of groundedness in what you know to be right.

Jupiter sextile Neptune is positive and optimistic. You are ambitious, confident, and energetic, brimming with original ideas and plans and possessing the dynamism and resolution to carry them out. You are as naïvely sanguine as the conjunction between these two planets, but are a bit more of a toughy, not taking everything that happens so much to heart. As a result, you do not permit setbacks, disappointments, or the opposition of others to deflect you or slow you down: if faced with unassailable obstacles, you just find a way to tack around them, or else blast your way through them without a second thought. Like the conjunction you take your own motives completely for granted, believing that you are always working for the common good, and that any disagreement or evidence to the contrary is merely the result of misguided thinking on the part of others. But you always do your best, and your winning enthusiasm is usually sufficient to carry the day.

Jupiter square Neptune is fastidious and uncompromising. You incline to strong beliefs and convictions, and you can be overly dogmatic, inflexible, and intolerant of dissenting opinion. You refer your behavior to a strict code of proper comportment and are quite judgmental of those who do not adhere to your exalted standards. You take no pains to disguise your likes and dislikes, and when you are up on your high horse your discourse can be short, curt, and withering. Your dismissive absolutism can be pre-emptive in nature, obviating reproof (particularly from yourself) by being the first to attack. Your cool nonchalance barely conceals a root self-doubt and defensiveness; and your apparent self-certainty can mask an underlying distrust of your own rationales and motives. Your need to maintain a stiff upper lip and unrevealing countenance at all times can wear thin when you are clearly outmatched or overwhelmed; your drive to control others is a projection of your fear of losing control of yourself. At your best you possess irreproachable impulses and the strong desire to be a paragon of disciplined rectitude.

Jupiter trine Neptune is idealistic but able to make allowances. You are soft-spoken and self-effacing, the sort of person who doesn't make waves or push yourself forward. You deal with people using good common sense, and you much prefer calm, reasoned negotiation to fruitless verbiage. This is not to say that you are a shrinking violet by any means: merely that your considerable inner strength and fortitude are not readily apparent to casual acquaintances. Where the favorable aspects of Jupiter-Neptune differ from the conjunction is in your bold directness which cuts across any sort of chicanery. You possess little patience for quibbling and have a realistic appraisal of realities rather than mere reliance on good hopes and keeping your fingers crossed. Opponents should not mistake your quietness for weakness, since you do possess a sharp tongue and an iron will when that is required by other people's bad faith or game-playing. On your negative side your ex cathedra judgments and highhanded self-certainty can be hard to take at times; but you are always true to yourself and you are not afraid to stand up for what you believe in.

Jupiter opposition Neptune gives a profound mental grasp. You possess a calm, thoughtful discernment which takes everything in detachedly (rather than reacting headlong); and you make your decisions with objectivity and true disinterestedness. You are nobody's fool: you have a shrewd grasp of human nature and the ability to see the underlying motivations and mechanisms by which your particular milieu and society operate. As a result your views have weight and your observations have meaning; however you generally tend to withdraw from taking a proactive role in affairs outside your immediate compass, preferring to armor yourself in your intellection with a smug, "I told you so" self-satisfaction. You prefer to play the critical sophisticate or cognoscente than have a real say in what will happen. This is not to say that you are lazy, or are not punctilious in discharging what you take your obligations to be – merely that you decline to bestir yourself beyond the minimum necessary for honorable acquittal. As a result you find yourself stranded at times in your own rationalizations, mistaking knowledge for wisdom. Nonetheless your analytical insight and ready wit compel the respectful attention of everyone who knows you.

Jupiter parallel Neptune is as optimistic and hopeful as the aspects between these two planets, but you are more realistic and shrewd. You don't just project an idealized fantasy and cross your fingers and hope it comes true; but rather you are skilled at manuevering and shifting as need be to adapt to the actualities standing in your way. You possess a sixth sense about other people's motives as well as a conscious recognition of your own (something the Jupiter – Neptune aspects lack); therefore you have an unerring feel for how best to trouble-shoot or ameloriate or do whatever is required to obtain what you want from people – usually by using your winning personality to seductively wheedle or cajole. Like the aspects, you set high standards for yourself and wouldn't think of resorting to underhandedness or double-dealing; but barring that, you have a way of insinuating yourself and your goals in such an enticing manner as to create as few waves or little blowback as possible.

Jupiter contraparallel Neptune is placid and accepting. The Jupiter-Neptune aspects tend to see the world through rose-colored spectacles: completely sold on their images and fantasies, and seemingly exist in their own insulated bubble. They are straightforward and direct (largely because they are incapable of dissembling). You contraparallels are as friendly and outgoing as the aspects and you can also be quite as blunt and removed. But you are more retiring, less inclined to need other people's support in the implementation of your own plans and dreams, and therefore you are less prone to meddle or presume too much. You are not particularly interested in convincing anyone of anything, but rather take pains to appreciate and learn from people rather than use them to validate your own schemes, or convert them to your point of view. On your negative side you can be the most self-contained and unreachable of all the Jupiter-Neptune types (which is the flip side of your unassailable integrity). As you float along in your bubble, you are unhurried, tranquil, self-possessed; and skillful at avoiding collisions.

Jupiter–Pluto Aspects

Jupiter-Pluto is objective, detached, and astute; and has considerable personal flair and élan. These natives are poised and skillful at manipulating people and situations to their advantage, possessing a penetrating insight, unswerving determination, and nerves of steel. They are impassive in the face of doubt or danger, and cannot be deflected from the path beneath their feet.

Jupiter conjunct Pluto is self-confident and jaunty. You possess considerable personal magnetism and flair, and you love to strut your stuff. You are candid and uninhibited, saying whatever is on your mind without the least concern about the possible consequences, and as a result your remarks (albeit usually right on the mark) can be blunt and bruising. You are not pugnacious per se (you don't go looking for trouble – nonetheless it always seems to find you); and in fact you delight in sharing your wisdom and knowledge with anyone willing to listen (and even with those who are not). You possess a practical, no-nonsense attitude towards life and relationships, and the ability to cut across rigmarole or obfuscation and get right down to brass tacks. You are guided by an internal surety which steers you unerringly towards the realization of your well-defined goals in life, and which you rely on instead of social sanction or fiat. You are saved from despotic arbitrariness by your noble sense of honor and duty, as well as your strongly-felt need to be of service and contribute something of value from your experience.

Jupiter sextile Pluto possesses all the self-assurance and swagger of the conjunction between these two planets, but you are more easy-going and sociable. You possess a sprightly, puckish demeanor and a waggish, tongue-in-cheek good humor. You are a good listener, and have the ability to see all sides of a question. Albeit very adroit when it comes to picking up on unspoken vibrations and group dynamics, you are slow to react and it is difficult to ruffle your feathers or knock you off your stride. You are deft at handling people, and are adept at winning them over to your way of thinking by putting matters on a basis of what is sensible and just (i.e., your way). You are the voice of calm reason in any milieu, striving to pour oil on troubled waters and reach a fair consensus. Although you can sometimes give the impression of being patronizing or putting people on rather than taking them seriously, your even-handedness and good cheer invite others to join the fun.

Jupiter square Pluto is indefinite and temporizing. You tend to drift through life without a strong sense of where you are going or how you will get there. You possess a rather blasé, effete air – a sense of world-weariness or "just can't be bothered". You are not lazy or irresponsible per se, but rather are touchy and exigent with regard to your own personal prerogatives. In the name of individualism you always strive to maintain your own space and neutrality, but this can mask an inability to truly commit yourself to anything outside of your own self-interest. Therefore it can be difficult to pin you down, or induce you to give more of yourself than the absolute minimum required. Others may see you as trifling, snooty, overly concerned with your status or other irrelevancies when it behooves you to be forthcoming or make some sort of stand. You retreat into vagueness and evasiveness rather than put your gumption on the line and perhaps subject yourself to reproach or unpleasantness. On your positive side you always follow your own star and do not rely upon the good graces of other people for approval or validation.

Jupiter trine Pluto has high ideals and ambitions, and the dedication and determination to see them through. You are by no means as effusive and demonstrative as the other aspects between these two planets: albeit friendly and willing to go out of your way to help, you always maintain your reserve, and you weigh your words carefully before speaking. You have a consciously articulated set of goals in life, together with a guiding philosophy and sense of integrity which guides your course and direction. You do not make your decisions without having first seriously considered all the ramifications and possible consequences. You are steadfast and true, and do not make commitments lightly or on impulse. As a result, it can be difficult to pull you down from your high and mighty perch, or appeal to your better instincts, when you are faced with distasteful realities (other people's problems and issues). Your disinterested adherence to the highest standards of thought and comportment – in its proper moment – is an assurance to the people who rely on you.

Jupiter opposition Pluto is inquisitive and unyielding. You possess a scrutinizing, skeptical cast of mind; are somewhat distrustful of other people's motives; and you cannot be rushed or forced. You accept nothing at face value – especially not other people's beliefs or opinions – but need to think things through for yourself and come to your own conclusions in your own good time. You have a searching intellect and a nonjudgmental attitude; and you keep your wits about you when others are confused or acting irrationally. You are a cool customer and an implaccable opponent – "When the going gets tough, the tough get going." You do not permit emotional considerations to take the place of logic, so people may regard you as obdurate and maddeningly impervious when they need some sort of spontaneous response from you. You are never at a loss but keep on an even emotional keel in all circumstances, so in times of stress and turmoil you are a rock of immoveable probity which others can rely on.

Jupiter parallel Pluto makes for a thoughtful conscientiousness. The Jupiter-Pluto aspects are alert, insightful and outspoken. They have a rough sense of humor and a cockiness which is superior and self-mocking at the same time. They possess an acute perception of human nature, but they also tend to feel that this puts them a notch above everyone else, which makes them mildly pompous and given to strutting. You parallels have the same mental clarity and discrimination as the aspects and you are every bit as jaunty and self-confident. But you possess a greater depth and delicacy of feeling than the flamboyant aspects. There is a greater self-awareness here; and a poignant sensitivity to the suffering and travails of others, together with the desire to do what you can to alleviate or ameliorate. You are humble and self-controlled, moderate and introspective, and given to dispassionate rumination instead of ostentatious self-aggrandizement. Your reach is for disinterested wisdom rather than self-dramatization: you feel a stronger need to appreciate the people around you than you do to dazzle or dominate them

Jupiter contraparallel Pluto has a penetrating intellect (like the opposition between these two planets), and possesses the same desire to get a philosophical handle on life. But in contrast to the reserved and self-cloistering opposition, your goal is to reach out to understand other people and connect with them on a heart (as opposed to mind) level. You are as outgoing as the aspects between these two planets, but are rather more serious and sincere – you are kindly, courteous, and decorous in contrast to the blatant aspects. You are a watcher and waiter rather than a mover and shaker; and you reach for abstract goals rather than merely that which best serves your own interests. On the negative side, there may be a tendency to vacillate, or to hem and haw, when decisive action or a bold stroke is required; but you are always able to hold your ground and stand fast in the face of doubt and confusion.

Saturn–Uranus Aspects

Saturn-Uranus natives are unvarnished and plainspoken, utterly lacking in pretense (and with little toleration for it in others). They are shrewd, alert, and take very little for granted: they do not abide sham or empty observance for the sake of form, and they are not given to tact or diplomacy. Of the planetary combinations which mean stubborn and inflexible determination, this one is about at the top of the list. Albeit superficially cordial, they have little warmth or empathy. They are wary and laconic, and when they do speak their mind they do so fearlessly, in good faith, and with good common sense.

Saturn conjunct Uranus makes for a no-nonsense toughness. You possess a subdued, impassive personality, which is not so much humble or self-effacing as it is utterly lacking in pomp or ostentation (or much humor, unless other horoscopic factors contraindicate). You are serious-minded, dedicated, and businesslike: you pride yourself on your competence and acumen, and you rely only on your own initiative and self-sufficiency. Fearlessly self-assured, you don't mince words and will not stand for doubletalk, but get right down to brass tacks with no dithering or fiddling around. You are logical, realistic, and hardheaded – like Missourians you have to be shown in order to be convinced, since you are not taken in by appearances or the conventional wisdom of your society; and you take no one at their word. You are not so much skeptical as wary, and you are not so much unsympathetic as emotionally self-contained. Since you indulge in little self-pity yourself, you possess little pity for others. Your unyielding stolidity can give the impression of callous indifference and thereby bruise the sensibilities of other people (though that isn't your intention). You are at your best under pressure and stress, when your imperturbable discipline and yeomanly perseverance provide an island of calm certainty in the midst of confusion.

Saturn sextile Uranus is feisty and irrepressible. You are lively, experimentative, and adventurous, with a bold willingness to follow your fancies wherever they may lead you. You have a restless spirit of enterprise; are rather bored by the routine and pedestrian; and you manage to stay on top of any situation or milieu with your limitless faith in your own abilities and your can-do optimism. You brim with original ideas, opinions, and plans; and you exhibit considerable brass and cheek. You take a rather jaundiced view of your fellow bipeds and their capacities; and you unabashedly speak your mind and let the chips fall where they may. On your negative side you can be something of the prima donna, regaling yourself with brazen self-delight and contumelious swagger. Your jaunty alacrity and unlimited self-assurance lighten the proceedings of any group of which you are a part.

Saturn square Uranus makes for disgruntlement and surliness. You are gruff, curt, concentrated on your own ends; and are highly suspicious of people and their motives. You carry with you a sense of onus or having a chip on your shoulder; and when you have that mood on, people know to stay out of your way. You are critical – even nitpicking – of others, and are impatient with their deficiencies and shortcomings. Your brusque, grumpy exterior serves to hold others at bay and thereby gives you the freedom to do as you will. You are politic, guarded and taciturn: close-mouthed about your feelings and intentions, and tightfisted with your resources. You let much pass without being fooled or creating issues where non-involvement will suffice, but you can unceremoniously slam down the portcullis when you've reached the limits of your forbearance. You prefer to avoid conflict and "stickiness", and will take a sinuous route to bypass any need for direct confrontation. Thus you can be very difficult to deal with since you are thick-skinned and deaf to entreaty, and possess little regard for other people's weaknesses or points of view. You are at your best when the chips are down and push comes to shove, and you are fighting for the common weal rather than your own personal goals.

Saturn trine Uranus is bold, forthright, and immoveable. You have strong opinions and are not afraid to voice them in any company. You know who you are and what you stand for, and you are always ready to back your convictions with decisive action. You are not especially pugnacious – you don't go looking for trouble if you can avoid it – but you don't dither or waste energy trying to temporize or ameliorate either. You have a calm demeanor which reacts to provocation or annoyance with impassivity, so it's very difficult to knock you off your pins. You quite consciously employ your tremendous resolution and self-possession to impress, intimidate, or dismiss those who you feel are not sufficiently respectful; and you are always ready to defend those who are not as strong-willed and self-assured as you are. You have a knack for being hard-nosed without being hard-edged: your disinterested and impersonal manner endows you with a noblity which wins people to your side.

Saturn opposition Uranus is single-minded and meticulous. You are not necessarily a leader, but are by no means a follower: you act only upon your own initiative and only in response to your own inner directives – the carrot and stick have no meaning for you. Insular and unattached even in the midst of a relationship, you are careful to maintain your personal space and distance at all times. You are not woolly or abstracted, and yet you're not really present either: you are wholly preoccupied with your own worldview and objectives. Your focus is always on yourself, yet you are not selfish per se, but rather are completely indifferent to the approval or rejection of those around you. Nor do you hear what anyone is trying to tell you, or accept responsibilities foisted upon you willy-nilly (rather than personally chosen). At your worst you blunder along like a bumper car mindlessly smashing its way endlessly around the same track; at your best you fix your eyes unwaveringly on the horizon and permit nothing to interfere with the fulfillment of your destiny.

Saturn parallel Uranus is democratic and nonjudgmental. The Saturn-Uranus aspects are diligent, steady, and thoroughgoing. They are extraordinarily tenacious and self-willed, and they make cold, hard, and unrelenting opponents. You parallels are as resolute and dogged as the aspects; and you are every bit as obstinate and unyielding. But you are more tender and humane than the intense, touchy aspects, and less inclined to overstep yourself or intrude yourself on other people. You have a strong sense of your own personal space; and as a result, you are meticulous in respecting the space of others. You are aloof and disinterested rather than self-obsessed; and you are quick to render assistance or support to fellow travelers on their journey (without entangling yourself in their issues or letting anyone bring you down). You are as outspoken in the defense of what is right and just as you are in proclaiming your own views and furthering your own interests. You are willing to grant other people the same rights and liberties which you insist on for yourself.

Saturn contraparallel Uranus is upright and gallant. Like the aspects between these two planets you are strong-willed and intent on the path beneath your feet, but you are by no means as hard-nosed and hard-edged. On the contrary, your willfulness is tempered by a painstaking dedication to what you conceive your duty to be; together with an ideal of correct comportment which you strive to uphold in your everyday dealings and relationships. You see yourself as the benevolent protector and defender of the people in your milieu (who are not as strong and capable as you are); and you address them with interested concern and respect. On the negative side, your pride in your own fitness and sense of responsibility for the common weal can verge on a know-it-all patronizing; and your high-horse superiority can insist that what benefits you personally must ipso facto be to the advantage of all. Your courage and readiness to stand up for your convictions are a reliance for everyone who knows you.

Saturn–Neptune Aspects

Saturn-Neptune aspect natives take their own measure in terms of how well they are living up to their ideals (and are indifferent to how they measure up in the eyes of others). They are solitary and possess great self-discipline in the service of higher aspirations rather than their own petty comfort or convenience. They are quite sensitive and vulnerable, with an air of pathos or anguish about them. They can be subjected to unmerited censure, or stumble into scandal or oppressive circumstances; and the particular aspect of Saturn-Neptune involved indicates how they face it and rise above it. There is often a strong spiritual or religious orientation which, on the negative side, can result in a holier-than-thou superiority.

Saturn conjunct Neptune is serious-minded and cautious. You have a grave, sober, dour demeanor and a weighty presence which overshadows the proceedings the moment you walk into a room. You are highly attuned to subtleties and nuances; are suspicious and mistrustful; and are quick to respond to any slight. You are conscientious and scrupulous, with a no-nonsense practicality; and you are incapable of dissembling or duplicity. You hedge and hesitate, are temporizing and tentative, and can even be something of a stick-in-the-mud, especially when boldness and spontaneity are called for. Because you incline to worry and brood, you need time to make up your mind before you commit yourself; and you can be mulishly obstinate (immune to second thoughts or other people's opinions) when once you have made a decision. You walk the straight and narrow with a resigned constancy, and follow through on your obligations even when they don't redound to your own convenience or particular interests. Your sincerity and earnestness are the hallmarks of a principled punctiliousness.

Saturn sextile Neptune is enterprising and imaginative. You are visionary, diligent, and willing to take complete responsibility for making your own dreams come true (relying on no one but yourself). You don't work well in harness (you chafe under supervision), and are the most productive and inventive when left to your own devices. You are able to follow a lifestyle uniquely your own without being assertive or rebellious just by quietly going your own way and doing your own thing without calling particular attention to yourself. You are not especially motivated by money, success, or applause; so you are free to follow your own inclinations without engaging in competitive one-upmanship (which you despise). You are able to avoid senseless conflict by being low-key and considerate without kowtowing or conceding to anyone. Since you attend primarily to the imperatives of your own heart, your matter-of-fact perfunctoriness in response to undesired burdens can frustrate those who put their own expectations on you. Your uncompromising pursuit of your objectives gives you an ingenious resourcefulness.

Saturn square Neptune is exacting and exigent. You possess a stern, forbidding demeanor and a staid and humorless gravity. You are cool, austere, and businesslike, with no time or patience for frivolity. You are thoroughly dedicated and make a virtue of self-limitation. You possess a nose-to-the-grindstone work ethic, and your eyes are always fixed upon some utopian goal. You possess genius in some sphere of activity or knowledge which gives you an authoritative voice and ensures that you will be believed and obeyed. You are competent and scrupulous; are severely self-critical; and are equally critical of others (particularly those under your direction). You can be overly fault-finding, needing to have everything perfect; and you do not hesitate to browbeat and humiliate those who fall short of your exalted expectations. Because you believe you are merely an instrument for some greater good and that you are relinquishing your own personal interests for the common weal, you may demand special treatment or dispensation as your due. On your positive side your spirit of willing self-sacrifice and fearless advocacy for the moral right is truly an inspiration for others.

Saturn trine Neptune is diligent and forward-looking. You are down-to-earth and unassuming, and therefore are able to relate to other people in a natural, unpretentious manner. You have high ideals and aspirations – and not particularly worldly ones: your aim is to better your own personal effectiveness and skills rather than to pursue specific expectations outside yourself. Like the other Saturn–Neptune aspects, you can be difficult to influence or convince. When once you have set your sights on an objective (which is rarely what the people around you are seeking), there is no stopping or deflecting you from your path. You don't so much fantasize about a perfect future (as most people do) so much as try to do your best in the present, keeping yourself on track with whatever resources you have at hand, and taking your satisfaction in your own proficiency rather than in the praise or approval of others.

Saturn opposition Neptune is irrepressible and quixotic. You are fresh, spunky, and you possess a highly individualistic and idiosyncratic point of view. You are candid and straightforward, and always attempt to put matters on a basis of reasonableness and logic. Perhaps because you are ingenuous and incapable of guile yourself, you tend to naïvely trust the motives of other people, and as a result you can be an easy mark for the unscrupulous. Or, you may enter in good faith into seemingly straightforward arrangements and relationships which in the end turn into convoluted imbroglios (although you do have a knack for extracting yourself from same with a minimum of wear and tear on your nerves by simply refusing to allow people to involve you in their issues or to bring you down – by rising above it all). You possess a whimsical, capricious turn of mind and are quite capable of "jumping the tracks" and steaming off in some new direction when circumstances become too cumbersome or involved. Since you don't take things personally you are able to emerge unsullied from even the most discomfiting circumstances without surrendering your composure and élan.

Saturn parallel Neptune is undeterred and optimistic. The Saturn-Neptune aspects indicate private individuals, concentrated and intent on their own designs and feelings. They are dutiful and obliging, but otherwise stay within their own shells. Although they possess a great depth of feeling they have an extremely narrow focus of interest – they shy away from harshness or conflict and tend to plod through life wearing blinders of self-protection or self-pity. You parallels are as emotionally self-cloistering and evasive as the aspects, but you have a great deal more joie de vivre. You are not as wrapped up in your past, but rather are always looking forward to a rosy future. You have utter faith in yourself and your own peculiar view of the world; and you are always engaged in some visionary scheme or other. You possess a single-minded doggedness and pluck which shakes off any obstacles and is deaf to any nay-saying (or entreaty). You have a knack for bouncing back after any defeat, or somehow turning it into a triumph or vindication (in your thinking). You maintain a positive and enthusiastic attitude towards life – the ability to confront rebuff without the constant sighing and *Weltschmerz* of the aspects.

Saturn contraparallel Neptune is plucky and adventurous. Like the aspects between Saturn and Neptune you have high ideals and the determination to realize them through dedication and perseverance. But unlike the rather staid, fond-of-the-old rut aspects between these two planets, you have a lighter spirit and a daring, cocky enthusiasm which is always willing to take an impulsive leap just to see where it lands you. You have a sharp, analytical intellect, and you speak your mind freely without worrying much about the consequences of such forthrightness – you dazzle people with your original insight and gall. You set a high mark for yourself, and you are ready and willing to extend the boundaries of your capabilities to the max to see if you can reach it. Where the Saturn–Neptune aspects tend to separate themselves from people by armoring themselves in sternness, you contraparallels express your individuality by pushing the envelope and inspiring those who have the courage to follow you.

Saturn–Pluto Aspects

Saturn-Pluto aspect natives possess a strong sense of integrity and probity, and they are indifferent to approbation or censure. They are fearless, dogged, and solitary – they wait for no one, and seek no one's support or succor. These natives are scrupulous in fulfilling their obligations, but must themselves choose where these obligations will lie (they cannot be forced, enticed, coerced, seduced, dragooned, or otherwise influenced from the outside – that just makes them more stubborn and contrary). They are candid and plainspoken, with nothing to conceal; and they pride themselves on being unbranded mavericks.

Saturn conjunct Pluto is willful and resolute. Stubborn, ornery and pigheaded, you stand apart from your background and upbringing (which you find limiting to your self-expression) and strike out on your own to make a life for yourself free of the dictates of others. You find no security or nurture in the taken-for-granted assumptions of your family and society; you bridle at authority and direction, and you are undaunted by the boogies which most people are taught to fear. You need very little in the way of support or encouragement since you have an inner conviction or sense of personal destiny which (rightly or wrongly) points your way and makes you indomitable – a law unto yourself. You are restrained only by your own conscience – your sense of what is right and honest – since the rewards and punishments of your social milieu have little meaning for you. Naturally, your hard-edged assertiveness thinks nothing of running roughshod over (or at least politely ignoring or evading) anyone who gets in your way; and unless other horoscopic factors (such as Venus rising) contraindicate, you are unabashedly unsociable (even rude). Your endurance in the face of overwhelming odds and your sureness under pressure – in the proper moment – make you a natural-born leader.

Saturn sextile Pluto is usually found off on your own tangent with your head in the clouds. You have the same unflinching determination as the conjunction between these two planets, but are less worldly, more inclined to go your own way following your dreams wherever they may lead you. You are judicious, astute, and economical, always seeking the path of least resistance to achieve your ends. You have an idealistic, philosophical bent but rarely share what you are thinking with anyone, since you tend to find effusiveness and emotional demonstration distasteful, and generally turn aside from dealing with other people's issues. While by no means anti-social, you don't go out of your way to seek allies or supporters, but have a cool, impersonal manner of relating which maintains your distance and independence of action without antagonizing people. On your negative side there can be something of a self-satisfied, holier-than-thou loftiness; but your conscientiousness and self-discipline bring you many admirers and devotees.

Saturn square Pluto makes for a noble martyr. You are concentrated, steady, and hard-working, with a grim demeanor and a no-nonsense, businesslike manner. You are cynical and pessimistic – ever ready to gird your loins and prepare for the worst; and in fact you do often find yourself under siege or facing overwhelming odds. You keep a stiff upper lip, possess great self-discipline and endurance, and have the ability to keep your cool under intense pressure. You tend to attract extreme situations which provide challenging tests of your mettle, as if to prove to yourself that "He who cannot obey himself will be commanded." – Nietzsche. You defend yourself by closing up emotionally and pulling your wagons into a circle, which makes you annoyingly impervious and unreachable in the face of uncertainty and confusion. You are reactive rather than proactive, taking the low road whenever possible and trying to steer clear of complications and entanglements. Thus you are a relatively simple person who strives to be aboveboard and keep things on an even keel, which makes you a rock of sobriety and good common sense.

Saturn trine Pluto is idealistic and determined. You are unobtrusive, soft-spoken, and low-key; but with unflinching resolve and beaucoup pertinacity. In contrast to the Saturn-Pluto conjunction there is less of the Great-I-Am hubris; a bit more humor and levity; and a willingness to adapt and adjust as necessary in order to realize your aims. You are a good judge of character and are able to relate well with people from different backgrounds and walks of life. You are a gifted speaker and teacher, and a good listener as well. You possess high ideals and noble motives (or at least that's what you believe), and you take pains to explain yourself and your ideas to other people in order to win them over to your way of thinking (rather than just elbow them aside). You couch your personal goals in terms of a religious, philosophical, or political creed, and thus you are able to identify your own ambitions with the social good.

Saturn opposition Pluto is acute and penetrating. You are perspicacious and insightful, with an ironic sense of humor and a wry outlook on life and other people. You possess a unique point of view – perhaps even a touch of genius – which makes you good at problem-solving, getting an objective view, seeing how to avoid obstacles (rather than butt through them, as the conjunction between these two planets is wont to do); and your impartial objectivity and good judgment make you the sort of person others instinctively look to for advice and guidance. Although you are quite shrewd, even cunning, you are more of a watcher and spectator than an active participant. You hold yourself above contention and all the hurly-burly (or try to – life doesn't always cooperate with your carefully arranged predilections); and you seek to make a comfortable niche for yourself off the beaten track from which perspective you can enjoy and marvel at the passing scene. It can be difficult for those in relationships with you to call your attention or pull you down from your cloud, since your natural tendency is to be uninvolved and noncommittal (although you stand firmly by your own personal code of honor at all times). Your fresh outlook and brisk derring-do animate and inspire those around you.

Saturn parallel Pluto makes for constancy and a willingness to serve. The Saturn-Pluto aspects have an intense energy combined with a great self-restraint and nervous control. Obdurate and stoical, they show a hatchet-faced unconcern for other people's feelings and limitations. You parallels are as focused and self-contained as the aspects; and you have the same analytical detachment in the face of adversity. But you are much lighter in spirit and don't manifest the inexorable sense of onus or begrudging which weighs down the aspects; nor do you put up so many protective walls. You actively seek company and are a boon companion – the anchor of stability and good common sense in any group. You are a patient teacher who is good at analyzing and unraveling complexities and explaining them to others. You are always glad to be useful, and you give of yourself unstintingly, expecting no particular reward in return. You are resolute, fearless, and ready for anything (albeit inclined to cockiness and cheek); but you greet life with eager élan rather than throw down your gauntlet at it.

Saturn contraparallel Pluto is positive and self-assured. Unlike the aspects between these two planets, who possess a "grin and bear it" fortitude, and are inured to (and even seek) hardship and challenge, you are able to keep your focus on ultimate goals without losing your sense of humor and irony. You possess the same ironclad sense of honor and integrity as the Saturn–Pluto aspects, but are not out to prove anything to anyone, least of all yourself. You are careful of other people's sensibilities; and just as you won't permit intrusions into your space, you are respectful of the feelings and limitations of others. You try to keep things on an even keel, and won't let anyone rock the boat with fussing or fuming. Your determination is to enjoy yourself, and the company you are in, right now; and (like the aspects) you won't let anything stand in your way.

Aspects between Uranus, Neptune, and Pluto

Although aspects between the trans-Saturnian planets do have implications for the personal choices which people make, nonetheless they indicate the Creative Mind or *Gestalt* of the times – the choices made by most people (or at least the vanguard) of that generation. Richard Tarnas has done an excellent job of pointing out the effects of world transits in his book *Cosmos and Psyche*. Since what we are concerned with here are natal aspects, we look at the *Zeitgeist* twenty to thirty years later, when the generation with a particular aspect came of age – that is to say, between the dexter Uranus square to its natal place when (presumably) the natives separate from their families and distinguish themselves as individuals; and the Saturn return when they are forced to renounce their individualism and make some kind of contribution to the greater weal.

Uranus–Neptune Aspects

Uranus–Neptune has to do with moral absolutes and certainties; with adherence to higher imperatives than quotidian exigencies. This combination is courageous and idealistic, with a philosophical turn of mind which relies upon thinking things through for oneself rather than depending upon established canons of social approval. It gives the ability to see ultimate purposes and designs, and to forgo immediate gratification for future betterment. Dr. Jones says that an absence of major aspects between Uranus and Neptune suggests "a tendency towards complete disinterest in the broader meanings of modern history with its underlying socioeconomic frictions and adjustment. ... they are likely to be the product of whatever mass psychology characterizes their formative years."

Uranus conjunct Neptune is earnest and intent. You are low-key, introspective, and wary: ever focused on your own feelings and the path beneath your feet. Reflective and self-critical, you have high standards of achievement for yourself and little tolerance for dissent. You are grave and stern, with no time for frivolity or much sense of humor. There may be a utilitarian, "end justifies the means" unconcern for other people's feelings or established canons of social acceptance in your solipsistic world-view; and your single-minded pursuit of your own goals can make you a law unto yourself. You are as obstinate and self-righteous as they come, particularly when you are under attack (and you do seem to become embroiled in your share of scandals, whether due to your own obliviousness or the belief that you are above the common herd). Your circumstances tend to carom from one extreme to the other – you take (or are forced to take) sudden decisions which veer your life in completely different directions – as if to test your grandiose theories of how things ought to be against the vicissitudes of harsh reality. Your uncompromising fidelity to your own vision and willingness to stand up for your principles lends you a commanding dignity.

The current Uranus conjunct Neptune generation (1990-96; also sextile Pluto) is coming of age as of this writing – a time when catastrophic climate change is just beginning to seriously manifest itself in human affairs and world governments are veering towards totalitarianism and re-arming with nuclear weapons. The previous Uranus conjunct Neptune generation (1818-25; this conjunction was also square Pluto) reached young adulthood during the famines and political turmoil of the 1840s, and produced political revolutionaries such as Karl Marx and Friedrich Engels as well as grim, severe, freethinking writers including Walt Whitman, Herman Melville, and Fyodor Dostoyevsky. Uranus conjunct Neptune also produces revolutionary thinkers such as Louis Pasteur, the father of microbiology and the germ theory of disease (who had the Sun and Venus within a close Uranus-Neptune conjunction); and in a previous cycle Petrarch, Father of Humanism, often credited for initiating the 14th-century Renaissance. The doggedness and authoritarian absolutism of this combination is shown by Thomas More, whose outspoken rectitude led to his being beheaded.

Uranus sextile Neptune is spontaneous and unpredictable. You are nonchalant and free-spirited; willing to fearlessly follow your hunches and impulses no matter where they may lead you; and you have a facility for serendipitously landing on your feet whenever you leap before you look. You are improvisational and resourceful – always able to change direction at the drop of a hat, and to make good use of whatever you find at hand. You possess an unruffled mentality – the ability to view yourself and your circumstances with cool detachment – which enables you to keep a psychological distance from day-to-day exigencies and insulates you from undue emotional wear and tear. You are off on your own tangent most of the time, pursuing your own quixotic images (or illusions); you will listen to no dissent or disproof, and you never say die. Your volatility and unswerving allegiance to your personal inspiration can render you vague and blasé in response to demands that you come down from your cloud. But your unflagging optimism and vibrant energy stimulate the enthusiasm of others.

The current Uranus sextile Neptune generation (1965-1969) came of age at the putative end of the Cold War and birth of the internet – a time of great economic and social expansion, opportunity, and optimism. The previous Uranus sextile Neptune generation (1850-1857) came of age during a long economic depression; however, Germany and Italy united now; the Second Industrial Revolution began, as well as the New Imperialism, when the European powers (and Japan) conquered almost all of Africa and parts of Asia. The preceeding Uranus sextile Neptune generation (1793-1798) came of age at the end of the Napoleonic wars, which led to the expansion of the English and Russian empires. The first Industrial Revolution was in full swing, and Spanish colonies in America were liberated.

Uranus square Neptune is purposeful but effete. You have good judgment and a strong conscience which guide your efforts and enable you to arrive at decisions with which you can feel justified at having done the honorable thing. You put your faith in moderation and restraint; in calm, reasoned discourse; but unfortunately you tend to find your adversaries playing some species of "heads I win; tails you lose". Your admirable resolve – which is based upon abstract considerations of what is right and just – lacks force in those not-infrequent situations which call for true grit and assertiveness. You are too preoccupied with not overstepping the boundaries of decorum to make effective use of your not inconsiderable perspicacity and powers of reflection. You tend to be more concerned with making an abstract point – with assuring yourself that you are in the right – than you are with actually influencing or convincing anyone; and your misplaced nobility prefers to suffer the slings and arrows of outrageous fortune rather than take arms against a sea of troubles and by opposing end them. Your conscientiousness and good faith win the respect of all who know you.

The current Uranus square Neptune generation (1952-1957) has thus far produced few notables (apart from Vladimir Putin); nor did they come of age in a particularly notable time. The previous Uranus square Neptune generation (1867-1872) also produced conflicted Russian leaders such as Nikolai Lenin, Czar Nikolai II, and Grigory Rasputin; as well Mohandas Gandhi (all of whom died tragically).

Uranus trine Neptune makes for a poised, unshakeable, self-adequacy. You are blithe and self-assured – never incommoded or at a loss under any circumstances. There is an economy to your actions and a muted understatement to your reactions, which are more convincing than words or deeds could ever be. You are cool, knowing, and in command: albeit sedate and undemonstrative in your personal manner, you dominate any proceedings by your sheer insouciance and the force of your presence. You are able to effectively communicate without speaking; and to enforce your will without especially appearing or trying to. On the negative side you can manifest a contumelious smugness and self-satisfaction which compensate for a psychological blind spot somewhere in your makeup: a magisterial absolutism which views things in black-and-white terms; a maddening imperturbability and concomitant disinclination to go much out of your way for anyone, or to involve yourself with other people's "issues". Nonetheless your calm self-certainty when others are given to doubt and despair has a stabilizing effect on any group, and induces people to rally around and rely upon you.

The Uranus trine Neptune generation born 1938-1944 produced most of the balladeers and troubadours (as opposed to hard rockers) of the hippie florescence – the Beatles, Rolling Stones, Bob Dylan, Lou Reed, Paul Simon. The previous Uranus trine Neptune generation (1879-1884), produced the leaders of the Second World War (such as Franklin

Roosevelt, Joseph Stalin, Benito Mussolini, Harry S. Truman), as well as the visionary Cubist painters and imaginative writers (such as Virginia Woolf, James Joyce, Franz Kafka) who created a totally new and modern aesthetic sensibility, just as Albert Einstein created a modern scientific sensibility.

Uranus opposition Neptune makes for an unrestrained imagination. You possess an incisive, probing intellect of considerable grasp and scope. You are good at problem-solving since you are able to see beneath superficial appearances and complexities, and decide matters in a logical and orderly fashion. You hold yourself above contention with an unswerving allegiance to the moral right. You are given to the grand gesture and the symbolic act – and you are unafraid to push the limits of the possible (or what you can get away with). You have an irreverent, sardonic sense of irony tinged with a Great-I-Am infallibility; which on the negative side can become a superior, patronizing noblesse oblige which is unwilling to compromise or to listen to the counsel of others. You are at your best when you follow your dreams and hold unswervingly to what you feel in your heart is proper and true.

The last Uranus opposition Neptune generation (1903-12) came of age in the Great Depression, and produced writers of despair and the meaninglessness of existence such as B.F. Skinner, Jean Paul Sartre, Jean Genet, Samuel Beckett, Jean Anouilh, and Eugene Ionesco. Previous cycles produced intellectual revolutionaries such as Thomas Aquinas (who epitomized, in the words of Richard Tarnas, "the rebellion against conservative or reactionary religious authority in the service of a new spiritual autonomy"); and in later cycles, the utopian Francis Bacon (the father of the scientific method), Galileo Galilei, and William Shakespeare. Many of the leaders of the American Revolution were also born with Uranus opposition Neptune. Historically it has signified generations struggling to free themselves from the limitation of the conventional wisdom of the times; whose standards exalt the rights of the individual at the expense of the church or state, and which put their faith in reason rather than unquestioning belief.

Uranus parallel Neptune makes for an even-handed probity. You are as staunch and untrammeled as the Uranus-Neptune aspects; can be as bullheaded in your insistence on your personal prerogatives and emotional privacy; and you possess the same unyielding staying power.

But in contrast to the super self-serious and standoffish aspects, you are breezy, light in spirit, and rather more humane. You are more disinterested than the partisan aspects, whose putative high-mindedness and impartiality somehow always seems to redound to their own benefit. You are honorable and upstanding, and cannot be deviated from your chosen path; which on the negative side can make you unduly smug and complacent. However here there is a democratic recognition of the rights and privileges of others as well as yourself, together with a willingness to include these in your reckoning in the name of fair play. Your basic decency and true-blue scrupulosity in all your dealings enable you to avoid compromising entanglements without any necessity for self-exculpation or regret.

Uranus contraparallel Neptune is staunch and self-sufficient. In contrast to the aspects between these two planets, who justify their actions with an appeal to the moral right or greater good, you are less inclined to self-justification, readier to fly with your innate sense of what is best for you (and at the same time will be best for everyone). You need little in the way of support or feedback to develop your plans and schemes, which are usually as abstract and humanitarian as those of the aspects between Uranus and Neptune. You just go your own way and do your own thing, looking neither to the left or right, and are not as interested in ultimate ends or proving your point so much as in enjoying the path beneath your feet. While you are as steadfast and true as the aspects, you are far lighter in spirit while being equally as serious about your task in life.

Uranus–Pluto Aspects

Uranus–Pluto gives a restlessness, a need to prove oneself in either other people's eyes or one's own by upholding traditional values of moral decency (or by establishing new – and more equitable and just ones). These natives possess a strong sense of social obligation and a desire to dedicate themselves to creating a better world, even when (especially when) this necessitates some sacrifice of personal self-interest. Their motto is: anything goes!

Uranus conjunct Pluto is purposeful and direct. You are concentrated, resolute, and businesslike, with no time for frivolity or hemming and hawing. You miss nothing of what is going on around you, and you get right to the point (brusque, indelicate). Indeed, you can be quite shocking in your acuteness, perspicuity, and explicitness; and you really don't much care whose toes you have to step on to assert your views and to get your own way. There is a plaintiveness about you; a feeling of onus or burden; a sense of struggle or being put upon – especially pronounced in those natives who have Saturn opposite this conjunction (1960s; and the generation which came of age at the start of the Thirty Years' War; or conjunct it in the 1850s) – which may be the residue of unfortunate early life experiences which you had no option but to endure. In any event you are driven by an incumbency – a need for vindication or self-justification – to fulfill a special destiny. Thus you are unyielding and indomitable (pigheaded and unstoppable), and ready to go to any extreme to outwit, outflank, or outwait. At your best you are a sterling example of unbending determination.

Uranus sextile Pluto gives a principled reasonableness. You are soberminded and sincere in your efforts, with a detached and philosophical take on life. You are high-minded and idealistic, and seek to establish the highest standards of correct comportment in your own behavior and in your relations with others. You tend to be nonjudgmental and accepting of people; and you base your actions on rational considerations and on what is best for everyone concerned (especially you). Glib and quick-witted, you are no less assured and authoritative than the other Uranus-Pluto aspects, but are far more subtle and persuasive. You are soft-spoken and low-key, and seek to influence other people by your example: by your earnestness and common-sense arguments, rather than by brute domination or manipulation. On your negative side your avuncular affability can turn patronizing or snooty: your lofty demeanor finds any discord distasteful, beneath you; and you can be something of a self-exculpating, self-righteous know-it-all. Your calm inner strength is a reliance for others in times of confusion.

The present Uranus sextile Pluto generation (1992-1997; Uranus also conjunct Neptune – see above) is coming of age at this writing. The previous Uranus sextile Pluto generation (1941-1945) overlaps Uranus trine Neptune (see above). The Uranus sextile Pluto before that (1867-1870) overlaps Uranus square Neptune (see above).

Uranus square Pluto is sharp and abrasive. You are stiff, touchy, and concerned with propriety – ever alert to insure that you obtain your moiety and that no one is infringing your prerogatives. You have a quick, nervous energy and a quick, incisive intellect which is fond of outdoing and outshining, and generally impressing people with your superior acumen and skill. You make a point of being on top of every development and dominating every proceeding; and indeed you do possess unique opinions and a sui generis philosophy which you willingly and daringly put to the test in your own personal life. You cultivate some area of expertise in which you are undeniably *it*; and you are picky and critical of lesser lights – smug in the knowledge of your own pre-eminence. You feel your supremacy grants you special privileges or dispensations, and you are at pains that everyone you know acknowledges and acquiesces in these and grants you your due. Thus you can be cavalier in your handling of people – outspoken to the point of brusqueness and insistent on doing your own thing come hell or high water. Your incisive perspicacity and penetrating insight – in their proper moment – are guiding lights for people who are doubtful or confused.

The last Uranus square Pluto generation (1930-1935) produced the astronauts who went to the Moon, and also irreverent, iconoclastic thinkers such as Richard Alpert, Andy Warhol, Ralph Nader, Woody Allen, Elvis Presley, and the Dalai Lama. The previous Uranus square Pluto generation (1819-1821; Neptune conjoined Uranus and squared Pluto now too) also produced revolutionary thinkers and writers (see above).

Uranus trine Pluto is poised and steadfast. You carry yourself with an ease of manner and a sense of comfortable belonging in any milieu; as *Desiderata* put it, "You have a right to be here." You are pleasant and democratic in manner, yet firm in your convictions – authoritative and self-possessed without being officious – as if you assume that everyone is on your side and agrees with you. You have a knack for balancing your own needs with those of other people, and for working out modus operandi without compromising your dignity or permitting encroachment upon your personal space. You are calm and composed even when under great stress and strain – you are able to contain your own feelings in the name of maintaining a tranquil environment and peaceful proceedings. You tend to turn aside from unpleasantness and studiously avoid becoming entangled in imbroglios, so at times your blithe breeziness can be frustrating rather than soothing; and you are quite deaf to anything you don't want to hear. You feel an obligation to be a model of immoveable constancy when times are tough.

Natives of this sedate and dutiful generation (born 1920-1923) were teenagers in the Great Depression and came of age during the Second World War; they had heavy responsibilities thrust upon them willy-nilly, and they were gifted with the ability to remain calm, collected, and "normal" in the midst of great chaos and uncertainty. The previous Uranus trine Pluto generation (1884-1886) came of age in the early 20th century and fought in the First World War; their charge was to maintain stability at a time when traditional social and political orders were dissolving and an uncertain future was emerging. The Uranus trine Pluto generation before that (1808-1812) included liberal politicians such as Gladstone, Lincoln, and Johnson; as well as writers sympathetic to the plight of the poor and dispossessed (Browning, Dickens, Stowe) and satirists of the existing social order (Thackeray, Gogol). Darwin was born now; also the romantic composers Chopin, Liszt, Mendelsohn, Schumann, Verdi, and Wagner.

Uranus opposition Pluto tends to be iconoclastic and sybaritic. Uranus opposition Pluto generations often come of age at the ends of major, destructive wars; and they enjoy the subsequent post bellum peace, plenty, and dissoluteness. The previous Uranus opposition Pluto generation came of age after World War I during the amoral, tradition-breaking, and thrill-seeking jazz age of the Roaring Twenties, and it produced writers who were anti-authoritarian and sympathetic to the marginalized and downtrodden such as Vladimir Nabokov, André Malraux, George Orwell, John Steinbeck, and Erskine Caldwell (and in an earlier cycle Percy Bysshe Shelley). Many of the founders of the revolutionary quantum theory and inventors of the (Uranium-Plutonium) atomic bomb, such as Werner Heisenberg, Enrico Fermi, and Linus Pauling, were also of this generation.

The previous Uranus opposition Pluto generation came of age at the close of the American Civil War and the unifications of Germany and Italy, as well as the Meiji Restoration in Japan (Emperor Meiji had a close Uranus-Pluto opposition) – all of which began major eras of economic and technological growth (the Second Industrial Revolution – this period in American history is referred to as the "Gilded Age").

The preceding Uranus-Pluto opposition generation came of age at the close of the Napoleonic Wars (and American War of 1812) – the gilded Regency period in England (according to Robert Southey, "the end of a more pious and reserved society, and … birth of a more frivolous, ostentatious one"). In short, Uranus opposition Pluto generations often reach adulthood at the ends of tumultuous, contractive eras and the beginnings of new, expansive, and optimistic ones which encourage innovation, thinking outside the box, and moral decadence.

Uranus parallel / contraparallel Pluto is visionary and impulsive. You possess all the adroitness and cocksure intensity of the Uranus-Pluto aspects; and you also have their fearless resolve to live out your beliefs in all that you do. But you are far more laid-back and tolerant than the dogmatic and self-certain aspects – intent upon doing your own thing, but willing to let other people do their thing as well. You are single-minded and uncompromising, but with a spirited alacrity in place of roughshod indomitability: imaginative and experimentative rather than complacently self-assured. You don't measure yourself against other people (or take much notice of their reactions) but follow your own intuition and assess your current status in terms of how true you are being to your own personal code of conduct. At times your blithe, unquestioning faith in yourself and your willingness to leap without looking can embroil you in dire, unanticipated consquences. Your unwavering optimism and hopefulness inspire everyone who knows you.

The last Uranus parallel Pluto occurred 1945-54 and gave rise to the psychedelic, peace-and-love hippie generation; and the last contraparallel in the mid-1970s gave rise to Generation X (described by Professor Christine Henseler as "a generation whose worldview is based on change, on the need to combat corruption, dictatorships, abuse, AIDS, a generation in search of human dignity and individual freedom, the need for stability, love, tolerance, and human rights for all"). The previous Uranus-Pluto contraparallel generation came of age during the First World War and were military leaders during the Second (and statesmen in its aftermath); the writings of its rebellious, nonconformist authors such as Henry Miller, Boris Pasternak, and Franz Werfel were concerned with free expression and human rights.

Neptune – Pluto Aspects

The planets Neptune and Pluto entered orb of a sextile aspect in the mid-1940s; and they will remain there through the 2030s. Normally aspects between Neptune and Pluto are within orb for only a dozen or so years at a time. However, Pluto is presently at a fast place in its orbit so that it is moving at about the same speed as Neptune, at the same time that the two planets are roughly 60 degrees apart; so they are both in the sextile pattern for about a century. Thus, there will come a moment in time when there is no one on earth who doesn't have Neptune and Pluto sextile in their natal horoscope.

Where aspects between the faster, inner planets symbolize relationships and roles to be played in everyday life, the aspects of the slower, outer planets – of which Neptune and Pluto are the slowest – symbolize people's adaptation to the social order and *Zeitgeist* of their times. Aspects of slow planets refer to the assumptions, activities, and beliefs which identify people with their generation, and which change but slowly over the course of a lifetime.

Neptune is the planet of Intuition, the receptor for all the impressions that hover just at the fringes of rational consciousness. It is the planet of belief, since anything which Neptune intuits has the appearance of truth (you believe what your intuition tells you).

Pluto is the planet of Clarity – analysis and discrimination – the sense of what is fit, just, and meet – in a word, the morality. If Neptune deludes because it makes its beliefs seems true, Pluto obsesses because it makes its judgments seem right.

Aspects between Neptune and Pluto produce generations for whom belief must be the instrument of morality. They are rather more idealistic and even revolutionary in pursuing their particular visions of utopia than are generations lacking Neptune-Pluto aspects, which basically just conform to the social codes instituted by the preceding Neptune-Pluto aspect generation. These generations are not necessarily more moral or spiritual than generations lacking Neptune-Pluto contacts, but they are more *self-consciously* moral and spiritual. They need to believe that the human race is progressing towards a goal, and that there is something which each individual must do in order to help it along. They demand that the social contract reflect and uphold universal principles. They feel a need to justify their actions before the throne of history. They need to believe that they were chosen, willy-nilly, to bring light to mankind.

The "hard" aspects between Neptune and Pluto (the conjunction, square, and opposition) tend to produce generations which are stern, disciplined, and controlled. People born under these aspects are constrained by their society to repress their own personal desires for the sake of the common weal. On the other hand, the "soft" aspects between

Neptune and Pluto (the sextile and trine) produce generations of individualists, for whom the only purpose society serves is to facilitate the happiness of its individual members. For example, the previous **Neptune trine Pluto** aspect lasted for most of the 18th century and produced The Age of Enlightenment, which "emphasized reason, analysis, and individualism rather than traditional lines of authority". The chief difference between the trine and sextile is (as we shall see) that the trine is intellectual, theoretical, idealistic, and just; whereas the sextile is pragmatic, unprincipled, and grabby.

The previous generation born with **Neptune square Pluto** (1814-1826 – note that Uranus conjoined Neptune and squared Pluto as well during much of this period) came of age during the political revolutions of the 1840s. These natives needed to believe in the better instincts of the great mass of humanity. The statesmen of this generation brought about the sweeping destruction of old social orders and class distinctions and the reorganization of society along vaster and more inclusive lines. Bismarck in Germany and Cavour in Italy welded clusters of small states into unified nations. Lincoln freed the slaves in America, and Alexander II emancipated the serfs in Russia (i.e. the square generation carried out in actuality the desiderata of the previous trine generation).

The current of these times was toward unification, broadening the social contract to bring more and more people into the governing process, and the supersedure of local political hegemonies by *Überstaaten* (a process common to all Neptune-Pluto aspect generations – e.g. the globalization override of national governments taking place during the present Neptune sextile Pluto period). In the vanguard were the suffragists Susan B. Anthony, Elizabeth Cady Stanton, and Lucy Stone; and on the more violent and revolutionary side, Marx, Engels and Bakunin. There was an intellectual tendency to view humanity en masse and to exalt the poor and downtrodden. Of the few notable painters of this generation, Courbet and Millet stand out with their realistic paintings of workers and peasants.

The literature of this generation also exhibited great compassion for the suffering of the common man in a world indifferent to him. The writing of Charles Dickens, Herman Melville, Fyodor Dostoyevsky, Edgar Allan Poe, and the Brontës tended to be dramatic, with an undercurrent of violence and an obsession with questions of morality and immorality. The sense of the time was that the cosmos, if not actually hostile, was at least disinterested in the fate of humanity. The theories of Charles Darwin, Gregor Mendel, and Louis Pasteur posited mechanistic models of nature which implied that the human condition was the product of largely impersonal forces.

The square aspect is forever trying to make sense out of the senseless and to rationalize the irrational. The square is an aspect of conflict, and with Neptune square Pluto objective, analytical mind was ever at war with intuition; so this generation – the generation of Queen Victoria – never really could trust its own personal instincts. Its morality had to be certified by the experience of humanity as a whole. Its only hope was that the entire human race would accept the responsibility for guiding its collective destiny.

The previous generation born with **Neptune conjunct Pluto** (1886-1898) needed to believe in the inspiration of the outstanding personality (focus on the Leader). Statesmanship in this generation often approached Caesar-worship. Its highly charismatic leaders governed by sheer force of personality, coupled with direct and absolute methods: Adolf Hitler, Mao Zedong, Francisco Franco, Charles de Gaulle, Juan Peron, and Josip Tito are examples. When each leader passed on, his work was largely dismantled by his successors.

The cult of personality even pervaded the sciences. The theories of Immanuel Velikovsky, Norbert Weiner, Wilhelm Reich, and T.D. Lysenko created storms of controversy with rabid partisans and opponents. Rather than building onto existing bodies of knowledge, the thinkers of this generation were lone visionaries off on their own personal tangents and out of the scientific mainstream.

The conjunction is the most subjective of aspects, and the Neptune conjunct Pluto generation took more stock in feelings than in reason or logic. The writers of this generation produced a highly subjective and stylized body of literature. Bertolt Brecht, William Faulkner, Eugene O'Neill and Thornton Wilder had intensely introspective, convoluted, and personalized slants on life; and their writing and characters tended to be artless and amoral.

Artless and amoral is also a good description of the art and morals of the Dadaist and Surrealist painters. The art of Marcel Duchamp, Jean Arp, Giorgio de Chirico, Max Ernst, Marc Chagall, and Joan Miró was highly personal and idiosyncratic, a revolt against conventional aesthetic sensibilities and a glorification of unbridled imagination.

The Neptune-Pluto conjunction tended to bring out the delusional side of Neptune and the obsessive side of Pluto because there was no separation of analytical mind from intuition, so anything imaginable was justifiable, and conscience could not be brought in as an outside check upon morality. The keyword for the conjunction aspect is Focus: this generation was too often eager to destroy all that had gone before in the name of a fanatical search for ideological purity. It was a generation of extremists with a narrow and intense focus, and it centered its hopes on certain personalities of severe morals and vivid imagination. It needed to believe in the inspiration of its prophets.

The previous generation born with **Neptune sextile Pluto** (1837-1851) needed to believe in the rights of everyman, and in a cosmos both sympathetic and infinitely pliant. It believed that it was the function of the state to serve the individual rather than vice versa, and as a result its statesmen were neither great innovators nor inspired leaders. Georges Clemenceau, Grover Cleveland, Paul von Hindenburg, and William McKinley were noted for their sterile conservatism and their defense of profit and privilege.

This generation was less interested in ultimate ends and meanings than in ways of getting things done. It loved to tinker, and it produced the great experimenters Alexander Graham Bell, Thomas Edison and Luther Burbank. Its scientists were not so much theoreticians as experimentalists: Albert Michelson, Georg Cantor, Ivan Pavlov, and Richard von Krafft-Ebing made great contributions to the methodologies of their respective disciplines; but they are most notable for the questions which their new techniques stirred up but left unanswered.

Even the literature of this generation was marked by technical refinement and scientific precision. Emile Zola, Henry James, August Strindberg, and Guy de Maupassant wrote about human behavior from the standpoint of objective psychology, reporting even life's sordid and seamy side with clinical detachment.

In art Neptune sextile Pluto represents technique rather than content, such as the transient light effects of the Impressionists Claude Monet, Pierre Auguste Renoir, Paul Cézanne, Paul Gauguin; or in an earlier Neptune sextile Pluto generation, the balance and geometrical perfection of High Renaissance artists such as Michelangelo, Raphael, and Titian. Impressionism is considered the beginning of modernism in art because these painters were the first to regard the act of painting as a technical process more important than an accurate depiction of subject matter.

Neptune sextile Pluto was usually more concerned with form than substance. It believed that form *was* substance, that technique was an end in itself. It loved to objectively analyze intuitive impressions, to give its instinctive feelings a whirl. The sextile is the most pragmatic and opportunistic of the aspects, and with Neptune sextile Pluto, anything realizable was justifiable: whatever seemed to work was considered good. This generation regarded the world as a laboratory in which to tinker, and it identified human progress with efficiency and technical advancement.

The previous Neptune sextile Pluto generation came of age in the 1860's through 1880's, a time of unprecedented economic and social expansion (earlier Neptune sextile Pluto generations came of age at the beginning of the Elizabethan era – considered the height of the English Renaissance; and the cycle before that came of age at the start of the three-century-long Ming dynasty – termed one of the greatest eras of orderly government and social stability in human history, as well as the Timur empire in Central Asia).

In late 19th century Europe imperialism was the vogue, and vast colonial empires were carved out of Africa and Asia. In America, the West was won. Everywhere western technological civilization gained undisputed hegemony over native peoples and cultures. Not only did this civilization spread out, it also began to assume a more and more complex character.

The Industrial Revolution was in full swing in the advanced nations, especially in America. In the words of historians Nevins and Commager, "No other generation in American history witnessed changes as swift or as revolutionary as those which transformed the rural republic of Lincoln and Lee into the urban industrial empire of McKinley and Roosevelt." The telegraph and rail networks put every part of the country into communication with every other part, facilitating the rapid movement of information, raw materials manufactured goods and food stuffs.

Great opportunities opened up, and great fortunes were made. Morality was a matter of individual conscience, and often great wealth was taken to be the outward sign of great spiritual worth. This was the era of the robber barons John D. Rockefeller, J. P. Morgan, Henry Clay Frick, J. J. Hill, and of the trusts and monopolies. Big Business was born and it quickly seized the reins of power in America. Labor unions under leaders such as Samuel Gompers and Terence Powderly arose as a counterbalance to the power of business combinations. For the first time, national and international factors were more important to the average person than local conditions.

Burgeoning industry tore at the earth and its resources with the same abandon with which it exploited labor. Pollution began to be recognized as a widespread problem, and wilderness disappeared at a fantastic rate before the onslaught of loggers, homesteaders, miners and railroaders. American civilization in the late 19th century exhibited a limitless optimism predicated upon a system of limitless expansion.

All generations born with Neptune sextile Pluto are particularly utilitarian; their watchword is practicality – "if it works, do it!" (and don't worry about traditional wisdom, or the consequences). Neptune sextile Pluto, like all sextiles, is poised to seize opportunities as they arise. Sextiles are technocratic rather than philosophical, pragmatic rather than theoretical. In contrast to the other aspects between Neptune and Pluto, the sextile generations produce few exceptional statesmen or social leaders because the emphasis here is on individual interpretations rather than reliance on societal fiat. These generations are not particularly interested in doing what they're told unless they can see how their own personal needs are directly served thereby, and they tend to be suspicious of leaders and authority. Thus in religion they tend towards individualism, such as the "priesthood of all believers" of Martin Luther and Ulrich Zwingli in an earlier Neptune sextile Pluto generation, which R.H. Tawney characterized as "the triumph of the commercial spirit over the traditional social ethics of Christendom. If the reformer did not explicitly teach a conscienceless individualism, individualism was, at least, the natural corollary of their teaching."

If the sextile resembles Neptune conjunct Pluto in its "end justifies the means" amorality, it also inclines to the Neptune trine Pluto faith in common sense standards of justice and fair play. The two faces of Neptune sextile Pluto are exemplified in an earlier generation by Niccolo Machiavelli (amoral practicality) on the one hand, and Sir Thomas More (Utopian humanism) on the other. In Neptune sextile Pluto generations each individual is expected to come up with his or her own answers, rather than to rely on experts or interpreters to intercede for them; to find purpose and meaning for themselves within the bounds of natural courtesy and respect for other individuals.

The present Neptune sextile Pluto generation – like the last one – is also in thrall to an amoral technocracy which is gaily despoiling the earth, devastating the natural environment, and creating a social order of vast inequality; as well as creating the technical means to implement a reign of Orwellian terror. The generation which will reap what is now being sown is the next Neptune square Pluto generation – born between 2055 and 2069 – who will come of age in the latter part of the twenty-first century. Like the previous Neptune square Pluto generation they will reach adulthood in a time of famine, plague, and universal political upheaval (an earlier Neptune square Pluto generation came of age during the Black Death of the 14th century).

The survivors, born under Neptune trine Pluto (2086 – 2096), who will come of age at the beginning of the twenty-second century, will be tasked with picking through the rubble and rebuilding society along more just and spiritual lines, as envisioned by their predecessors of the Enlightenment.

The manner in which each individual Neptune sextile Pluto native adapts him or herself to their generation's ideal of taking personal responsibility for making one's own choices is shown by the *value* of the Neptune sextile Pluto aspect in their birth horoscope. The value is simply the orb of inexactitude: if Neptune and Pluto are within one degree of exact sextile (59°01' to 60°59' angular separation), then the value is one; if greater than one and less than or equal to two degrees from exactitude (58°01' to 59°00' or 61°00' to 61°59' angular separation), the value is two; if greater than two and less than or equal to three degrees from exactitude (57°01' to 58°00' or 62°00' to 62°59' angular separation), the value is three; and so on. This technique was explained by Dr. Marc Edmund Jones in his Lecture - Lesson on *Pythagorean Astrology*, from which the keywords for the values were also taken:

DR. JONES' KEYWORDS FOR THE VALUES (Aspect Orbs)

1 = EMPHASIS (Doing)   4 = HABIT (Limitation)
2 = CHANGE (Thinking)   5 = EXPRESSION (Skill)
3 = GROWTH (Relating)   6 = EXPANSION (Self-enlargement)

1. EMPHASIS (Doing). All aspects within one degree of exactitude reveal their meaning in its purest, knee-jerk-responsive form – "as near impersonal as it is possible for them to be and yet be individual experiences." Thus natives with Neptune sextile Pluto within one degree of exactness are the most compulsively pragmatic and individualistic – not in the sense of being rebellious or flaunting your independence of spirit, but rather that you are a self-contained, lone wolf. You are an idealist off on your own tangent, hence you are not especially successful in mundane affairs unless the rest of your chart is dynamic. You have considerable self-discipline, are self-motivated and self-starting, and are conscientious and dedicated. On the negative side you lack perspective: you are too focused on the path beneath your feet and easily become mired in your thinking. Your individualism manifests as a naïve doggedness and scrupulosity which inspires others with its unassuming honesty and integrity.

2. CHANGE (Thinking). All aspects between one and two degrees of exactness indicate flexibility: the ability to adapt oneself to changing conditions – "universals are only to be perceived in terms of constant flux." This means that you natives with Neptune sextile Pluto greater than one but less than or equal to two degrees from exactitude are the most experimentally pragmatic and individualistic: you are eager to learn new things and to examine situations and other people's ideas and motivations from different points of view. Like the ones, you twos are hardworking and competent (all Neptune sextile Pluto natives are – Dr. Jones' keyword for the sextile is PRODUCTION), but the reach here is more towards understanding than psychological independence. You are thoughtful, introspective, and arrive at solutions to problems by thinking them through rather than bulldozing ahead. On the negative side, lacking the single-mindedness of the ones, you can come across as being indecisive, bland, and wishy-washy: too lacking in firmness to be masterful (unless the rest of the chart cooperates). Your individualism manifests as a naïve intellectual curiosity which inspires others with its unpretentious open-mindedness.

3. GROWTH (Relating). All aspects between two and three degrees of exactitude symbolize friendliness – "the expanding element of simple co-operation in being. It is the basis of pure social relationship, the emanation of ... self to the point of fellowship with other selves." Accordingly, you natives with Neptune sextile Pluto between two and three degrees of exactitude are the most socially pragmatic and individualistic:

outgoing, gregarious, eager to please; yet still original – fun-loving and mischievous, with a true sense of irony. You are cheerfully optimistic, and enjoy other people instead of analyzing them (twos) or ignoring them (ones). You live and let live, and try to turn aside from conflict and unpleasantness. On the negative side you are inclined to sidestep or slough off problems, to let things slide until they build to a crisis (rather than tackling them directly or thinking them through). Your individualism manifests in a detached, light, unconcerned manner which inspires others with its graciousness and buoyant hopefulness.

4. HABIT (Limitation). All aspects between three and four degrees of exactitude symbolize a tenacity and sagacity which must "observe and classify and understand." You natives with Neptune sextile Pluto between three and four degrees of exactness are the most eccentrically pragmatic and individualistic – highly self-attuned and self-assured, with great depth and delicacy of feeling. You are calm and knowing, with good intuition and the ability to stop to listen to what your heart is telling you. Where the twos reach out for intellectual comprehension, the outreach of the fours is less cerebral, more a passionate (and compassionate) lust for life. For you fours understanding is not so much a matter of formulating ideals as it is living your ideals to the fullest, of drinking life to the dregs. On the negative side you are stubborn, self-willed, convinced of your invincibility and rectitude, and inclined to go to the extremes of human experience (and endurance). Your individualism manifests in your ability to stand up for yourself with utter disregard for the social consequences, and you inspire others with your nobility of spirit and your can-do resourcefulness.

5. EXPRESSION (Skill). All aspects between four and five degrees of exactitude are ingenious and straightforward – "the clue to a man's heart lies in his artlessness – simplicity, smooth functioning in little things." You natives with Neptune sextile Pluto between four and five degrees of exactness are the most candidly pragmatic and individualistic: you are not particularly humble or self-effacing, but rather waste little energy in affectation or posturing – you are plain vanilla with no frills, and just get down to the real business at hand. The striving here is towards reasonableness, fairness, and clear communication with others. You possess a good-natured bonhomie, which on the negative side inclines you towards talking rather than doing; you can be noncommittal or hedging when what is needed is fairness and taking a stand. Your individualism manifests in

your unvarnished outspokenness – saying what you think without fear. You inspire others with your optimism, frankness, and impartiality.

6. EXPANSION (Self-enlargement). All aspects between five and six degrees of exactitude show a no-nonsense practicality: "bending of outer factors to inner convenience; smoothness in the accomplishment of things." You natives with Neptune sextile Pluto between five and six degrees of exactness are the most dispassionately pragmatic and individualistic: you are cool, down-to-earth, purposeful, and realistic – ready to roll up your sleeves and get to work. You are deft at processing – whether this be people or problems – and you are willing to take on more than your fair share of responsibility, which on the negative side can lead you to deliberately multiply your burdens and then feel put upon; or to push into areas where your counsel is neither needed nor appreciated. Your individualism is manifested in your ability to meet and even exceed your own (rather than society's) expectations; and you inspire others with your thoroughness and selfless dedication.

Neptune parallel (1916-19; 2005-7) / **contraparallel** (1966-1969) **Pluto:** Intuition obliquely bolstered by Clarity makes for a visionary intrepidity. The aspects of Neptune and Pluto produce natives who – in one fashion or another – are creatures of their culture and times. They toe the line, play by the rules (or try to establish new ones); justify their doings by referring them to prevailing canons of social acceptance. You parallels also feel a deep sense of responsibility for humanity and a need to contribute what you can; but you possess a spirit of errant adventure, and are always off in pursuit of your own dreams. You are incapable of following anyone; nor do you seek followers – you are at your best and freest when you are acting alone in obedience to your idiosyncratic (eccentric and quixotic) world view – and you are quite willing to go the limit to prove your mettle (to yourself – you don't care what anyone else thinks). You are a pioneer who fearlessly ventures forth on your own, with no need or desire for support or succor; thus to be involved in an intimate relationship with you can be very trying: albeit well-meaning, most of the time you simply aren't there. At your best you are the ballast who is able to bring a sense of calm, immovable reassurance in the midst of general uncertainty.

The Moon's Nodes

The Moon's nodes (intersection points of the Moon's orbit with the ecliptic, which have a cycle of about 18 years and move retrograde roughly 3' of arc daily) can be considered to indicate karmic lessons to be learned in this lifetime. The North node (where the Moon crosses the ecliptic moving north) symbolizes good karma: it shows where natives have a positive attitude, where they are open and trusting and willing to just let things happen by themselves – instead of sweating and stewing and bending things; and people; and themselves; out of shape. By its house position and aspects it indicates where they face life directly and take full responsibility for themselves, the feelings of other people, and the situations in which they find themselves; and thus are open to receive the blessings all around them. It shows where they are free of any need to make excuses, and therefore where they are able to take advantage of lucky opportunities as they arise.

By contrast, the South node (where the Moon crosses the ecliptic moving south) indicates bad karma left over from other lives and realities which still needs to be worked out in this one. The South Node is the bête noire: it shows where its natives have a bad attitude; where they close up, defend, and salve themselves; where they are caught up in issues of control or being controlled. Conjunction with the South node burdens the natural action of a planet by overlaying it with an agenda of self-pity which gravitates towards situations and relationships in which its natives will have do battle and win at all costs; or else crash down in flames. Where the North node reaches out to others, the South node closes up into (and vaunts) itself. A planet conjunct a node is similar to having that planet posited in its exaltation sign (North node) or in its fall (South node).

In using the interpretations that follow, you should allow 6 degree orbs from exactitude in measuring conjunctions with the nodes.

Preponderance of planets conjunct North node (3 or more): You are a simple, straightforward person who is utterly incapable of guile or artifice.

Attuned primarily to otherworldly realms (or at least not altogether centered in this one), you are thoughtful and abstracted, absorbed in your own musings most of the time, and are not temperamentally suited to dealing with the convolutions and politicking of everyday society. You are a trusting soul who is a better listener than talker: you try to take all viewpoints and possibilities into account before making a decision, and as a result it's fairly easy for the unscrupulous to fool or take advantage of you. You tend to be a passive watcher rather than a decisive leader; but when you do act or speak out it is with a calm, reasoned assurance which springs from inner certainty, from conscience, from your heart's core; and you can quite immoveable when once you have made a stand.

Preponderance of planets conjunct South node (3 or more): You love to be the leader or center of attention – the one calling the shots; and you possess a do-or-die insistence on getting your own way come thick or thin: "my way or the highway"! Frank and outspoken (even brazen to the point of rudeness), you are incapable of tact or diplomacy but must bull your way through at all costs and devil take the hindmost. You are nobody's fool and have few scruples about using any people or opportunities which present themselves to advance your self-interest. You take pride in your uncompromising independence of spirit, and are contemptuous of shilly-shallying and beating around the bush. In the name of principle you put your ego on the line with every decision you make, and you will not retreat or modify your objectives in response to limiting actualities or the sensibilities of other people – when stymied, you merely go off half-cocked in some other direction.

Sun conjunct North node: You possess a stout heart and good instincts, which guide you unerringly through the vicissitudes of life. You are impetuous, vivacious, and unabashedly frank; and you receive blessings from father and superiors / bosses / authorities (observe that the term "blessings" doesn't necessarily imply a happy relationship, particularly if Sun-node is afflicted; rather, it means one through which spiritual benefits accrue – i.e. those which redound to your *ultimate* good; the most important relationships for your self-definition; for learning life's main lessons; for fulfilling your true destiny – the reason you incarnated in this life). Your charming alacrity disarms other people – they are won over by your geniality, your honorableness, and your disinterested practicality. You are not so much self-effacing as you are earthy and real.

You possess a self-certainty which is patient and humane – you respect other people because you truly respect yourself. While you are not particularly rebellious per se, you make your decisions by following the call of your own personal destiny (rather than relying upon the customary mores and canons of social acceptance); thus your life and opinions likely take directions very different from the dictates of your upbringing, your family, your society. On the downside you are headstrong and willful – unabashedly pig-headed, contrary, and impossible to deflect once you've set your sights on a goal. Your good-spirited faith in yourself is a steadying influence on the people around you – they look up to for guidance and trust your leadership unreservedly.

Sun conjunct South node: You are blunt and bluff: proud of your fitness and capabilities, and always ready to charge full-steam ahead regardless of the consequences or the sensibilities of others. You are unyielding, uncompromising, and can be quite perverse in going off on your own tangent – indeed, the wronger you are, the more confident in yourself you become. In particular you tend to trip yourself up with regard to father and superiors / bosses / authorities. Your self-certainty is the product of a bull-headed stubbornness rather than a true seriousness of purpose; and you are given to a self-righteous, self-coddling complacency that tends to slow you down so that you lose a beat or tempo, and often find yourself stranded alone in your self-congratulations. Because you are so unconcerned and invest little of yourself in your relationships with others, you are able to shrug off inconveniences and walk away from any imbroglio or debacle with a minimum of sweat or pother. Thus you are able to maintain a coolly indifferent – unfazed and unfeeling – emotional equilibrium no matter what is going on outside of you.

Moon conjunct North node: You are natural, spontaneous, and unassuming – able to relax and be yourself at all times and in any company. You have a rough-and-ready simplicity of manner: you feel no need for pretense or putting on airs because you are comfortable within yourself (at home with your own feelings); therefore you can be comfortable with others, and they in turn feel relaxed and at their ease with you. You appeal to people with your unapologetic outspokenness, which is neither superior nor officious but thoroughly apropos, insightful, and to the point (and often wryly humorous). You are not fooled by superficial appearances, nor do you feel any incumbency to go through the empty motions of obligatory social niceties, or put up with people you dislike in the name of politeness (hence on the negative side you can be quite brusque and rudely dismissive). Blessings flow to you from women – especially mother – and the general public. Yours is a soothing, reassuring presence; and your unadorned sincerity calls forth the better impulses of others.

Moon conjunct South node: You are broody and given to incessant indwelling and rumination. Because you are overly sensitive, easily affronted and quick to take offense, it is difficult for you to see other peoples' points of view, or acknowledge that their feelings are as important to them as yours are to you. You get huffy and go into a sulk whenever you believe (as is your wont) that you have been slighted; and as a result it's hard for other people to reach out to you through your screen of pouty, self-salving sulkiness. You are moody, with an air of long-suffering, of being unfairly put upon or unduly burdened by life – perhaps in reaction to let-downs due to mother (or unseemly coddling by her), or by women generally. You seem to demand a special dispensation due to all you've been through. On the positive side you hold your head up high, and have no qualms about standing fast and standing alone; thus you are at your best in confusing or threatening situations in which most people lose their heads.

Mercury conjunct North node: You are alert, lively, a good raconteur or showman; and you are quick to pick up on and address the mood of the moment and the feelings of other people – especially young people and students (you are a good teacher). You're actually quite a character: perceptive, forthright, and saucy. You possess an unflagging élan; a cocky strut; and an irreverent, impish sense of humor. Although you can be pugnacious (even caustic) when thwarted, you are usually able to take dissent in your stride without becoming unduly ruffled by it – you have a facility for objectively detaching yourself from (being emotionally uninvolved – not taking personally) limitations and failures, which enables you to keep yourself on an even emotional keel even when everything is falling apart all around you. Your images and beliefs arise from a true inner conviction – thinking things through thoroughly for yourself rather than relying upon other people's belief systems – and your meticulousness and upstanding comportment result from a broad, accepting philosophy of life and respect for other people's ideas (rather than from unquestioning allegiance to prevailing social norms).

Mercury conjunct South node: You are curt, brisk, short, and strident: no one is ever in doubt of your opinions on any subject since you love to lecture and hold forth; and you interact with other people in an objective, businesslike fashion. Your cold reserve and bold, autocratic manner are designed to (and succeed at) making others defer to you (although you are unquestionably idealistic; and you adhere to the highest standards of honorable – if self-serving – behavior). However, you are also a bit of a know-it-all, and you believe that you're so sharp – have taken every imaginable factor into your calculations, and so must be unalterably in the right at all times. In fact, you *are* rather astute up to a certain point; but you often fail to see when this point has been reached and whimsical absolutism or dictatorship begins. You're at your best when inflexible and unyielding determination is the order of the day, since you have great staying power in adversity, and are an inspiring rock of conviction whom other people listen to in times of doubt.

Venus conjunct North node: You are soft, gentle, and gracious, with a knack for being tender and patient without becoming a pushover or sucker. You are able to be intimate with people (show them your true feelings) because you know what your true feelings are: you are in close touch with your inner desires, and your social acts are based upon a humane fairness – a genuine (if credulous) sense of peace and goodwill towards men (although your blessings tend to arrive by means of women – female family members / friends / lovers / coworkers). You are sincere and disarming, so people are inclined to indulge you your eccentricities and forgive you your whimsical peccadilloes or gaffes. You carry yourself with poised self-possession under any circumstances because you know that at root your own impulses are good; and you have the unshakeable hope and optimism that you'll be able to handle anything that may come in the future. Because you trust in your own feelings, you are able to trust in other people; and your openness and emotional accessibility invite them to relax their defenses in turn.

Venus conjunct South node: You are extremely sensitive and easily discomfited and put out (grudging). You are fastidious and particular – even a bit snooty and sniffy – and you need to have everything around you (including the people) arranged perfectly. Because you don't really have a clue as to how to just relax with people, you are easily disappointed or hurt (particularly by women). You may have betrayal or abandonment issues, and you quickly close up like a clam at the slightest hint of rejection. Although you are sociable and gregarious outwardly, inwardly you hold yourself apart: your spontaneity and childlike, boyish (or girlish) naïveté and playfulness are cultivated to charm and wheedle people as a defense against them, precisely because you don't quite trust them or their motives. You derive your main enjoyment in life not so much from intimacies as from arts, crafts, and social activities in which you can excel and demonstrate your prowess (worth) to others.

Mars conjunct North node: You are bold, self-certain, relentless, and indomitable once you have set your sights on a goal. You lack much in the way of social grace or suavity (or tact, diplomacy, or patience with folderol), but your honorable and principled views and vision carry the force of a disinterested and highly original insight behind them. You are brash, experimentative, and animated by an enthusiastic spirit of adventure and discovery, which makes you a natural-born leader and organizer. You thrive on challenge and the opportunity to push yourself beyond your own limits; and on the negative side you evince little tolerance for dissenting opinions. Your unhesitating decisiveness is the product of a true moral courage: you know who you are and you know what you stand for. You are a model to others of self-discipline, loftiness of purpose, and right-minded determination.

Mars conjunct South node: You tend to be smug and self-satisfied, unconcerned with the opinions of others, and zealously protective of your own personal comfort and convenience. You become crotchety and easily ruffled at having to compromise yourself or go out of your way, and you resist any threat to your comfortable accustomed routines. You have your own rules and lines which are not to be crossed, and you will not bend to the rules of anyone else. You do not shrink from confrontation or conflict, especially with men; and you will not kowtow to anyone who challenges your fond predilections. Thus you can be too inflexible when improvisation and adaptation are required; and too complacent and indifferent when it's time take a stand. On the other hand, like Eeyore, you possess a dogged independence, true grit, and a sardonic view of life which keeps you going in any rut. Ultimately, you are capable and content and compelled to do your own thing irrespective of the social consequences, and to revel in your independence of spirit.

Jupiter conjunct North node: You possess zest, sparkle, and an infectious joie de vivre. Your utter artlessness and frankness are disarming and endearing, and your presence is soothing and reassuring. You strike an easy, relaxed pace in life and push neither yourself nor other people. You are an interested listener and nonjudgmental confidant, and you are the voice of reason and a calming influence in any milieu. Although you are by no means a shrinking violet, you find conflict distasteful and seek harmony and accord whenever possible. You possess a knack for spreading oil on troubled waters and for finding common grounds for agreement. On your negative side, there can be something of a prima-donna tendency – a lofty hauteur or disinclination to take sides when real commitment is called for. You are a perceptive and articulate conciliator and facilitator – a voice of reason and sanity – and you bring a fresh, open viewpoint to any group interaction.

Jupiter conjunct South node: You are composed and collected, and you maintain an above-it-all sang-froid at all times. You pride yourself on your perspicacity and competence, and you like to feel that you are in a leading position in the race of life. You stay on top of things by not permitting yourself to become bogged down in other people's emotional issues or quagmires, so you are able to remain indifferent and unruffled and keep yourself tuned in to your own wavelength. You maintain your individualism and blithe savoir-faire with an incessant busyness and preoccupation, which can make you seem annoyingly remote and impassive when an emotional response is called for. You are detached and businesslike in your personal relations, briskly processing people and situations with little sweat or pother on your part, and moving right along to the next item on your agenda. At your best your imperturbability and ability to hold fast to your own convictions are a surety in times of confusion.

Saturn conjunct North node: You are stolid, stable and steady as a rock. You are not given to demonstrativeness or show, but are unvarnished, straightforward, and plainspoken in any company. You always cut across doubletalk and equivocation and get right down to the business at hand because you are guided by strong integrity and sense of justice, and a fearless willingness to stand up for what you know is right and true. You do not take setbacks or rejection personally: you possess inner control and the ability to accept things evenly, as they come, without feeling that your ego is on the line in the outcome. You are capable of measured advance or strategic retreat, as circumstances require, without working yourself into a lather or giving needless affront. Your level-headedness is born of a sense of self-acceptance which in turn endows you with an acceptance of other people and life in general. Your sobriety and detachment make you a dependable, reliable person who can always be counted upon when the going is tough.

Saturn conjunct South node: You are volatile and reactive – quick on the indignation trigger, and quick to commit to the warpath. You have a restless energy, and are never quite satisfied with the situation at hand. You must always take the lead or call the shots: you drive yourself (and other people) relentlessly, and you take great pains to make your point or to get your lick in. You are easily offended; disdainful of tact or temporizing; and proud of your penchant for calling a spade a spade. You rely on bowling people right over and brushing obstacles aside in order to make your own will prevail. When it doesn't, you coddle yourself with an affected unconcern and indifference; or else you withdraw from the proceedings in a pouty, sulky moodiness. Your brazen pigheadedness and obstinacy, on the positive side, make you idealistic, dauntless, and tenacious to a fault; and you possess considerable personal flair and bravado.

Uranus conjunct North node: You are meticulous, responsible, and thorough, and take pride in your competence and diligence. You possess a shrewd analytical faculty – a mental clarity which sees through pretense and goes right to the heart of matters – but you are a disinterested and private person who doesn't readily share your insights with anyone. You are intelligently curious and non-judgmental, and are motivated by a deep-felt need to try to understand other people and their points of view. You are quite centered within yourself (need little in the way of approbation or support from anyone), and you studiously avoid involving yourself in other people's issues and turmoil. It's difficult to sway you or to knock you off your pins; and intimates may complain of your aloofness and non-reactivity. You have a benign sense of humor which is ironical in a resigned, self-deprecatory way, and your fairness and impartiality are an inspiration to other people.

Uranus conjunct South node: You are daring, cocky, and prefer to strike out on your own and explore new avenues and frontiers rather than to passively accept the boring routines and humdrum lifestyles favored by most people. Your indomitable persistence and originality can be admirably staunch and noble in their proper moment; but your perverse self-will often isolates you in your bumptiousness and self-congratulation. You are imperious, supercilious, and inclined to prance and posture. In fact you *are* rather amusing, what with your affectedly blasé insouciance and your droll outlook on the passing scene. You have a mocking view of your fellow bipeds and a dry, snide sense of humor. You have little patience for what you consider paltry trifles (i.e. anything you don't want to bother with); you simply tune out anything you don't care to hear and ignore anything you don't want to see. Your jauntiness and flippancy add spice to any group of which you are a part.

Neptune conjunct North node: You are ruminative and philosophical, soft-spoken and considerate of others. Albeit outwardly sociable and dutiful in discharging your worldly obligations, you are something of a loner who quietly and conscientiously pursues your dreams without seeking any special recognition or calling undue attention to yourself. You are inspired and visionary, and unhesitatingly follow the beckoning of your own feelings wherever they may lead you (distracted, otherworldly). You are able to pause, tune out static, and listen to your inner voice; which on the negative side can make you woolly, absent-minded, or indifferent to constructive criticism. Because you are so self-attuned you find it easy to tune in to other people, which makes you a good listener and sympathetic interlocutor, and other people in turn feel unthreatened and willing to open up to you. Your moral probity embodies the highest aspirations of humanity in your own life and personality.

Neptune conjunct South node: You are cheeky, impatient, and capricious: inclined to shoot from the hip and react with knee-jerk reflexivity (rather than exercise caution or think things through). You take a great deal for granted in your relationships because you are overly casual and presumptuous in your assessment of what others will accept (or will stand for). You are perfunctory in your handling of people, as if everyone agrees with you ipso facto. You assume that your thinking is prima facie valid; that your motives are irreproachable; and that your desires are unselfish and in the best interests of all concerned. You fancy yourself to be shrewd and cunning, but in fact your "objectivity" is extremely naïve and self-interested. Your stealth barely conceals a heightened facility for seeing the world through your own rose-colored glasses, which no intrusion of outside reality or differing shade of interpretation is ever permitted to disturb; and as a result it isn't that difficult to rip you off by playing on your fondest hopes and fancies. At your best you are spontaneous, impulsive, and possess an unshakable faith in yourself.

Pluto conjunct North node: You are ingenuous, unassuming, and don't vaunt yourself or put on airs. You are sprightly and mischievous, with a conspiratorial twinkle in your eye, and your spirited freshness is knowing rather than naïve. Although you are quite perceptive and nobody's fool, your low-key, laissez faire manner and good-natured tolerance for human foibles and frailty conceals a strong will and determination. Through thick and thin, you know who you are and what you are after – you never lose sight of your goals, and your perseverance is an engine that never rests. You are able to go your own way and do your own thing by slithering around obstacles rather than butting through them; and you win people over with a live-and-let-live bonhomie which inclines them to cede to you or abet you. On the negative side you are single-minded, unyielding and impossible to influence or deflect. You are resourceful and ingenious at making do with whatever's at hand, and are able to enjoy yourself and other people come what may.

Pluto conjunct South node: You have a forbidding demeanor and an acerbic manner which aims to intimidate or overpower rather than encourage intimacy or solicit collaboration. You are reticent and secretive – never sharing what is really on your mind with anyone – and you feel freest when you are on your own and don't have to answer to or for anyone else. You drive yourself ruthlessly and are formal and stringent with other people: when someone has earned your displeasure you voice your disapprobation in no uncertain terms, so people are afraid to cross you. You are rather taken with your own cleverness and discernment, and are convinced that you are one up on everyone else. Thus you neither need nor want anyone's endorsement or blessing; and you run roughshod over anyone who stands in your way. You are a stickler for minutiae, intolerant of foibles, and succeed whenever stiff-necked discipline is required. On the positive side you are mettlesome, decisive, and don't wait for anyone's approval before acting.

Appendix: The Natural Disposition

According to the Yaqui Indian sorcerer Don Juan (quoted in *The Power of Silence* by Carlos Castaneda), the entire human race falls into three categories. Although he describes the three types in negative terms, nonetheless the most likely astrological correspondence shows through quite clearly:

> "People in the first class are the perfect secretaries, assistants, companions. They have a very fluid personality, but their fluidity is not nourishing. They are, however, serviceable, concerned, totally domestic, resourceful within limits, humorous, well-mannered, sweet, delicate. In other words, they are the nicest people one could find, but they have one huge flaw: they can't function alone. They are always in need of someone to direct them. With direction, no matter how strained or antagonistic that direction might be, they are stupendous. By themselves, they perish.
>
> "People in the second class are not nice at all. They are petty, vindictive, envious, jealous, self-centered. They talk exclusively about themselves and usually demand that people conform to their standards. They always take the initiative even though they are not comfortable with it. They are thoroughly ill at ease in every situation and never relax. They are insecure and are never pleased; the more insecure they become the nastier they are. Their fatal flaw is that they would kill to be leaders.
>
> "In the third category are people who are neither nice nor nasty. They serve no one, nor do they impose themselves on anyone. Rather they are indifferent. They have an exalted idea about themselves derived solely from daydreams and wishful thinking. If they are extraordinary at anything, it is at waiting for things to happen. They are waiting to be discovered and conquered and have

a marvelous facility for creating the illusion that they have great things in abeyance, which they always promise to deliver but never do because, in fact, they do not have such resources."

These three different types of personality were described by Dr. Marc Edmund Jones (in somewhat less caustic terms in *Essentials of Astrological Analysis*) under the rubric of a simple yet powerful technique known as the *Natural Disposition*. What the Natural Disposition reveals is the aspect of everyday life which excites the greatest interest and enthusiasm, whether this be for people (mutables – Don Juan's first class), projects (cardinals – the second class) or ideas (fixed – the third class). The differences between the three types are most apparent in the kind of conversation each prefers: mutables tend to talk (and gossip) about other people and their lives, and shyly avoid talking about themselves or their own feelings. Cardinals tend to eschew conversation altogether unless they can talk about themselves, in which case they become animated and voluble. Fixeds tend to keep conversation on a formal, abstract, or intellectual plane; and in any event, they keep their distance.

What the Natural Disposition shows is a person's everyday expectations; the source of their self-esteem; the sorts of things to which they pin their hopes – whether this be relationships, ideals, or projects. These three archetypes are often recognized in psychological literature. For example, in the best-selling self-help book *I'm OK, You're OK* author Thomas Harris describes what he terms "life scripts" or "life positions", which correspond to the three types of Natural Disposition – fixed, cardinal, and mutable respectively – as follows: "The script may call for a life of withdrawal, since it is too painful to be around OK people. These people may seek stroking through make-believe and engage in an elaborate wish-life of *if I* and *when I*. Another person's script may call for behavior which is provoking to the point where others turn on him (negative stroking), thus proving once again I'M NOT OK. This is the case of the 'bad little boy.' ... A more common way to live out this position is by a *counterscript* ... This person is eager, willing and compliant to the demands of others."

Divergent Natural Dispositions can become a perennial source of friction in close relationships: each person comes to believe that the other one occupies him or herself with trivial matters (projects, ideas, or people) rather than taking care of business and attending to the truly important stuff of life (people, projects, or ideas, as the case may be).

Although the Natural Disposition is an easy technique to learn and apply, it provides a great deal of insight into natives' slants of interest in everyday life: what animates them, spurs them to action, and provides them with the feedback that nourishes their self-esteem.

N.D.	Area of Everyday Interest	Impulse to Action
Cardinal	ACTIVITIES	DYNAMIC
Fixed	IDEALS	REFLECTIVE
Mutable	RELATIONSHIPS	ADAPTIVE

VALUABLE TIP: it's often useful when looking at natives' progressions and transits to keep their Natural Dispositions in mind, since the doings in a cardinal native's life (no matter whether by positive or negative indication) tend to manifest as outward events – triumphs and defeats; the doings in a mutable native's life tend to work out through relationshipsx (their own; and also those of other people with whom they identify); and the doings in a fixed native's life tend to be inward, psychological realizations. Thus it is easier to predict future events for cardinal and mutable Natural Disposition natives than it is for fixed N.D. natives since the lives of the former are "eventful", and these events can be dated; whereas the effects of progressions or transits for fixed N.D. natives may be subtle changes difficult to appreciate while they are occurring, but recognizable in retrospect as: "Oh yes, that was about the time in my life when I began such-and-such a change in my life direction (progressed Sun) or outlook (p. Mercury) or feelings (p. Venus) or commitments (p. Mars) etc." – that is to say, subtle yet important changes or new beginnings or tendencies (rather than concrete "events") whose significance in the life is only apparent upon reflection long after the fact.

A horoscope has a simple Natural Disposition whenever there are oppositions in only one of the three quadratures – cardinal, fixed, or mutable (there can be more than one opposition – as e.g. in a Grand Square – but all oppositions must be in the same quadrature). For this analysis we will use wide orbs: 17° when the Sun is involved in an opposition aspect; 12° 30' when the Sun is not but the Moon is; and 10° when neither of the lights participates in the opposition. Oppositions are to be taken only between planets (i.e. Chiron, asteroids, angles, Moon's nodes etc. are not considered). Oppositions between planets in different quadratures (across the line of the sign, e.g. from 29° Aries to 1° Scorpio) are disregarded.

The opposition is the basis of the Natural Disposition technique because it is the paramount aspect – so much so that Dr. Jones considered the absence of oppositions in the horoscope to be a definite handicap in the life of a native. Natives lacking oppositions shy away from commitment and contention (i.e. opposition) and prefer not to involve themselves directly (allow themselves to get too carried away about projects, ideas, or relationships).

If your horoscope has oppositions only in the cardinal quadrature (i.e. between planets in Aries–Libra or Cancer–Capricorn) then you have a **Cardinal Natural Disposition**. You pay attention primarily to projects, activities, situations – the transient business of life. You thrive on excitement and challenge, and are the least cautious of the three types. You are cocky and self-dramatizing, and love to make a big impression. You have boundless optimism and self-confidence, and considerable swagger and panache. You tend to see the world as spoils to be seized and enjoyed. You are restless, impatient, and opportunistic. You are not big on subtleties or nuances, but you can quickly spot any opening that will further your personal ambitions. In relationships you are gregarious but impersonal. You have a dominating, challenging presence. You may have a tendency to pigeonhole people, or to regard them in terms of the use to which they might be put. You cherish your independence, and therefore shy away from entangling commitments. Since you shoot from the hip, you often lack a sense of the consequences your actions might have on the feelings and sensibilities of others, so that the other types tend to see you as being unconcerned and callous. You are coolheaded and unflinching, and never feel yourself to be compromised even in defeat: you merely pick yourself up, dust yourself off, and gird once again for battle.

If your horoscope has oppositions only in the fixed quadrature (between planets in Taurus–Scorpio or Leo–Aquarius) then you have a **Fixed Natural Disposition:** your slant of interest in everyday life lies in its ideals or potentials; hence your life tends to be more psychological than eventful. You prefer a grooved or routine existence to a constant stream of happenings. You have a deep sense of dignity and pride, a firm sense of direction in life, which consists not so much in consciously articulated goals as in an unswerving fidelity to your own inner voice (your sense of private destiny). Albeit a bit eccentric, you are highly attuned to your own feelings, hence your moods don't go up and down with the world quite as much as those of the other two types; and you have by far the richest inner life. At the same time, you are the most self-obsessed and the least responsive to the now moment, except when the spotlight happens to fall upon you. You are detached, calculating, and hold yourself firmly in check. The other types tend to see you as being an inhibited, stuck-in-the-mud fuddy-duddy. You tend to idealize the world and your role in it: you see the world as merely the ongoing confirmation of your own hopes and fears. In relationship you are introverted and reserved – not relaxed in a group. Usually you don some social mask or hide behind some wonted stereotype or posture in dealing with other people. You can be disarmingly frank, perceptive, and intense when you are dominating the proceedings, but maintain a rather dainty or supercilious reserve otherwise, as if you were somehow exalted above the common hustle and bustle of everyday existence. Albeit brusque and aloof in manner, you are patient, tenacious, and have a deep sense of integrity.

If your horoscope has oppositions only in the mutable quadrature (between planets in Gemini–Sagittarius or Virgo–Pisces), then you have a **Mutable Natural Disposition:** your slant of interest in everyday life lies in people and relationships. You are spontaneous, artless, candid, and have a childlike sense of wonder and delight. You are genuinely interested in your fellows and are solicitous for the well-being of others. Casual conversation with casual acquaintances is your staff of life (whereas cardinal and fixed types find this sort of chit-chat utterly boring unless they are talking about themselves); and your home soon becomes the neighborhood hang-out. You possess an innate humility and a true desire to serve; perhaps you have no real life of your own, but rather live vicariously through the lives of others (such as your children or grandchildren). You have a soft quality, a feeling of good will, and an attitude of nurturing and cherishing. You are by no means as egocentric as the other two types: you are instinctively self-effacing rather than self-promoting. You possess refinement and delicacy of feeling, and are quite susceptible to emotional undercurrents. You are easily hurt or disappointed. You tend to view the world as both a refuge and an obligation, rather than as an object of control. Because you define yourself in terms of relationships and the measure of acceptance or rejection you receive from others, you tend to lack the robustness of the other two types. Your life lacks cohesion and a sense of direction beyond vague yearning and hope; hence the other types tend to view you as flaky, with a hummingbird's attention span. But you possess a deep trust in the essential goodness of things, and a faith in the ultimate triumph of virtue.

If there are no oppositions in your horoscope; or when there are only oppositions across the line of the sign; or when there are oppositions in all three quadratures (as might happen, for example, in a Grand Sextile), then you have **No Natural Disposition,** i.e. no consistent slanting of interest in terms of projects, ideas, or relationships. You are self-contained, with little need to assess your current status in terms of your interactions with the world around you. This means increased inner stability and self-adequacy; less inclination to be constantly putting your ego on the line; relative freedom from nagging doubts or the painful apprehension of failure. You tend to see life in its chess-game aspects, hence you are more effective in manipulating the world to your own ends than are natives who possess Natural Dispositions. You have an air of extreme gravity or seriousness, but none of the intensity of the three types of Natural Disposition, and nothing of their spirited joie de vivre. You are bent upon your own purposes, hence tend to be detached from and out of tune with your environment. You are the abashed or perplexed spectator of the drama of life rather than the eager, whole-hearted participant. You are the loneliest, most anguished of the types, but also the most steadfast and quietly determined.

When oppositions occur in two different quadratures but not the third one, there occurs what Dr. Jones terms a Natural Disposition by Negative Indication. In this case the slant of interest in everyday life is shown by the third, unaccented quadrature, but with a twist. The difference between the positive and negative indications is that the former show a free, unconditioned channeling of interest and attention (towards projects, ideas, or relationships); whereas the latter show a conditioned response motivated by ulterior objectives, as if these natives were trying to compensate for a felt psychological lack or need. They try to resolve the conflict for their attention created by the competing demands of the two emphasized (by oppositions therein) quadratures by responding through the neutral, unemphasized quadrature. Thus the negative indication reveals an intellectualized or conscious construct, a balancing or juggling, where the positive (simple) indication reveals a spontaneous, knee-jerk response to a given stimulus. The delineations for the three types of Natural Disposition by Negative Indication are largely the same as those for the positive types, except here there is an exaggerated self-consciousness. The symbolism (thought form) stays the same, but the *feeling* (light fiber) reverses: i.e., if the positive indication is heavy, then the negative indication is light; if the positive indication is nasty, then the negative indication is nice; and vice versa. These are far more complex individuals than the positive types, possessing an odd mixture of innate wisdom, clear intuitive perception of human nature on the one hand, and a flagrant self-indulgence and self-stroking on the other. At the same time there is an air of world-weariness or effeteness about these natives which contrasts markedly with the eagerness and expectancy of the positive types.

When oppositions occur in both the fixed and mutable quadratures (but not in the cardinal quadrature), then you have a **Cardinal Negative Natural Disposition**. Your focus of interest (as that of the positive type) is in the excitement and clatter of everyday life; you have same the cockiness and love of challenge; but you have a decreased ability to just shrug things off and remain unaffected by the consequences of your behavior. Rather, life cuts you right to the bone. You possess the idealism of the fixed types together with the warmth and humanity of the mutable types, and the result is a desire to plumb life to the depths and to experiment with the more extreme possibilities of human experience. You are attracted to the foreign and exotic and dangerous; as a result, your life exhibits unusual features and you frequently find yourself on the brink of being overwhelmed and swept away by the situations you encounter. The conflict going on inside you reveals itself in your shifts between blithe, nonchalant insouciance and intense self-justification and defensiveness. Like the positive cardinal type you find your psychological equipoise in the feeling that you're on the inside track of life, or one step ahead of the game; but the difference is that while the simple types *know* it; you self-consciously cross your fingers and assume it.

When oppositions occur in both the cardinal and mutable quadratures (but not in the fixed quadrature), then you have a **Fixed Negative Natural Disposition**. Your interest in everyday life (like that of the positive type) lies in meanings and potentials, but in contrast to the extreme dignity and self-absorption of the positive types you have a lighter spirit which seeks meaning in the moment, in whatever is at hand. You possess the headlong adventurousness of the cardinal type together with the sensitivity of the mutable type, and the result is a species of "I do my thing and you do your thing" guiding philosophy, which neutralizes the competing demands on your attention and places you on a plane above the confusion. The conflict going on inside you is shown by your alternation between straightforward reasonableness and pig-headed quixotism. You view life as a drama in which you have the leading role, and you find it all rather amusing and entertaining.

When oppositions occur in both the cardinal and fixed quadratures (but not in the mutable quadrature), then you have a **Mutable Negative Natural Disposition**. Your focus of interest (like the positive types) is in people and relationships, but without the warmth and tenderness of the positives; rather, there is here a detachment and cunning. You are genuinely democratic, sympathetic, and attuned to the feelings of others, but with an element of artfulness and shrewdness absent in the positive mutable type (who is more like a puppy). This is because the two emphasized quadratures – cardinal and fixed – are concerned mainly with the manipulation of power; you resolve the competing demands for your attention by placing yourself at the disposal of other people. The conflict going on inside you reveals itself most clearly in your mood swings: you are alternately charming, ingratiating, of service; and then thorny, brusque, and vain. You're a bit of a rascal, and you know it and are proud of it. Though you tend to preen yourself you have a winning alacrity and assurance.

Bibliography

Charles E. O. Carter, *The Astrological Aspects*, Fowler, London 1930

Geoffrey Dean, *Recent Advances in Natal Astrology*, Astrological Association, 1977

Dr. Marc Edmund Jones, *The Essentials of Astrological Analysis*, Sabian Publishing, Stanwood WA 1970. All unattributed quotations from Dr. Jones are taken from this book.

Dr. Marc Edmund Jones, *Pythagorean Astrology*, Sabian Assembly 1929

Leo, Alan, *The Key to Your Own Nativity*, Fowler, London 1969

Robert Pelletier, *Planets in Aspect*, Para Research, Rockport MA 1974

Richard Tarnas, *Cosmos and Psyche*, Plume-Penguin, 2006

Books by Bob Makransky

Intermediate-Level Textbook on Horoscope Interpretation from The Wessex Astrologer:

Planetary Strength – a commentary on Morinus

An essential contribution to natal horoscope interpretation. Taking as its point of departure *Astrologia Gallica* by Jean Baptiste Morin de Villefranche (1583 – 1656), *Planetary Strength* explains the differences between the strengths conferred upon planets by virtue of their sign placements (celestial state); house placements (terrestrial state); and aspects (aspectual state). A detailed system of keywords is augmented by insightful "cookbook" interpretations for each and every planetary combination. The depth and quality of the analysis – as well as the hundreds of practical examples and tips – make *Planetary Strength* an essential reference work which both neophyte and experienced practitioners will consult every time they read a horoscope.

> "The book is beautifully written. With Makransky, whether you agree or disagree is not the issue – you will always get a good read. It is clear. He has done his homework. He makes the genius of Morinus accessible to English speakers. He shows us how to 'think astrologically'."
>
> – JOSEPH POLANSKY,
> *Diamond Fire* magazine

> "What's fascinating about Planetary Strength is that the author is using his own prose to describe the planets' conditions. In the introduction, he advises readers to study Morinus, but clearly Makransky's efforts are the better source. ... Try them in practice and compare these interpretations to what you might otherwise think about a planet. It may just sharpen your ability to make accurate statements about character, a person's history, and even to make predictions. And what more do you ask of astrology?"
>
> – CHRIS LORENZ,
> *Dell Horoscope* magazine

"We have found this book invaluable to reading natal charts. The author describes methods that are forgotten for too long. His contribution to analyzing a horoscope is remarkable. For the first time in the astrological literature, you will find reliable delineations of stationary planets, well-placed or 'afflicted' planets, angular planets, unaspected planets and the Ascendant rulerships, among others."

– Astrological-Compatibility-Advice.com

"This is certainly an interesting addition to reading and interpreting the translations of Morinus' original work. It is detailed and considered, and the author's knowledge and experience are evident throughout."

– Helen Stokes,
AA Journal

"Presenting a mixture of discussion, detailed cookbook offerings and chart examples as well as keywords and tables, this fascinating book also addresses the fixed stars. ... This fascinating book assumes a fair knowledge of astrology as well as some experience in preparing charts."

– Margaret Gray,
ISAR

"This is a book that every beginner as well as advanced student of astrology would do well to possess. The author is extremely perceptive in his descriptions of the planets in their various strength and weaknesses ... this book would be a helpful aid to the researcher, as it would point him in the right direction."

– Wanda Sellar,
Correlation

Published by The Wessex Astrologer - Swanage - England

paperback – ISBN = 9781902405506 – 150 Pages

from: **https://www.wessexastrologer.com/product/waps001/**

* * * *

Planetary Hours

The Planetary Hours are an ancient astrological system for selecting favorable times to act (and avoiding unfavorable times), by assigning planetary rulers to the twenty-four hours of the day. This book has easy-to-follow instructions for finding your birthday and birth hour rulers, and clearly explains how these determine your personality and your luck. A chapter on electional astrology explains how to use the Planetary Hours to find lucky times to act (to ask for money; to ask someone on a date or to marry; to go on a journey; to begin a new business). The chapter on How to Cast Spells gives the low-down on how to make magical spells (and prayers) *really* work, using simple astrological techniques. The use of the Firdaria, an ancient astrological prediction system which indicates positive and negative periods during a lifetime, is illustrated with a detailed analysis of events in the life of Theodore Roosevelt. Complete Tables of Planetary Hours at the end of the book allow you to find favorable times to initiate activities for any day of the year, and for anywhere on earth from the Equator to 58° North and South latitudes.

> *"Usually the subject of planetary hours gets a chapter (and usually less) in a larger book. Usually the subject is dealt with very superficially. How refreshing to have a whole book on the subject and one that goes very deep! How refreshing to have someone who knows his subject inside out, explain it. ... Bob Makransky has written the definitive book on Planetary Hours. It's the best book on the subject out there. It will be read and studied by future generations of astrologers. It's not just something that you read and discard. You want it in your bookshelf to refer to again and again."*
>
> – JOSEPH POLANSKY,
> *Diamond Fire* magazine

> *"Bob Makransky's new book ably taps the rising vogue for traditional astrology, though eschewing the fatalism often assigned to so-called 'magical' ancient approaches. He describes Planetary Hours (PH) as the "astrology of luck" and a method of finding empowering life moments for the proper exercise of freewill – to be yourself and not an enslaved cog of convention, Makransky explains in this*

admirably lucid guide book. Having talked us through the system he then examines PH's application in natal charts, electional astrology and magical spells before tackling the Firdaria system – which divides a person's life into periods...of time ruled in turn by each of the planets in Chaldean order'. As an introduction, this book is highly accessible."

– AA JOURNAL

Published by The Wessex Astrologer - Swanage - England

paperback – ISBN = 9781910531051 – 130 pages

from: **https://www.wessexastrologer.com/product/waph001/**

* * * *

Topics in Astrology

A delightful cornucopia of over three dozen essays on a wide variety of astrological topics ranging from practical, hands-on advice to technical issues to humor and satire. *Topics in Astrology* is chock-full of original tips and guidelines for experienced practitioners (it may be a bit advanced for beginners, but even they will find parts of the book fascinating).

Partial Contents:

The natal horoscopes of Philadelphia hippie guru-cum-murderer Ira Einhorn and polygamist Mormon guru-cum-murderer Ervil LeBaron are thoroughly analyzed; as is the abortive romance between Nobel laureate William Butler Yeats and the unattainable beauty Maud Gonne. The subject of synastry (horoscope comparison) is explained with detailed information on how to determine if someone is sexually turned on by you (and vice versa); and how a marriage will go. Exhaustive, in-depth discussions of how transits, primary directions, and secondary progressions work are illustrated with scores of examples taken from the horoscopes of notables. How to use astrolocality (employing astrology to find favorable and avoid unfavorable places to live or visit) is described in detail. The traditional rules of horary astrology are examined and evaluated in the cases of the Titanic disaster and the Nixon resignation. The rules of electional astrology are illustrated in a chapter on how to pick winning lottery tickets. The validity of eclipses and comets is examined; and technical issues such as how house systems are constructed are discussed in depth. Oh yes – Bob pokes fun at astrology too, with convincing analyses of the natal horoscopes (including predictions which came true!) for a couple of fictional characters.

> "The sheer scope of the work is mind boggling. Bob Makransky has thought deeply and cogently on the subject and it shows. He is one of our most prolific of astrology writers. ... In typical Makransky fashion he takes an axe to some of our most cherished assumptions. After the shock wears off, we are forced to consider what he says and go deeper in our own understanding. .... He is a beautiful writer and as always, you get a good read regardless of whether or not you agree with him. He shows aspects of Astrology that are outside the current mainstream. A very recommendable book for the serious astrological student."
>
> – Joseph Polansky,
> *Diamond Fire* magazine

> "Makransky's plainspoken writing style is direct and thought-provoking. Beginners will enjoy and frequently refer to many of the articles. With his wide-ranging interests, Makransky offers something for everyone."
>
> – Chris Lorenz,
> *Dell Horoscope* magazine

Published by Dear Brutus Press

paperback – ISBN = 9781519765871 – 312 Pages

Kindle edition

from: **http://www.amzn.com/1519765878**

* * * *

Bob Makransky's *Introduction to Magic* Series from Dear Brutus Press:

"In this series, not only do we get an author who knows his subject inside out, but also a directness of approach often not seen in works of this kind. Not for Makransky the wishy-washy approach that attempts to soothe and reassure the reader with false promises of magical success - something about which many customer complaints arise on the Amazon website - but, rather, an honest and uncompromising study of what Magic really entails.

– JAMES LYNN PAGE
author of *Celtic Magic, Everyday Tarot* and *The Christ Enigma*

What is Magic?, the introductory book on witchcraft, can be sampled and purchased at:

paperback: http://www.amzn.com/1499279418
Kindle Edition: https://www.amzn.com/B0079K8X9O

Magical Living, the second volume about paganism, can be sampled and purchased at:

paperback: http://www.amzn.com/1499279337
Kindle edition: https://www.amzn.com/B0041843ZU

Thought Forms, the third volume about cognitive psychology and the Mercury cycle, can be sampled and purchased at:

paperback: http://www.amzn.com/1499267444
Kindle edition: https://www.amzn.com/B00439H1F6

The Great Wheel, the fourth volume about reincarnation and the lunar cycle, can be sampled and purchased at:

paperback: http://www.amzn.com/154416355X
Kindle Edition: https://www.amzn.com/B00CD958PS

* * * * *

Volume I of Bob's Introduction to Magic series:

What is Magic?

Magic is a spiritual path which is not very well understood in our society. This is because the theory and practice of magic have never before been explained clearly and convincingly, in a way that makes sense to intelligent and thoughtful people. Written in a sassy, irreverent style, *What is Magic?* discusses how such otherworldly concepts as demons, casting spells, and bewitching are just the hidden underside of everyday society – the skeletons in everybody's closet. *What is Magic?* answers the questions which all serious spiritual seekers, no matter what their spiritual path, ask at one time or another, but can never find satisfactorily answered:

1) What is the difference between faith and fooling yourself?

2) What is the relationship between altered states and normal, everyday life?

3) If you lose your desires, as many spiritual paths advocate, what zest or spice does life have left?

4) If the world is an illusion or dream, as it's said to be, then why does it seem so real?

5) Where does the world of magic – the shaman's world – take off from the world of everyday life? What and where is the interface?

6) Why is it so difficult to achieve real, permanent spiritual growth?

Contents:

Spirits, Intent, The Nature of Reality, Spells, Charms & Rituals, Science Debunked, Demons, The Nature of the Self, Bewitching, Magic & Money, Death, Black Magicians & Vampires, Power Places, The Magician's God, Magical Time, Magic and Morality, Dreaming & Stalking, Magic and Sex.

> *"There is a certain no-nonsensical feel to his presentation that is both refreshing and a bit disconcerting. Makransky's writing style is very*

different from other New Age authors, and that alone should appeal to readers looking for a bit more substance in their study of magic"

– J Byrne,
Psychic Magic magazine

"Bob is daring, willing to be offensive with his truths, and wise in the ways of words and magic. ... Bob Makransky, I feel, has written a great treatise on magic. I urge you to enjoy it as much as I have."

from the foreword by
Michael Peter Langevin,
publisher of *Magical Blend* magazine.

What is Magic? – ISBN 9781499279412 – 202 pages

paperback: http://www.amzn.com/1499279418

Kindle Edition: https://www.amzn.com/B0079K8X9O

* * * * *

Volume II of Bob's Introduction to Magic series:

Magical Living

Winner of the Sacramento Publishers' Association awards for Best Nonfiction and Best Spiritual book; and Reader Views Reviewer's Choice Award, *Magical Living* is a collection of essays which give detailed, how-to instructions on channeling spirit guides, communicating with plants and nature spirits, developing your psychic vision; together with inspirational essays on managing love relationships, handling oppressive people, and dealing with hurt.

"I love this little book! ... Carry this book with you, read and reread the essays, and connect with joy."

– Kathryn Lanier,
InnerChange magazine

"He writes beautifully, clearly, elegantly ... he is incapable of an unoriginal thought."

– Joseph Polansky,
Diamond Fire magazine

"If learning how to live magically appeals to you, you'll love this book. This is not only an interesting book with some different ideas, it's also a fun book that can be used to lighten the readers' hearts, minds, and spirits."

– Krysta Gibson,
New Spirit Journal

"It's a beautiful little book to carry around for when you just want something to read at odd moments, but I suspect that, for some, it will be a book that's picked up over and over again. At times, I find myself ruminating over something I read or glance at the contents page to have something jump out at me that's relevant to the moment. I highly recommend this book to anyone with an open mind and a real willingness to look at themselves and their surroundings."

– J Byrne,
Psychic-Magic magazine

"I could not get enough! I actually read some of the essays 2 to 3 times and discovered new insights each time. ... A great book to revisit more than once!"

– Susan Violante,
Reader Views

Magical Living – ISBN 978-1499279337 – 173 pages

paperback: http://www.amzn.com/1499279337

Kindle edition: https://www.amzn.com/B0041843ZU

* * * *

Volume III of Bob's Introduction to Magic series

Thought Forms

Astronomical and astrological explanations of Mercury's synodic cycle – its cycle of phases as it circles the Sun, with tables 1900-2050.

Complete delineations for Superior and Inferior Conjunction, Greatest Eastern and Western Elongation, Stationary Retrograde and Direct, and their intervening phases in the natal, progressed, and transiting horoscopes.

Explanation of the astrological / magical view of mind (the theory of Thought Forms): what consciousness is, how it arose, and whither it is going.

Basic course in white magic with detailed instructions on: How to Channel and Banish Thought Forms; Creative Visualization; How to banish the Black Magicians in everyday life; How to Cast out Demons; How to use Tree Spirits.

"Bob Makransky is a knowledgeable, purposeful and entertaining writer."

– Paul F. Newman,
The International Astrologer

"Steady Diamond Fire readers are well acquainted with the genius of Bob Makransky. Highly recommendable."

– Joseph Polansky,
Diamond Fire magazine

"Considerations Readers have become familiar with [Makransky's] fresh insights into different facets of astrology. In this book Thought Forms he is especially provocative and I strongly recommend its purchase and study."

– Ken Gillman,
Considerations

"I will fully agree with the statement that 'You've never read a book like this before!' The material is fresh and woven very skillfully to conclusion. I look forward to his next installment of the trilogy."

– Marion MacMillan,
SHAPE

Thought Forms – ISBN 9781499267440 – 323 pages

paperback: http://www.amzn.com/1499267444

Kindle edition: https://www.amzn.com/B00439H1F6

* * * * *

Volume IV of Bob's Introduction to Magic series:

The Great Wheel
– a commentary on W.B. Yeats *A Vision*

The Great Wheel is the wheel of karma;
of reincarnation – of death and rebirth.
It is the wheel of the law;
the wheel of retribution.
It is number and it is measure.
It consists of wheels upon wheels,
and wheels within wheels;
and it is symbolized by
the phases of the Moon.

"On the afternoon of October 24th, 1917, four days after my marriage, my wife surprised me by attempting automatic writing. What came in disjointed sentences, in almost illegible writing, was so exciting, sometimes so profound, that I ... offered to spend what remained of life explaining and piecing together those scattered sentences."

– WILLIAM BUTLER YEATS

It is often said in spiritual literature that time and space are an illusion, *maya, samsara*. But what exactly does this mean? And what implications does it have for how you should live your everyday life? *The Great Wheel* is an explanation of the System of birth, death, and rebirth which Nobel laureate William Butler Yeats' described in his masterpiece, *A Vision*.

Starting out with a discussion of how you can connect with your true purpose in this life – the reason why you incarnated on the earth at this time – *The Great Wheel* describes simple techniques you can use (such as past life regressions, probable reality progressions, and recapitulation of present life memories) to glimpse different facets of your *Daimon* (your oversoul; the totality of who you are), in order to understand clearly how you got to where you are at right now. To live your true life's purpose rather than drift along helplessly, it is necessary to see how your present life situation is the end result of decisions which you, yourself, made in other lifetimes and realities.

An in-depth discussion of twenty-eight personality types (depending upon where you were born in the Moon's monthly cycle of phases) illuminates your individual true purpose in incarnating in this life, and helps you to understand where you belong and where you are going.

The Great Wheel concludes with a fascinating explanation of what reality is all about: Mind and Memory, Waking and Dreaming, Change, Familiarity, and the Akashic Records.

"This new work in Bob Makransky's excellent and thought provoking 'Introduction to Magic' series ... is a fascinating and illuminating take on the meaning of the Moon and I learned a great deal, but there is much more, particularly a discussion of the Daimon, the part of you that encompasses all your human memories past present and future. It's truly a Moon book unlike any other and is guaranteed to alter you perception of yourself and the world." -

PAUL F. NEWMAN,
author *LUNA: The Astrological Moon*

"[Bob] has written what I consider some of the best books on magic published in recent years. Bob has a very keen mind and understands connections between many levels of realities. ... I truly loved this book. If you want to better understand yourself and how to function better in your life I advise you to take the time to study it."

– MICHAEL PETER LANGEVIN,
Echo magazine

"Bob Makransky ... is directing the reader to access the higher consciousness. He gives many wonderful techniques for it . ... This is not the kind of book you just read and it's finished. It's really a work book. You have to practice the exercises he gives. You have to apply the lunar phases to your own chart and to others. Many statements require thought and reflection. Not beach reading material. Be prepared to be educated and also shocked!"

– JOSEPH POLANSKY,
Diamond Fire magazine

"To use a 1960's term, this is a heavy book. It is very deep, thorough and forces one to step back and start looking at the big picture. What picture of your life is in need of help? What aspect of your personality could use some help? This book has the tools to help you."

– PEGGY MATHIAS,
Psychic-Magic magazine

The Great Wheel – ISBN 9781544163550 – 335 pages

paperback: http://www.amzn.com/154416355X

Kindle Edition: https://www.amzn.com/B00CD958PS

* * * * *

www.ingramcontent.com/pod-product-compliance
Lightning Source LLC
Chambersburg PA
CBHW050348230426
43663CB00010B/2039